Of Rivers and the Sea

Of Rivers

Other Books by HERBERT E. FRENCH

My Yankee Mother
My Yankee Paris

and the Sea

by HERBERT E. FRENCH

G. P. PUTNAM'S SONS, New York

Copyright © 1970 by Herbert E. French

Library of Congress Catalog
Card Number: 71-97078

PRINTED IN THE UNITED STATES OF AMERICA

To my *almus pater* John R. Tunis, guru William Targ,
cicerone Don Gold, and merboy/companion Peter French

Further grateful acknowledgments:
For assistance and guidance, from the U.S. Geological Survey,
National Park Service, Scripps Institute of Oceanography, U.S.
Army Corps of Engineers, Woods Hole Oceanographic Insti-
tution, and many other national and international organiza-
tions, offices, and individuals—especially in the area of travel,
many of them members of the Society of American Travel
Writers

33818

Contents

Introduction

All the rivers run into the sea; yet the sea is not full; unto the place from whence the rivers come, thither they return again.

Twenty-one centuries ago a wise man named Koheleth traced the watery mystery of our planet's continuous circulation in the Book of Ecclesiastes, and we wonder about it still. Many of the ultimate explanations seem likely to become clear during the 1970's.

The ancients sought an original source for Egypt's Nile River, always unsuccessfully. In modern times, two sources were discovered, one for the White and one for the Blue Nile. In the United States, one may visit Lake Tear of the Clouds, called the source of the Hudson, and Lake Itasca, supposed source of the mighty Mississippi River; there are plaques that proclaim this to be so; and yet it simply is *not* so, because the hydrologic cycle of our planet does not have a beginning or an end, any more than could the human bloodstream.

The two circulation systems are remarkably similar, as are the contained watery motions within all living things. Our living planet should, of course, be called Water, not Earth. Its living quality, like our own, is made up of and depends wholly on the presence and participation of water. Salt-water oceans occupy more than 72 percent of its surface.

The hydrologic cycle is deceptive. What appears to our limited vision as a massive exchange of watery elements among oceans, land and sky—in the continuing precipitation-evaporation-condensation cycle—is in fact the active movement of a mere fraction of the planet's total waters, not more than 3 percent, just as our own bloodstream (more than 60,000 miles long) represents a mere 7 percent of the waters that make up 70 percent of our human body.

"Water thou art and to water returnest" is a more exact description for the living human condition than the more familiar "For dust thou art, and unto dust shalt thou return" of Genesis. Cementing our dear dead ones into sealed coffins is outrageous—their bodies ought, more properly and meaningfully, to be thrown naked into the sea, in order to rejoin the chain of life.

Water is life, and life is water. Perhaps if one could explain water, which is no way as simple as it appears to be, it would also be possible to explain life itself. Is *water* perhaps the living element, life itself, and are all of the so-called living things—plankton, people, plants, pachyderms—mere peripheral capillaries on the outer fringes of the great inner living flow of the planet's true anima mundi, the living body and spirit of Planet Water, the water that pumps so endlessly and tirelessly throughout all of our world's infinite tissues and stream beds? Is man himself merely one additional aqueous environment and landscape through which water pulses freely, creating its own passageways and detours?

Through their leaves trees immediately transpire back up into the atmosphere more than 99 percent of the water they have drawn up through their roots and trunks, and forests are called the oceans of the continents because of this vast, invisible flow of water vapor. Man achieves his own similar kind of hydrologic happiness by dispersing five pints of water a day that escapes in feces, urine, sweat and also whenever he breathes out —visible as mist on a cold day.

All living things have a close hydrous family relationship to one another that dates back to their origin in the aqueous cradle—or more exactly the aqueous womb—of the planet's oceans which gave birth to all life. Human blood today contains the same salts as the waters of the seas, in the same ratio but fivefold more dilute, an indication of the saltiness of the mother sea when she begat our ancestors and of the gradually increasing salinity of the oceans.

To view the Planet Water most properly, one must turn a globe upside down, so that Antarctica, the only "continent of peace"—so declared in 1959 by a dozen nations at the height of the cold war—is at the "top" of the world. More than 90 percent of the planet's permanent ice rests here, nearly 3 miles thick, more than 5,000,000 square miles of it. If we are in the midst of an *interstadial* between ice ages, then this strange world of ice is an indication of the future, sometime after A.D. 11970. If instead the deepfreeze of Antarctica should melt, then all the lowlands of the planet would be inundated, drowning millions of inhabitants. Freezing occurs with remarkable swiftness, whereas defrosting is a slow process that might allow plenty of time for New Yorkers, Londoners, Yokohamans and San Franciscans to escape to the hills. No one knows for sure which alternative is to be.

Around the coldest continent swirls the Ocean Sea or World Ocean, of which all other oceans—the Pacific, Atlantic, Indian and even the tiny Arctic at the nether end of the globe—are mere arms and extensions. If UFO's were truly inhabited flying saucers from other worlds, then this three-fourths watery surface would cause them to name our planet after the unknown cosmic miracle liquid. If they were to "land," it would be most likely by a splashdown on water, just as our own astronauts return from space. The greatest expression of oceanitude is this great Antarctic World Ocean, where gigantic Cape Horn rollers—"graybeards" with a crest-to-crest length of more than a mile—billow endlessly around the globe, some up to 200 feet high. This is the world of albatrosses—the great bird with a wingspread of 11 feet that superstitious sailors once believed could sleep on the wing "in cloud-rocked slumber"—and of the planet's largest animals—herds of giant blue whales (up to 100 feet long, weighing more than 150 tons) that browse on endless great marine-meadow sea pastures of microscopic plankton.

Eighty-five percent of all the Planet Water's inhabitants live in the seas and are perpetual wanderers, drifting plankton. Evidentially, householders, stay-at-homers, the sessile members of establishmentdom, are an infinite mini-minority. The Aquarian Age—which began in August, 1969, when the rains came down to bless with holy waters a half million celebrants of an Aquarian Exposition—has been proclaimed as an era of peace and love. Aquarius' other name is Ganymede, that "most beautiful of all mortals" who serves the gods on Mount Olympus as cupbearer and the rest of us as waterbearer to the Planet Water. Yet we must face the fact that all life is change, just as water is life and life is water, and the most terrible fact of life/ water is that life *feeds* on life; that life *must feed on other life* in order to live. In the oceans, violence and cannibalism are the natural, expected way of life.

Ever since Alfred Wegener's first island of land poked up above the surface of the World Ocean, about 3 billion years ago, a great "seasaw" battle royal has been waged between sea, land and sky at every land edge or seashore, which may be seen at its present unrelenting utmost at such way-out places as Big Sur, west, or Acadia Park, east. The tops of today's highest mountains contain fossilized remains of former sea-bottom creatures, just as one may see, with awe, snowcaps on the peaks of mounts Kilimanjaro, in Africa, and Ixtaccihuatl, in Mexico, both practically on the Equator.

The planet's number one sight-see *water* goal is still Niagara Falls, which deserves the applause and honor. Niagara was once a "receding" falls, slowly retreating upriver, destined in time to turn into flat, fluvial rapids. But because of the vast international power plant down below, Niagara Falls must now be forever preserved at its present site, above the hydroelectric facility. Before long, it will be rimmed with a permanent "device," like a capped human tooth.

The water planet is overrun with thousands of tumbling, rioting waterfalls, of which the peer is the highest, Salto Angel, in a lush, jungly South American wilderness, named not after diaphanous celestials but for Jimmy Angel, the American airplane pilot who discovered it. Africa's greatest wonder is Musi-o-Tunya, "the smoke that thunders," which is usually called Victoria, named by the missionary for the little old lady back in Buck House, London, who of course never saw it; North America's most dramatic "natural" falls are in the Rockies and in the Sierra Nevada. The United States is especially blessed with numerous *artificial* waterfalls, ranging all the way from a million-dollar mini-wonder in mid-Manhattan, New York, Paley's Percolation, to well over 3,000 other artificial cataracts leaping down over the spillways of high dams—most outstanding, the Grand Coulee. All waterfalls, natural or artificial, should be viewed in the late spring, when they are at their best/highest, rather than in mid- or late summer, when most travelers usually see them.

Man first became aqueously civilized when he learned to create fountains, the artificial opposite of waterfalls, *up*shooting waters. The original fountains of Rome, half a thousand of them, were first set in motion by the greatest fountaineer of all time, Marcus Agrippa, imperial edile to Octavian Augustus, Rome's first emperor, in 30 B.C.—both to provide pure, clean water for the citizenry and for beauty. Today we can view many of the fountains, reinstalled by Pope Sixtus V A.D. 1588.

Americans, raised on tight-up training about turning off faucets, combine visual pleasure with disestablishmentarianism by viewing the freely flowing fountains of Rome, and also in visiting-viewing seventeenth-century flowing-water gardens (same vintage, different makers) of Kashmir and India, notably the Taj Mahal memorial of Shah Jahan to his beloved Mumtaz Mahal.

Every major capital has classical imitations of Rome's fountains. Holiest fountain may be the remains of the ancient Castalian Spring, at Delphi, Greece, or maybe the pool in Cairo, UAR, where the sun used to bathe himself daily; for fun, there is the Manneken-Pis statue of *Petit Julien*, who has been relieving himself—*making water*—now for more than 700 years, in a Brussels, Belgium, square. Classical-modern is the Prometheus fountain, Rockefeller Center, New York (the golden lad bringing fire to earthlings from the gods, but doing a splashdown with it in the midst of fountain jets). Psychedelic-modern, the Lincoln Center fountain, also in New York. In Portland, Oregon, the Halprin cascade achieves the finest extreme—an artificial fountain resembling the wild-water cataracts of the upper Sierra Nevada. Rome's modern ediles forbid the kids to play in fountains; in Portland, they're encouraged to do so.

Rain—gently merciful April showers to tropical torrents—is nature's most constant skywater show; most rained-on spot is Mount Waialeale, on the Hawaiian island of Kauai, up to 624 inches a year; Mount Olympus, at the top of the rain forest, receives the most U.S. snowfall; perhaps some mid-ocean point receives more of both, unmeasured. When rain and wind unite in storm, the planet's surface is lashed and buffeted with hurricanes and typhoons; tornadoes, passing over water, become waterspouts, their most malevolent form; the worst recorded hurricane was in 1969, Camille, a billion-dollar disaster. After the storm, in seven sacred living colors, comes the rainbow, usually seen as an *arc-en-ciel* whose ends touch down, but from a plane, one may occasionally see the complete circle.

The Planet Water's volume of water doesn't vary. When water vapor rises up to about five miles, it's seized, "grabbed" by gravity, turned into picturesque clouds and returns back down as rain.

Snow is water's most poetic form, "frolic architecture" that turns our ordinary world into a fairyland of unbelievable strange domes and pagodas. Modern man emerged exactly with the end of the last Ice Age. Did he acquire his intelligence (and sense of fun) from rolling and sliding in snow, his inventive skills from making skis to pursue game, his artistry from drawing holy pictures on cave walls? This part we may see and wonder whether.

Today we still play with water in its every form—swimming, skiing, surfing, sliding, skating, scuba diving and locomoting over snowy surfaces cross-country in the most remarkable of vehicles, the snowmobile. More and more automobiles are topped with symbols of man's return to water pleasures—surfboards in summer, skis in winter, with almost as many sail- or motorboats towed behind.

Ponce de Leon searched where the fountain of youth *was* to be found, for Florida has the planet's greatest water springs, most notable the 800,000,000 gallons that pour forth at Silver Springs daily. European man's first encounter with an eruptive hot spring was the Great Geysir, in Iceland, which is today quiescent (a daughter erupts nearby). All other geysers, notably Old Faithful, in Yellowstone Park, which remains faithful, are named after it. Medicinal hot springs, with their hideous brimstone odors, are back in favor, and spa water cures will be much sought during the 1970's. Greatest of water cures is, of course, the thalassatherapy of bathing in the salt waters of the seashore, where the healthy bromide- and iodide-laden atmosphere just above the surf aids in the health cure. Holiest river journey is the six-year sacred pilgrimage the length (and back) of Ganga

Ma, Mother Ganges, in India. Perhaps most sacred is a journey up and back, along the planet's greatest river, the Amazon. Or a quiet voyage through the greatest freshwater reservoir, the Great Lakes—the greatest water phenomenon of all in North America.

Water is life, and life is water. We still do not know just what water really *is*, because it is more than the simple chemical combination of the elements hydrogen and oxygen into H_2O; already it is known that there are at least thirty-three diferent combinations of isotopes and ions of the two elements, in what we call water. Tasteless, odorless, colorless, there is no such thing as pure water. When water vapor, far up in the sky, begins to turn into liquid water, it also starts to acquire star dust, carbon dioxide and even sky microorganisms.

Some creatures—toads, frogs, cats, dogs, even monkeys—can actually *taste* water; man can't. When water "tastes good" to man, it is because of the flavorsome minerals added. Each of us needs five or six pints of water a day. Today, the American economy uses 400 billion gallons a day, which will reach up to 500 billion a day by 1980.

The oldest U.S. reservoir is Croton Dam, built in 1842, "modernized" in 1906, and not so very different from a 5,000-year-old dam discovered in Egypt, either version. Then Boulder/ Hoover, and Grand Coulee. Still the need grows. The North American Water and Power Alliance has proposed a $100 billion project, involving thirty years of construction, to bring the far-north headwaters of the Yukon River, in Alaska, south for use by the western United States and Mexico.

Man needs water to drink, to wash (himself, his dishes, his sheets), even for such psychological needs as weeping and wailing. The flush toilet is perhaps man's greatest invention, perfected by a watchmaker named Cummings (memorialized in WC) and an engineer named Crapper (also memorialized, lower case).

A sea creature gone ashore, man is constantly "moisturizing" himself, never more fulsomely than when he orders an alcoholic drink to be poured "on the rocks."

1 Water Wonders

To experience water is to experience life itself. For water is life and life is water. Life on our planet, which I suggest should be renamed Planet Water, is due solely to the presence and use of water. The great poet of the skies, Antoine de Saint-Exupéry, once said, "Water, thou hast no taste, no color, no odor; canst not be defined, art relished while ever mysterious. Not necessary to life, but rather life itself, thou fillest us with a gratification that exceeds the delight of the senses. Of the riches that exist in the world, thou art the rarest and also the most delicate: thou, water, art a proud divinity." A briefer statement, by the Greek writer Nikos Kazantzakis, equates wonders: "Happiness is a simple everyday miracle like water, and we are usually not aware of it."

The 1970's are likely to give us a basic, comprehensive understanding at long last, and for the first time, of the waters we live by, in the perpetual seeking after man's not-so-remote liquid origins. For wetness is life, just as dryness is death. The springtime leaves on the trees speak (the sound they make when the wind moves them) the watery richness of life, and in the fall the dried-out leaves declare the death rattle of waterlessness. When you take a seat on a bus (I live in New York City), you will at once note the difference between leathery male visages and "moisturized" female faces. Men follow the local customs of shaving or not shaving, leaving their faces to deal with the local elements; contrastingly, the ladies work on their faces so constantly that one cannot imagine how the original face might have turned out if it had been left alone to deal with the elements. There are local weather things—for example, the British climate, which gives all citizens pink cheeks, so delicately pink that when I first nuzzled one, during World War II, I wondered if perhaps all English girls were tubercular—the Dresden-china effect is exactly so fragile, tremulous, dewy.

"The more a man drinketh of the world, the more it intoxicateth." Francis Bacon stated the watery wonder for any student of our planet. In asking you to follow me on my peregrination, which should more properly be called a paddle, I take the place of guide only, introducing many of the scientists, scholars, social scientists, statisticians, spiritual interpreters, and poets who have examined, studied, loved, praised, and played with water. For the Planet Water is first of all *to be enjoyed*. George Leonard, in *Education and Ecstasy*, admonished that ecstasy, joy, *ananda*, "the ultimate delight," should be a natural part of our everyday living. Trapped between diaper-sogged babes and weeping old folks, ecstasy? Yes, "the natural condition of the human organism is joy." Then maybe we are being daily swindled of our happy birthright. One reviewer of Leonard's book wondered, ecstatically, whether joy "*does* threaten things-as-they-are. Ecstasy, like nuclear energy, *is* dangerous. The only thing that may turn out to be more dangerous is shunning it and clinging to the old ways that clearly are dragging us toward destruction."

The "new ways" very often are concerned with water in one of its many forms: an increasing number of automobiles are equipped for carrying either surfboards (summer) or skis (winter); other cars drag boats behind them on trailers, even an increasing number of iceboats in winter, all bound for play, joy, fun, and sometimes the ecstasy attained by moving about on water, snow, or ice. The 1970's will bring about the broadest breakthrough of all, as increasing numbers of adventuring landsmen break through the looking-glass surface of water to delve about in the previously unknown world of underwater.

Many individuals, as they age, also ossify in their outlook and demands. Having found a good thing, they wish it to remain the same forever, or at least for the duration of their lifetime. Thoreau expressed it incompletely: "Things do not change; we change." In fact, *everything* must change constantly. Intransigence is the important machinery of living nature, and nothing on our watery planet contributes more immediately and constantly to the steady transformation of life, landscape, and latitude than does water, that busy, liquid, unknown stuff that moves so determinedly and restlessly through everything and everybody, to its own rhythm and regulation. Sometimes the fact seems all too obvious that water, of and by itself, is the livingness, perhaps even the *only* living thing present, and that we people and plants, rocks and hills, are merely its environment and landscape.

Hornification, fossilization, all this hardening of life forms, this drying out, is some form of advance indication of death and desiccation, which must overtake all of us at the ultimate, final, unwatery moment when we go rigid, dry, and lifeless. But why must so many people and institutions dry out long before their time? Generation gaps happen perhaps not so much because of youth's lack of appreciation of the rich wonders of the previous generation's accomplishments (especially those of immediately previous parents) as because of the advance senescence and decrepitude which arrive as a grand climacteric at a time when a man or woman should be just maturescing into rich enjoyment: Sophocles shouted it, "Nobody loves life like an old man." But life is change, just as life is water and water is life, and the old man who truly loves life is also expressing his love for *change*.

We have just entered a new age, which is being proclaimed ever more widely: "This is the dawning of the Age of Aquarius," James Rado and Gerome Ragni have been telling us in that great "American tribal love-rock musical" *Hair*.

Many astrologers assure us that the age has already begun and will last an approximate 2,000 years, but the exact commencement date hasn't ever been stated so far as I could discover, up to now. Let me now do so.

In August, 1969, an "Aquarian Exposition" was held in Bethel, an up-state New York town, at which a half-million youthful enthusiasts gathered to celebrate rock and folk music, but perhaps mostly just to celebrate themselves, which is about the most joyful thing a mortal being can engage in.

"The largest number of people ever assembled for any event other than a war lived together, intimately and meaningfully and with such natural good cheer that they turned on not only everyone surrounding them but the mass media and, by extension, millions of others, young and old," Ellen Sander reported in *Saturday Review.*

"It" also was expressed in a poem by Arthur Schreibman in the *Village Voice:*

> It was weird,
> and it was wild.
> It was freaky,
> and it was freedom.
> It was lunacy,
> and it was love.
> It was beautiful.

The celebration took place for about three days, during which the skies also let go: The *Village Voice* reported, of the celebrants down below: "The Catskills rocked and rocked and rocked," and as for the clouds above, *"it rained and rained and rained."*

The Aquarian Age began, inevitably, at Max Yasgur's farm, and it was, obviously, blessed by Aquarius, Cup Bearer and Water Bearer, whose sign is eleventh in the Zodiac and whose symbol ≈ represents a stream of running water. "When the sun is in this part of the heavens, the weather is rainy."

Who is this Aquarius? Surprisingly, his other name is Ganymede, that "most beautiful of all mortals" who once served or, for all we know, still serves as cupbearer to the gods on Mount Olympus. As Aquarius, he works also for you and me, as water bearer to the Planet Water; he is the divinity who distributes drink to the gods in heaven and presides over the supply of water to men.

Thor Heyerdahl's *Kon-Tiki* voyage is the most beautiful example of landsman's rediscovery of the living quality of the surface of the sea. I was fortunate in spending a few quiet moments with Heyerdahl in the summer of 1969 just after he had been to the United Nations to give a horrified report on the miles of petroleum pollution he had observed in the mid-Atlantic during his just-completed crossing in the *Ra*. This was a journey to prove that Egyptians may have once crossed the

North Atlantic in papyrus boats. To hell in a basket, it turned out to be, for the papyrus steadily absorbed more and more water, the men could not very well go overside to make repairs in shark-infested waters, and how does one repair a papyrus boat?

The vessel was named *Ra,* after the ancient Egyptian god, and the papyrus was genuine, just as the stuff of construction on the *Kon-Tiki* was genuine South American balsa logs. But what Heyerdahl proved is something else again. His diary of the *Kon-Tiki* voyage is the best sea-level experience that any-one may vicariously share. This has nothing whatsoever to do with whether South American primitives actually once crossed into the Poly-Micro-Macro-nesians, or whether men rode the ocean currents in the opposite direction. These seemingly un-provable theories are as disputable as the Bering Straits east-ward crossing concept; someday, it would be fun to hear the countertheory that man and mammoths both moved *westward* from Alaska into Siberia, across a *wonderful land bridge,* to people the empty Orient, during one of those 500,000 B.C. peri-ods that so many astrological scholars have begun writing "histories" about.

The *Ra* was *not* the first world voyage with an international crew. In fact, most commercial sea travel has been managed by vessels manned with gentlemen from all over, all too often by the forced labor of shanghaied landsmen who didn't intend to go to sea. Heyerdahl, who garnered his international crew carefully, has his own report on how these men from varied backgrounds got along together—an Italian, an Egyptian, a Russian, a Mexican, even an American, and an African from Chad (who speaks only French), living the confined life of a human-menagerie Noah's Ark at sea.

I trust this is not too much introduction to my quote from this greatest ocean adventurer of our time, who was so tired when I interviewed him that I was almost ashamed to be so pressing-quizzing him: first I questioned, standing up, and then, most apologetic, asked if we could sit down, please, so I could write. This remarkable, assured oceanic traveler then repeated exactly what he'd remarked so casually a few minutes before, so profoundly is this a part of his personal philosophy: "You feel at home with yourself and with nature in a beautiful way at sea—a sort of undisturbed entity which is difficult to experience ashore.

"You may find it also in a desert, or on a glacier or on the peak of a far mountain. You find it much less in a farm, though there is still some there—but it is absent in a city: there are so many disturbing elements there—everything split up, *and so are you yourself.*"

Always we come back to the great central mystery of our planet—*water.* Dr. Will Mayo pondered, "We know much about the solids, but very little about the seventy percent water in the body—which is the element vital to life." And his brother, Charles Mayo, said, "There is very little that medical science knows about the effect of water of varying chemical composition that will benefit the human system." Ernest Borek described the mystery of human life in un-Biblical but more exact watery terms: "What have the generations of biochemists found in living things? First of all, they struck water. Lots of water. About 70 percent of the human body is water. 'Water thou art and to water returnest' would be a chemically more accurate, if less euphonious, description of our corporeal denouement."

"Life as we know it is not limitless in its capacities, above all, in the higher organisms," Loren Eiseley has said. "Actually, its manifestations are confined to a small range on the thermometer. Moreover, life demands water for the maintenance of its interior environment, in quantities hard to come by, if this solar system can be taken as a typical example."

In July, 1969, a suitcase-sized aluminum box arrived at the Manned Spacecraft Center in Houston, and a typically Texan bit of braggadocio was broadcast immediately: that the first samples of lunar soil it contained were "worth twenty-five billion dollars, more than all the gold in Fort Knox." And yet a small growler of Adam's ale, *aqua pura,* ordinary water, is so valuable as to be priceless, and so unrealized by Texans and the rest of us that we rarely worship it and respect it sufficiently. Nobody has yet announced, "This pailful of ordinary water is worth five hundred billion dollars." Even this is putting a very low price on our planet's most precious commodity. The moon, meantime, is so damned dry that the fact was announced, also out of Texas, that man's first footprints on it will undoubtedly last for at least a half-million years. Why that exact time dimension was used, rather than a million or quarter-million, remains a lunar or even lunatic mystery.

1969 was a remarkable year in terms of its number of watery discoveries. The most dramatic was that water vapor was for the first time found way out in space. In January, 1969, radio astronomers began observing what could presumably prove to be the "births" of several new solar systems elsewhere in the Milky Way, accompanied by the remarkable emission of the prime life factor, water vapor. *This was the first time that scientists were able to find evidence of water in space.*

Walter Sullivan, science writer for the New York *Times*, suggested, in March, 1969, that the discovery of formaldehyde clouds in the Milky Way "reinforces the growing suspicion that evolution of the complex chemistry of life, as it exists on earth, began in space between the stars." He went on to suggest that locating certain amino acids in space "could confirm that life's evolution began out there, rather than on earth. Such a discovery would strengthen the view that life has arisen on many other planets in the Milky Way."

Dr. Harold Urey, the Nobel-prizewinning chemist, in August, 1969, was encouraged by the findings of man's first lunar landing to tentatively resurrect his first belief that the moon is probably infinitely older than the Planet Water—"a single relic of objects formed in the earliest period of the solar system's creation. If so, it is far more interesting than if it were merely a daughter of our planet." Before we leave the dry (prewater) luny business, let us remember that there are all of 32 moons revolving about various planets within our solar system. Few citizens of Planet Water realize that we have not one but *three* moons. The other two are massive deadly-dry dust clouds that move in Moon No. One's orbit, held by gravitational attraction, one a quarter-circle ahead and the other a quarter-circle behind. Dead, dusty moons, making for increased human gratefulness that our planet is watery.

Gratefulness for wateriness? What about vegetative gratefulness? Of "the lifeblood of our planet," Herbert Wend exclaimed in romantic worship in his *The Romance of Water:* "About two-thirds of every bundle of hay or wheat or oats, of each potato or beetroot placed in the countryman's barn or store, consists of water and the soluble nutriments it carries. Vegetals need between two hundred and fifty and one thousand grammes of water to produce one gramme of vegetable tissue. It has been calculated that roughly two hundred and fifty million tons of the world's annual crop of grain correspond to an intake and transportation of a hundred and fifty thousand million tons of water. All terrestrial life depends upon this continuous cycle."

The hydrologic cycle has no beginning and no end. The evapotranspiration of water through *plants* and back into the main cycle of sky-to surface-to-sky precipitation-evaporation-condensation represents a tiny trickle, and the flow of water through man and all the other *beasts* an even smaller flow. It is as though all of us, the so-called "living" plants and people, were mere peripheral capillaries in the great, living flow of the planet's true anima mundi, the water that pumps endlessly through all of the living orb's tissues and stream beds.

We refer to urination as "making water," and yet we truly do "make water," as much as two quarts a week of H_2O, in the process of metabolizing, or converting, our food into body protoplasm and energy. In the mere physical act of living, we thus are important in a watery sense, as one more diverse channel through which water passes, before returning to the central hydrologic sky-surface cycle.

Of course, water—H_2O—is not simply a molecule made up of two hydrogen atoms bound to a single oxygen atom: thirty-two other components are also present, in minute quantities. Harold Urey, in 1934, discovered "heavy water": molecules made of oxygen atoms and of atoms like hydrogen but having an atomic weight of two (H^2); such atoms combine with oxygen to form deuterium oxide (D_2O). Deuterium is present in water from all sources, in a consistent amount of 1 part to 2,500. Another isotope, tritium (H^3), has been found; it is formed in the upper atmosphere by the bombardment of cosmic rays and falls to earth as rain or snow. In September, 1969, Professor Ellis R. Lippincott and Gerald L. Cessac, of the University of Maryland, investigating reports in Soviet journals a half-dozen years before by N. N. Fedyakin and Boris V. Deryagin of a "new" form of water, verified the discovery of polywater. Polywater has the same chemical composition as ordinary water, two hydrogen atoms and one oxygen atom, but it does not freeze at 0 degrees Centigrade; at 40 degrees below 0 Centrigrade, it solidifies to a glasslike state unlike the "crystal" state of ordinary ice. With a density about 40 percent greater than ordinary water (about the consistency of Vaseline), it remains liquid to 500 degrees Centigrade, whereas normal water turns to steam at about 100 degrees Centigrade. Polywater has never been found in nature. In laboratories, it has as yet been produced only in minute quantities.

Heavy water is presently used to control nuclear reaction in some nuclear power plants. Perhaps polywater will replace heavy water and prove a still greater improvement toward plant safety because it is so much denser than heavy water; meantime, scientists have begun searching for its possible natural occurrence, then will follow further research into its function in the chemical processes of life on the Planet Water. There may even be further undiscovered water variants that will be dowsed and diagnosed during the 1970's.

Ordinary H_2O isn't even the best thing for putting out fires. Today firemen reduce the surface tension of water with chemical additives to make water "wetter." A single gallon of chemical will make a hundred gallons of ordinary water into "wet water." These "water stretchers" require less water, and put fires out far more quickly.

At the 1967 Winter Olympics, in Grenoble, France, skaters skimmed over "softened-water" ice made of demineralized water—which was found to be faster and smoother-surfaced.

Is there such a thing as "pure" water in nature? Perhaps at that exact moment when water vapor first begins to condense into droplets to form clouds and, later, rain. But even up there, are carbon dioxide, star dust, and many microorganisms: by the time the rain hits the ground, it has become a mildly diluted carbonic acid solution.

The human body, which is seven-tenths made of water, requires a steady flow of water through it, both for the many kinds of vital dissolved minerals and trace elements it contains, but also for the sheer liquid flow of the water itself, from five to six pints daily for the aqueous adult—for respiration, cooling, flushing away of body wastes, and even for such important "extra" psychological watery functions as weeping and wailing.

Two-thirds of our water comes from the ordinary food and drink consumed. Man does not, like a dog, automatically take in his body's specific "required" daily amounts of water, because his more sophisticated senses get too wound up in drinking's many delicious tastes and flavors and because he is more concerned with whether he "likes" a drink or not. The simple dog knows better, waterwise, quaffing his exact requirements without question or partying with other drinkers. The children in a human family would be furious if parents left out a water dish for them, as is done for Rover or Polly. Yet it is notable that in aqueous man, as with the planet's hydrosphere, only a small proportion of his contained waters are taking part in the great in-out hydrologic cycle and that, as in the upward constant transpiration of water through trees, the greater part is simply flowing through the human body as one more kind of available water passageway.

Up to 85 percent of American water supplies are hard, chiefly made so by calcium and magnesium, though iron, manganese, and other metals play a lesser role. In a 1968 study of the chemistry of water purification, *Water Is Everybody's Business*, A. S. Behrman explained: "It isn't enough for us that our drinking water be safe. Our highly civilized tastes demand much more. We insist that the water be inviting enough to make us 'want' to drink it, it must be clear and colorless with no objectionable taste or odor, without excessive salts, cool. Water should not be too 'hard' to make a lather with a reasonable amount of soap.

"New York City water is only about a seventh as hard as Chicago water; accordingly, it takes much less soap to form a good lather. The common complaint of people used to hard water is that they 'can't get rid of the soap' when they wash with very soft water for the first time. Conversely, New Yorkers coming to Chicago complain of the extra amount of soap they have to use to get a good lather. They would complain even more loudly in some of the suburbs west of Chicago where the water is five or six times as hard as Chicago's."

A biochemist describes us: "We are all chiefly systems of aqueous solutions containing electrolytes and various polar molecules which behave in a unique manner." Poet John Masefield, somewhat more simply, said: "Life is a thing of watery salt." In a 1969 examination of the water within our bodies, *Sea of Life*, Dr. William D. Snively found that "our body-fluid tides, flowing from plasma to interstitial fluid or from interstitial fluid to plasma, are still objects of mystery and of intensive investigation by scientists. We do know that they are of prime concern in certain diseases, and that disorders in their ebb and flow can prove fatal. Our biologic clock injects the dimension of time into our study of body fluids. The intensity of almost all your body actions varies every twenty-four hours, metered by this inborn clock. Scientists have just begun to break the surface in learning how we can make use of our expanding knowledge in this field."

There's a tendency to think that "body fluid" is mostly blood. Although more than 70 percent of total body weight of an adult is fluid, only about 7 percent of this is blood. "The greatest portion of our fluid is a syrupy liquid cloistered within the billions of cells of the body," Dr. Snively stated the division. "Since many different substances are constantly being transferred back and forth through the cell membrane, the composition of this fluid within the cells is really regulated by the contents of the fluids we find outside the cells . . . Fluid *within* the cells comprises about three-fourths of the body fluid, or about 45 percent of the total weight of an average adult. Extracellular fluid constitutes the remaining one-fourth of body fluid, or 15 percent of total body weight, and has two main subdivisions: interstitial fluid and plasma.

"No harbor, seaport or stream accommodates the volume of traffic that plasma does. Constantly, it transports pounds of minerals, and carries all of the various foods absorbed from the digestive tract; millions, perhaps billions, of antibodies race through it to combat infections; more than a hundred hormones carrying messages to the organs travel this route; it conveys gases and countless numbers of enzymes, which regulate the body's endless chemical reactions; it collects pounds of wastes, which result from those reactions; it ships a variety of proteins, in great numbers, which aid in healing wounds."

Later in this chapter, I shall get to the question of man's increasing endeavors to control and direct our planet's natural supply of water, as the human need and use of water continues to increase drastically. When a town in southwest Africa, Windhoek, began recycling sewage for use as drinking water in mid-

1969, the purified product was widely acclaimed by United Nations water experts: "The result is better water than the residents ever had before!"

Exactly how life processes transform polluted, undrinkable runoff into clear, fresh drinking water is still unclear. The most important problem facing "Homo pollutans" today is to quickly discover how to speed up the self-cleansing capabilities of our increasingly poisoned rivers, lakes, and great reservoirs.

In nature the flow of waters often seems directed for a specific purpose as part of the round-trip hydrologic cycle. This is never more obvious than within living plants and animals. Tracing *The River of Life* within each one of us, Bernard Seeman found: "The flow of the blood is no haphazard tumbling of vital fluids along an unchanging course. Unlike the usual rivers which are open systems, beginning one place and ending someplace else, this strange river is a closed system that constantly returns to its source. Its total course, its channels and the direct mechanisms of its propulsion are known as the cardiovascular system. This includes the pumping heart which thrusts the blood out on its surging way; the arteries and their small branches, the arterioles, which carry the blood outward; the capillaries where the blood performs its destined function; then the venules and larger veins that carry the blood back to the heart." The human heart is the superwaterpump: in an average human's lifetime of seventy years, his 11-ounce heart will pump 46,000,000 gallons, thump some 2,500,000,000 strokes, at 72 times per minute, self-mending and repairing without ceasing operations! The pump's thumps, an alternating heavy and light beat, are related to and descended perhaps directly from the beat of the planet's own rhythmic tides created by sun and moon. When man, the salt-water-fueled creature, began stumbling about on land, his most important luggage brought ashore was his salt-water-washed eyes, which are still not wholly unlike those of octopuses. The brain's most important outpost, the eyes somehow acquired lids, so that, pools set on the edge of the head's proscenium, they are as constantly bathed and lubricated as if man were still swimming in the sea.

Eyes are the greatest, and also most unbelievable, means of communication among sea creatures which have made the decision to go ashore and reside in the alien environment of air-above-earth. No one has ever been able wholly to understand how two liquid-reflective pools first learned to "get together," to communicate across space with each other. Their first function was and is to watch out for danger and to find food. Somehow, sex, casual friendship, art appreciation, and ever so many other things have got into the visual act. John Walker, of the National Gallery of Art, once pleaded that "museums are for the eyes what concert halls are for the ears," and urged that "we only want to stop the viewer before the art for 'x' seconds of contemplation." This is, of course, comparable to the limited observation time that each one of us has for taking in the innumerable momentary impressions by which we must live.

We also "communicate" with birds and our animal brothers, with whom we exchange "eye smiles" by means of our strange, vertical, saltwater reflecting pools.

Eye intimacies—"it caught my eye"—between humans and parakeets, between humans and goldfish, or even between humans and walking catfish are often startling.

There is, simply, too much to "see," and too little chance to truly *observe*, to take it all in. Our watery eyes are rather like periscopes; through them our sea-dwelling ancestors perhaps first glimpsed life on land, and then followed their eyes ashore. Our eyes are said to bring us 83 percent of all our knowledge and to guide 90 percent of our actions.

Eyes: Watery mirrors to reflect self-discovery, acquaintance, friendship, love, hostility, hatred; all expressed from beginning through fulfillment to end, via the remarkable space-bridging interchange of sentiments between two sets of light-reflecting *saltwater pools* on the proscenium fronts of living creatures (the only ones upon whom the pools have moved all the way around to front stage).

"Women's weapons, water drops," and "Tears are the noble language of the eye." Just as the nighttime madness of our dreams is supposed to make daytime activities more rational, many women find that a personal rainstorm of tears will bring them surcease and relief, and set the world once more in balance.

Jellyfish, with the oldest eyes like ours, swim in the salt sea which bathes their glims conveniently. Ours are bathed fully as adequately by lids. Our tears are sterile, pure, but salt. Anthony Smith says, in the *The Body* (1969): "Laughing, yawning, coughing, vomiting, cold wind, foreign objects, certain chemicals, and crying all step up tear production, and the traditional 'good cry' will certainly produce in excess of .017 oz. All vertebrates living in air produce tears, and all humans over a few weeks old do. No animal other than man has yet produced convincing evidence that it can weep in response to emotional stress." There are no wild bears in England, where Dr. Smith pursued his studies, but in North America some scientists have suggested that when sorrowful, bears also weep.

Man is essentially a water creature who has somehow learned to live ashore. His final death, each generation of him, takes place inevitably with the departure of water from him. Think of the aged and dying: they lose half their watery weight in that terrible terminal time, becoming part prune, part mummy, then finally dry cadaver. The human spirit is a watery thing, an undine that requires moisture. And yet our natural environment, the thing we live by, water, is also a human killer. Death by water comes to about 7,000 people annually—sailors, swimmers, and unfortunate folks who just happen to tumble in.

Drowning is small cess compared and contrasted with the massive evil of mass suffocation that is now facing and threatening to abolish all of us, forever. Hark to astronaut Walter Schirra. In warning about our self-poisoning of our living place, he says, "You can only truly appreciate when you look out on earth from a seat in outer space the *frightening* problem of air and water pollution." Schirra pleads, "When you're out there looking back, you want to come back to the planet and help to neaten it up, want to do something also about the pollution of minds and ideals, as well as air and water pollution. After all, humans and natural resources are the only *true* wealth on earth." Geographer Millicent Todd Bingham rated the two-legged bastard very low: "Man can be ranked with earthquakes and tidal waves as a geological agent of destruction . . . the people in this country must realize what is happening, *for the hour is late.*"

In spite of the increasing anti-man outcry today, he, like earthquakes or seismic waves, is not all that bad. His inventive uses of power and materials drawn from nature to provide ever more creature comforts and conveniences are the most remarkable development and miracle of our living world. But suddenly he is confronted with the need to undo the destruction wrought by his inventiveness. The automobile, most universally useful of all mechanical workhorses, turns out to be the most ecologically destructive, via the poisonous fumes from the incomplete firing of the internal-combustion machine. Phosphates, so wonderful in detergents for cleaning clothes, foster excess growth of algae, leading to the death of all other life in our lakes and streams. Hard pesticides, notably DDT, so wonderful for removing insects, also end by killing the rest of us.

A Hydrological Decade was announced by the United Nations Educational, Scientific, and Cultural Organization in 1964. At the end of 1969 suddenly the entire world seemed to be becoming aware of the hydrological crisis. UN Secretary-General U Thant warned, in the 1969 study *Problems of the Human Environment,* that "the future of life on earth could be endangered if current trends continue." President Richard Nixon's first State of the Union message pronounced "the great question of the 1970's: Shall we surrender to our surroundings or shall we make our peace with Nature and begin to make reparations for the damage we have done to our air, to our land and to our water?" Many state governors joined the outcry.

In 1970 the youth of the nation has joined in the public fury against "ecocide"—the willful destruction of the environment. Groups are forming on campuses all over, among them North American Habitat Preservation Society, Environment!, Student Council on Pollution and the Environment (SCOPE). Many new adult groups have strengthened the longtime conservation societies: Society Against Violence to the Environment (SAVE), Group Against Smog and Pollution (GASP), Citizens for Clean Air, Environmental Defense Fund, Sierra Club, Friends of the Earth, Nature Conservancy. The new U.S. Council on Environmental Quality, set up in 1970, "authored" by Senator Henry M. Jackson of Washington, should, in his words, "play an independent and aggressive role in defining the threat to our environment and developing programs to combat it."

Stewart L. Udall, now head of the Overview Group, environmental consultants, and former U.S. Secretary of the Interior, has urged the startling new viewpoint that we must *stop grow-ing*—in population, industrial production, everything: "We have to get off this train of galloping growth." Perhaps this almost Gandhian approach is the right one? Secretary-General Thant has welcomed "a new era of international cooperation" against the universal menace of terminal pollution and an-nounced a twenty-seven-nation Conference on the Human En-vironment to take place in June, 1972.

Words, words, words, while our watery world is being rapidly poisoned to death! Yet here is a beginning of *action* and perhaps even of salvation.

An average adult American requires about 5 or 6 pints of water a day for his personal bodily needs. But in a civilized soci-ety there are all kinds of additional uses for water, from wash-ing dishes to watering plants to operating industrial plants. In a typical household, each member of the family uses about 60 gallons per day for domestic purposes. Even the gasoline that runs your car, which we'd better stop using, even if it means get-ting out and walking for a change—if the exhaust from it can't be corrected to keep from poisoning the atmosphere—requires 770 gallons of water for the refining of a single barrel of petro-leum. The U.S. Geological Survey estimated, in 1965, that Americans then used about 1,600 gallons per day per person, to-taling about 310 billion gallons a day. Most of this water is used "for" us in such widely disparate activities as operating air-conditioning plants or printing newspapers. For 1970 the indi-vidual figure is probably up to 2,000 gallons per day, and the national figure 350 billion gallons a day, which can be expected to rise to around 450 billion gallons a day by 1980. William Laas and Dr. S. S. Beicos, in *The Water in Your Life*, say that it took 10,000 gallons of water to build your car, including not only processing steel, rubber, and gasoline, but also paint, painting, cooling, and many other manufacturing processes. "It takes 300 gallons of water to produce just one loaf of bread, and 4,000 gallons to provide one pound of beef."

"New water" has to come from somewhere, and the planet's skilled engineers steadily continue to construct new dams all over the world, hydroelectric wonders that will give power but that will also furnish flood protection and, first of all, provide a steady supply of fresh water. Recently, I rode a bus over the top of one of the historic monuments of water supply in the United States, the Croton Dam, in New York State's Westchester County. This dam has been supplying water to New York City since 1842. When the "new" dam was built, in 1906, it was at the time the largest and most expensive dam in all North America. It is a pleasant, unimposing engineering triumph, with no contained or visually evident dynamic impression of industrial accomplishment. A contrast is noted, for example, when driving over the top of the Hoover Dam, where one can sense an inhuman, unhuman feeling, up from below, of titanic water power at work, what the power of moving water, in vast turbines, pushing, pumping, forcing, actually *is*. To me, Croton Dam, an American project, is our own home version of the planet's oldest known dam, in Egypt, built of rock some 5,000 years ago to store water both for drinking and for irrigating crops. Building it must have seemed a vast job for its times; it was all of 40 feet high and 355 feet long. Water "won," of course (it *always* does), by flooding the Egyptian job till it toppled, just as one of these days water will either topple or silt up *all* of the dams we have been and are presently constructing. Water *always* wins. But build we must, if future Americans are to have enough water to drink and live by (not necessarily "beside"). And some of today's "plans for the future" are truly fabulous. The California State Water Project is the first statewide development. When completed, it will move more water a longer distance than any other man-made distribution system ever tried on the Planet Water. Water deliveries to the San Joaquin Valley first began in 1968; they will reach Castaic Lake, Los Angeles County, in 1971, and Lake Perris, Riverside County, by 1972. Crossing the Tehachapi Mountains, the Edmonston Pumping Plant of the California aqueduct will pump more water higher than any other pumping plant in the world—110,000,000 gallons per hour, more than one-third of a mile up.

A few years ago, a top hydrologist with the U. S. Geological Survey, Dr. Harold E. Thomas, suggested that most Americans are "hydroschizophreniacs," because we tend to concentrate our interests, efforts, and hopes only on the *visible* water resources, making no plans for adequate use of the *invisible* ones, "whereas there are on the one hand flow resources, chiefly surface waters, visible, renewable, fairly well-known, but on the other hand there are also the ground waters, invisible, constituting most of the total fresh water resources, but only partly renewable and comparatively unknown."

Today's dreams and poetry sometimes prove to be a surprising advance indication of the scientific and industrial realities and fulfillments of tomorrow. No such dream is more dramatic or remarkable than the continental watery vision of a Los Angeles engineering firm, the Ralph M. Parsons Company, for a means to feed water endlessly and forever to Canada, the United States, and Mexico, a vast and unending flood of living water for drinking, irrigating, and all the other civilized and industrial purposes which the expansive uses of water make possible.

NAWAPA, North American Water and Power Alliance, has dimensions on the truly monumental, continental scale that American engineering is just beginning to attain, from proposed reservoirs and vast new lakes dammed up behind the headwaters of the far-north Yukon River all the way south to a Chihuahua aqueduct, delivering some 25,000,000,000 cubic meters of water and 2,000,000 kilowatts of power southward to include Mexico.

"The question of how much it will cost and who pays for it can only be answered by rule-of-thumb estimates until such time as extensive studies of physical and economic features have been made," the firm's literature sensibly proclaims. Even the astounding working figure is introduced most sensibly: "The North American Water and Power Alliance program could cost up to $100,000,000,000 and would require a tremendous amount of preliminary study . . . and thirty years to complete."

Dr. Raymond L. Nace, research hydrologist with the U.S. Geological Survey's Water Resources Division, has the sense to trace our trouble to people pollution: "Current projections of population growth indicate 6 billion within a few decades, or 3 billion more than at present: does anyone actually advocate that the planet *needs* 3 billion more men? *Or even three more?* Has anyone advanced a plan that will make it worthwhile for 6 billion people to put up with each other? Just try to imagine what the pollution load on water supplies could be with that

many people around! Especially if the 'advanced' countries succeed in teaching the retarded ones all of their technologically
ingenious ways for adding new and weird pollutants to the environment!" Dr. Nace expressed himself vigorously at the
International Water Quality Symposium in 1966 on big water
redistribution: "NAWAPA is one of the biggest water
'thoughts' yet generated. At present it has developed no water;
it has generated some heat but no power; and it has the sanc-
tion of no alliance. . . . We already have electrical power
link-ups; why not hook up the plumbing systems in the same
way? NAWAPA's huge reservoirs would place new load stresses
on the earth's crust . . . in this case, along the 400 miles of the
900-mile Rocky Mountain Trench. What would be the effect of
this loading?"

Dr. Nace then wondered about the visible-invisible water
sources, as Dr. Thomas had, finding that the total surface-water
drainage for NAWAPA would be about 1,300,000 square miles,
yielding about 195 cubic miles per year, 190 controlled by NA-
WAPA. But the total discharge of *all* North American rivers is
1,540 cubic miles, so NAWAPA would be controlling only
about 13 percent of the total water crop. "Considered in these
terms, the NAWAPA plan is not so enormous after all."

More immediately usable pure water *must* come from somewhere, and this is perhaps our leading problem today. It will
obviously be solved, and is in the process of being solved. We
need freely flowing fresh, pure water on a grand, an unprece-
dented, scale, and it will come.

Man has advanced ever so far as a land creature on the Planet
Water. Water carriers in the early cities of the Near East were
benefactors of their cities. A *saqi* in ancient Cairo had to qual-
ify for his trade and profession by first carrying a skinful of
water weighing 67 pounds *for three days and nights without
pause.* "Once enrolled," Desmond Stewart stated in his history
of Cairo, "the *saqi* had to be ready to play the role of municipal
fireman; to assist him in this work, a law required householders
to keep Ali Baba-sized jars filled-to-the-top with water in case of
fire." This is still the purpose of all those wooden tankards that
stand so like Martians atop skyscrapers everywhere: emergency
water in case of fire.

Richard Bissell has described a water phenomenon at the

McCloud Lumber Company cafeteria at McCloud, California, "one of the wonders of the modern world." Bissell let himself go to exclaim that "the simplicity of this natural marvel is dazzling: there are two drinking watertaps side-by-side. They are *tied open*, and twenty-four hours a day, they *gush forth* streams of cold, crystal-clear diamond-pure *water!*" This is part of American "doingness," that the water has to come through a *tied-back* faucet, in contrast with a Roman fountain, where the water flows steadily, is fresh, pure, and usable, and reaches the parched drinker via lovely statuary, not a probably faulty (leaky) plumbing device.

II Variety and Dimensions of the Ocean Sea

TOO much of our lifetime is spent pacing the paved world of cities, mechanically obeying the stop-and-go directions of automatic signals. There is a stretch of Park Avenue, in the heart of Manhattan Island, just north of Grand Central Station and the "new" Pan Am Building, that is the utmost expression of total urbanization: on all sides are great skyscraper towers of glass that stretch up into infinity. Everything here is squared and impersonally rectilineal: sidewalks, buildings, windows, entranceways. The pneumatic sound of the automobile traffic is enhanced by the flat fronts of the buildings into a defeaning, steady, deadly, baneful roar. If you pause near a grated opening in the sidewalk, you can also hear from below the metallic, subguttural sound of trains moving along the Penn Central tracks down below.

The paved world is a wonderful place. I live in it and love it, for it is the place where men build and do, where creative power dwells, a place where one can also best study the latest achievements of mankind as a city-dwelling race, which he most universally is. It is a place almost totally alienated from nature, but not necessarily therefore from life—for here is the life of ideas, today's dwelling place of human mental creativity.

Someday, perhaps 50,000 years from now, if the basic structure of these buildings were not so perishable, this area would make a splendid ruin—comparable to the Roman Forum or the Athenian agora, or even to Angkor Wat—wrapped, however, not with great jungly vines but highly appropriate glassy tentacles of ice. In a recent wonderment about the future which speculates whether we may now be in an *interstadial* period (a short interval of mild climate during an ice age), David B. Ericson and Goesta Wollin have suggested, in *The Ever-changing Sea*: "If New York is spared a flooding, the alternative will be the advance of a glacier, which creeping forward like an irresistible bulldozer will topple the tall buildings one by one, that is, if there are any buildings left at that time. If the past is a key to the future, our 'interstadial' probably has another 10,000 years to run."

The extreme opposite of the paved world is the untamed sea, and the best place to view this planetary wonderment is anywhere one is at last out of sight of land. One may view the vast ocean surface from a high-flying transoceanic jet plane, but up there the ocean of the sky with its population of clouds becomes visually far more important. Or one may view the surrounding sea from the deck of an ocean liner. Here again, there are too many accompanying distractions that may hinder the direct contemplation of the surrounding sea.

The best place to study the sea is as close to sea level as one may attain. Many ocean travelers have stated the scientific evidence of their study of the ocean's surface, and many of the poetic utterances which nonscientists have made concerning their findings have caused the great waters to become even more comprehensible to us than the words of the scientific scholars. Another category of interpreters, who are often the best explicators of all, astonishingly, are the fictionalizers: the men who may not even have been there themselves, but who make the place live for us through their lively make-believe.

Since we must travel to many of the way-out places in both space and previous time chiefly on the written words of others, there isn't much actual difference between the actual-factual and the lively-fictional, in creating for us the chance to imagine that we are participating in ever so many delightful but vicarious voyages. Herodotus' so-called *Histories* (Greek *istor*, learning) are as "real" to me—even their curious monsters—as Caesar's diaries. All that one asks of the fictioneer is that he create a tale that reads like fact.

The greatest sea saga of all time was written by a British inlander who never saw a real ocean (the height of his "voyaging" was the crossing of the English Channel to the Continent, once each way), Samuel Taylor Coleridge. His "Rime of the Ancient Mariner" (published in 1798 as one of a collection of *Lyrical Ballads*) is still quoted at length by all oceanophiles.

The tale is told by the Ancient Mariner himself; he insists upon telling the history of his punishment for killing an albatross (the biggest creature that flies—with a wing spread of up to an astonishing 11 feet) to a group of urbane wedding guests in the heart of London. Coleridge succeeded in making real the experience of a sailor all alone in the midst of earth's largest sea, the great Pacific Ocean:

> Alone, alone, all, all alone,
> Alone on a wide wide sea!
> And never a saint took pity on
> My soul in agony.

The most famous oceanic lines of all time are:

> Water, water, every where,
> And all the boards did shrink;
> Water, water, every where,
> Nor any drop to drink.

His words express in stark poetry what later explorers of the Pacific Antarctic were to discover in stark reality. Sir Ernest Henry Shackleton, who led 28 men on a fantastic walk-row-sail journey across the Weddell Sea in 1915–16 (292 days in the icebound ship *Endurance,* 165 days parked on bare ice, a month of rowing and sailing to achieve safety at last on the solid land of South Georgia Island, one of the way-outest places ever occupied by man in the god Oceanus' territory) encountered an albatross (you only do when you sail these remotest seas) that hovered, curious, over the crew of lost land creatures in wonderment: "It soared with an ease and grace that was poetic, riding the gale on wings that never moved, sometimes dropping to within ten feet of the boat, only to plunge downward again in beautifully effortless sweep." Biographer Alfred Lansing, an American Coleridge who also wasn't there, described the reality more vividly than Sir Ernest himself could have.

This way-out place is the uttermost area of oceanitude: Shackleton's small vessel crept over the line separating the Raving Fifties from the Screaming Sixties across the Drake Passage, the "most dreaded bit of ocean on the globe," where, according to *Sailing Directions for Antarctic*, U.S. Navy, the winds "are often of hurricane intensity and with gust velocities sometimes attaining to 150 to 200 miles per hour. Winds of such violence are not known elsewhere, save perhaps in a tropical cyclone." Lansing stated of the waves thus created that "they are called Cape Horn Rollers or 'graybeards.' Their length has been estimated from crest to crest to exceed a mile, and the terrified reports of some mariners have placed their height at 200 feet."

In this remotest sea, the Great Southern, the albatross, which might accompany a ship for days, was considered a good omen. Albatrosses regularly ride the storm-force westerly winds of the screaming sixties around the world (no intervening continents, here). A banded bird was recaptured ten days after: He'd just casually flown around the Planet Water! Since it was never seen to alight, sailors often believed that it accomplished the miracle of sleeping on the wing, what one poet beatifically described as "cloud-rocked slumbering." Its wing bones, for the unsuperstitious, made excellent tobacco pipestems. A modern mariner, Harold Dixon, who made a fantastic journey on a rubber raft after his World War II scout bomber was downed in the Pacific in 1942, suffered an ancient-mariner kind of encounter with an albatross shot down by one of his companions. They hauled it aboard the raft, skinned it with a pocketknife, and quickly ate the heart, liver, and other organs, including the entrails. The rest was set aside.

During the night, Dixon awoke to undergo a visual orgy of supernatural horror: "I noticed a glow of light so strong that it illuminated the entire boat, and the sea around. When I held it up, the albatross glowed like a flashlight." And so, though they were near starvation, they decided that phosphorus was poison and threw the carcass overboard. "Later I found out that it wouldn't have been dangerous to eat the albatross. Its flesh *is* phosphorescent, I learned, because it preys largely upon luminescent fish." What an unusual feast for true gourmets *that* would be, served without candlelight, of course: pressed luminescent albatross!

Adventurers, explorers and simple travelers all tend to believe in an extreme sort of anthropomorphism in nature. It's cruel enough to attribute to your pet dog the human emotions and behavior which it doesn't possess, but it's downright sacrilegious against Poseidon to suggest that in man's struggles against Nature she fights back, moved by vengeful, human (unnatural) instincts. Part of the lovely albatrocious myth is that there's a gigantic interwoven plot among all natural forces (combined with supernatural powers) to bring evil cess to the man who dares to combat Nature.

I encountered this personally several years ago, when I had gone into the sea naked and alone from the Great South Beach on Cape Cod, an area now called a national seashore, but as yet only partially properly nationalized, and found that I could not get back to shore. To this day, I still believe that the ocean had decided to take me. When I'd finally, painfully, won my way back to the shore, by then uncertain whether my choice and struggle were right or not, I could still hear the tempting voice calling me back in. Not a sweet young mermaid voice, but the summoning command of the great ocean sea itself.

There were many old sea-gods and sea-goddesses, mostly of the narrow Thalassic Sea—Xenophon's homesick Greek soldiers, reaching the Black Sea on their way home from Persia, shouted joyfully, *"Thalassa!"* when they first sighted it. Poseidon and Neptune and the 3,000 Oceanid nymphs—daughters of Oceanus and Tethys—were respectfully and fearfully worshiped when it was believed that most of the flat earth was land, surrounding the Mediterranean Sea, but that all this terrestrial island was in turn surrounded by the all-encircling Ocean River.

The old gods and goddesses are as forgotten today as the flat earth, but in their place we have a brilliant new hierarchy of modern oceanic gods and goddesses. Chief modern goddess is Rachel Carson, whose *The Sea Around Us* burst upon the world of terrestrialite worshipers of sea things like a breath of fresh sea air in 1951.

Two sea kings who occupy thrones alongside Miss Carson are Captain Jacques-Yves Cousteau and the late James Dugan, for their intelligently poetic penetration of the living world of the underseas.

Of all the new sea-gods, the most veracious is perhaps William Willis, who began his sea adventures by turning himself loose in a rowboat at the age of eight in the Hamburg harbor and ended by disappearing in the mid-Atlantic at the age of seventy-eight, when he'd probably gone briefly overside to make some minor but necessary repair. Willis was a true sea observer. In *An Angel on Each Shoulder,* he described what oceanitude (obviously a kind of beatitude to him) meant in terms of blessed escape from the rest of us on land: "As mind and body became used to the work and solitude, an increasing sense of freedom came over me. The sea was bringing out what was necessary to survive. The world I had lived in, the companionship of my fellow men, had faded and appeared more and more like a dream through which I had once wandered without having really been part of it." He found that "the solitude had really closed down on me, for I began to hear voices . . . echoes of my innermost craving for companionship. Solitude chastens a man, for he sees himself in his true stature whether he wants to or not. 'What am I really doing out here?' I asked, and answered, 'I am on a long and wide trail, a trail made by millions of dreamers, and so I am not alone. How small I am and yet so bold.' "

The first man to sail alone around the world, Joshua Slocum, must also have immensely enjoyed his solitary life at sea. (He always took a large number of books along on his voyages.) Van Wyck Brooks has called Slocum's classic *Sailing Alone Around the World,* written in 1899, a "nautical equivalent" to Thoreau's *Walden.* An unlettered man, in that he had little schooling and spelled poorly, Slocum was nevertheless a great scholar of the sea: "I consider the human mind above all else that we know of in this world. . . . At any rate, I could trust even my poor head to find my way about independent of the machine we call a chronometer. I sailed scientifically, too, I was in touch with nature as few have ever been. I was aware of it all the time and had never a doubt of the outcome of my voyage."

What a journey it was! He crossed the Atlantic; then, warned of pirates in the Mediterranean, recrossed the Atlantic, passed three times through Magellan's Strait, then across the South Pacific, the Coral Sea, the Arafura Sea, the Indian Ocean, around the Cape of Good Hope, and across the Atlantic a *third* time—a journey of 46,000 miles that lasted three years, two months, and two days. When he entered the Pacific, he wrote: "Then was the time to uncover my head, for I sailed alone with God. The vast ocean was again around me, and the horizon was unbroken by land. A few days later the *Spray* was under full sail, and I saw her for the first time with a jigger spread. This was indeed a small incident, but it was the incident following a triumph. The wind was still southwest, but it had moderated, and roaring seas had turned to gossipping waves that rippled and pattered against her sides as she rolled among them, delighted with their story. Rapid changes went on, those days, in things all about while she headed for the tropics. New species of birds came around; albatrosses fell back and became scarcer and scarcer, lighter gulls came in their stead, and pecked for crumbs in the sloop's wake."

More than a half-century before Slocum's 1898 solo circumnavigation, Richard Henry Dana, Jr., wrote his great *Two Years Before the Mast,* which expressed his lifelong dichotomy of feeling toward life at sea. "Its reality is privation, hardship, tyranny, and irksome and disgusting details. Habit and familiarity wear away all romance. Perhaps it may be different with passengers and those who have nothing to do but be romantic." His good friend and "sea-brother"—as they called each other—Herman Melville, who also recognized that the sea wasn't "romantic," said: "With Dana, the world was God's great ship, and his place was always 'before the mast.' " With memories still of irksome details, many years later on a journey around the world, when he himself was a *passenger,* Dana exclaimed, "I was made for the sea and all my life on shore is a mistake. How marvellously content I am at sea! The worse the weather the better I feel!"

Dana's worst experience of bad weather occurred during his first night out of Boston on the 15-man-crew *Pilgrim.* "There is not so hopeless and pitiable an object in the world," he described himself, "as a landsman beginning a sailor's life. The heavy head sea was beating against the little brig's bow with a noise and force almost of a sledge-hammer, and flying over the deck, drenching us completely through. The topsail halyards had been let go, and the great sails were filling out and backing against the masts with a noise like thunder." Rookie Dana was ordered aloft for the first time to reef the topsail. "How I got along I cannot now remember. . . . I could not have been of much service, for I remember having been sick several times before I left the topsail yard, making wild vomits into the black night, to leeward."

Perhaps the greatest paean to any ocean was a laudation of the Pacific delivered by Herman Melville in *Moby Dick*. Arriving beyond the "Bashee isles" (the Philippines), the writer says, "Now the long supplication of my youth was answered." Melville wrote: "We emerged at last upon the great South Sea . . . that serene ocean rolled eastwards from me a thousand leagues of blue." One must hastily reorient, or reoccident, oneself: Yes, eastward from Asia all the way to the Pacific's eastern shore in California! "There is, one knows not what sweet mystery about this sea, whose gently awful stirrings seem to speak of some hidden soul beneath; like those fabled undulations of the Ephesian sod over the buried Evangelist St. John. And meet it is, that over these sea-pastures, wide-rolling watery prairies and Potters' Fields of all four continents, the waves should rise and fall, and ebb and flow unceasingly; for here, millions of mixed shades and shadows, drowned dreams, somnambulisms, reveries; all that we call lives and souls, lie dreaming, dreaming, still; tossing like slumberers in their beds; the ever-rolling waves but made so by their restlessness.

"To any meditative Magian rover, this serene Pacific, once beheld, must ever after be the sea of his adoption. It rolls the mid-most waters of the world, the Indian Ocean and Atlantic being but its arms. The same waves wash the moles of the new-built Californian towns, but yesterday planted by the recentest race of men, and lave the faded but still gorgeous skirts of Asiatic lands, older than Abraham; while all between float milky-ways of coral isles, and low-lying, endless, unknown Archipelagoes, and impenetrable Japans."

Eastward across Melville's Pacific, at Monterey, in 1879, a young wanderer from Scotland was meantime composing a pirate tale, *The Sea Cook* (the title was later changed to *Treasure Island*), in which he created a novel admixture of his Highlands boyhood (his father was secretary to the commissioner of northern lighthouses), the California coastal scenery of nearby Point Lobos (transferred to a tropical island), and fearful piratical derring-do of heroic Jim Hawkins against the buccaneers. It is interesting that throughout the voyage of the *Hispaniola* there is little *sea* activity. Only when Jim takes off in Ben Gunn's goatskin coracle, which "was like the first and the worst coracle ever made by the ancient Britons," does Robert Louis Stevenson give us a beautiful description of the tiny vessel's gentle motion through the high seas: "I found each wave, instead of the big, smooth glossy mountain it looks from shore, or from a vessel's deck, was for all the world like any range of hills on the dry land, full of peaks and smooth places and valleys. The coracle, left to herself, turning from side to side, threaded, so to speak, her way through these lower parts, and avoided the steep slopes and higher, toppling summits of the waves."

The Ocean Sea, we call it, or the World Ocean, this all-embracing watery carpet that covers 71 percent of the Water Planet's surface. Half the planet's surface lies a mile or more below sea level. Though the World Sea contains 97 percent of the earth's water (excluding the waters held within the pores of sedimentary rocks, and not counting the massive amount of water not yet released from within the earth's crust), the 330,000,000 cubic miles of ocean water, even if we were to view it all alone from a small raft in mid-ocean, nevertheless represents a tiny entity in earth's immensity. M. Grant Gross states in *Oceanography*: "Geophysicists studying the physics of the earth, or geochemists investigating the earth's chemistry, consider the earth to consist of concentric shells, each shell having a distinctive chemical and physical composition. When viewed from this perspective, the earth's metallic core and the rocks of the mantle constitute 99.6 percent of its mass. The rocks of the continents and ocean basins, the oceans, and the atmosphere, amount to only 0.4 percent, of which the ocean and atmosphere are only a very small fraction. Thus in terms of the earth as a whole, the oceans constitute an insignificant fraction of its mass —a thin film of water on a nearly smooth sphere."

Perhaps, if iron is the great mass at earth's center, and since iron and its chief alloy, steel, make humanity's present state of civilization possible, our planet should be called "iron," instead of "earth." On the other hand, Leon Bertin has suggested: "Earth is a singularly inapt name for a planet covered over 71 percent of its surface by oceans." A better name, for a splash-down visitor from space who gets a planetary panorama surface view, would be, simply, "water." Bill Laas expressed this beautifully in his *The Water in Your Life*: "If invaders from another world really are hovering about in those flying saucers, looking us over, the most astonishing sight to meet their eyes—if they have eyes—must be *plain water*. So commonplace on earth, so abundant that we take the oceans for granted, liquid water is a cosmic miracle."

Most of us, even when we go to the seashore, still retain the ancient continental concept that our world is chiefly land. Modern transoceanic travel, shifting to rapid jet flights in the air, goes far to continue this misconception. We fly more and more swiftly, as jet speeds increase, from earthport to earthport (mistakenly we began calling these launching pads "airports"—which soon *will* exist, but up in the sky).

Our jet planes, and the rockets which one day soon will succeed them, fly through the atmosphere, which is a great sea of air far more immense than all of the planet's surface oceans. But don't be trapped into therefore suggesting that our spaceship home should be called the Planet Air, for much of the sea of air is also *water*. "When you go to the window and see some sort of weather," meteorologist James G. Edinger has reported in *Watching for the Wind*, "chances are you're looking at just water . . . water in a great variety of forms: raindrops, snowflakes, cloud droplets, and ice crystals. Most of the 'weather' we see is water in its gaseous form, water vapor. Typically, we are surrounded by water, invisible gaseous water. Were it visible, we would be able to see nothing else. We'd be like fish in a turbid sea, unable to see anything but our gaseous environment." Oh, yes, our planet should be called "water."

The oceans combine with the atmosphere to form an immense, interacting *tourbillon,* in human terms a sort of potter's wheel—what Dr. Columbus Iselin, of Woods Hole Oceanographic Institution, has called "a huge heat engine in which currents, winds and weather are only a means of dissipating the energy received from the sun." To which Hawthorne Daniel and Francis Minot, in *The Inexhaustible Sea*, have added: "The winds, of course, are vital in the operation of this 'heat engine,' but equally important are the less apparent currents of the sea. There is no simple pattern to the movements of the sea. Waves and tides and currents, familiar though the words may be to us, are far more complex than first glance might suggest. Every storm at sea—every submarine earthquake—every volcanic eruption that has taken place beneath the surface of the ocean—has etched a kind of record in the waves. They have appeared—and passed—and disappeared. As new storms and quakes occur, they appear again."

The romantic poet forever clashes with the informed scientist. "Light as any wind that blows," Tennyson repeated the untruth most of us believe. But Frank Lane, in a terrifying compilation called *The Elements Rage,* began his study of hurricanes, the most destructive of all windstorms, by explaining: "Air is surprisingly heavy, a cubic yard of it—a large bathtubful—weighs two pounds. It is the very heaviness of air which accounts for the tremendous force it exerts when it is moving at high speed."

In 1492, Christopher Columbus sailed into the very eye of the region that gives birth to hurricanes, at the height of the hurricane season, when today's meteorologists are busily giving ladies' names to the storms as they follow one another at an average rate of eight a year (in the Atlantic—but up to twenty-eight annually in the Pacific). After describing the balmy weather of this potential hell's kitchen as "always like May," Columbus landed gracefully on Guanahani, later called Watling, and presently San Salvador, on October 12. Or possibly he landed on Cat Island, to the northwest. We'll probably never know for sure.

The naked natives who received the resplendently dressed discoverer believed that a miracle had taken place and that these future destroyers of their innocent way of life had arrived from heaven. The miracle, of course, was how the three tiny caravels had made it at all. The best supposition I've met is stated by Thomas Helm in *Hurricanes: Weather at Its Worst:* "It is possible that 1492 was a freak year in which no hurricanes blew, or perhaps the divine hand of Providence steered them around the little fleet."

Not until 1503 did the great admiral encounter his first hurricane; he wrote in his diary (one trusts somewhat later): "For nine days I was lost without hope of life; eyes never beheld the seas so high, angry and covered by foam. The wind not only prevented our progress, but offered no opportunity to run behind any headland for shelter; hence we were forced to keep out in this bloody ocean, seething like a pot on a hot fire. Never did the sky look more terrible."

A present-day oceangoing yachtsman, Weston Martyr, could have been describing some other aspect of Columbus' encounter, only this was 434 years later: "You cannot breathe with a hurricane blowing full in your face. You cannot see, either; the impact on your eyeballs of spray and rain flying at over 100 miles an hour makes seeing quite impossible. You hear nothing except the scream and the booming of the wind, which drowns even the thunder of the breaking seas."

This Cerberus creature made of violent winds is, like the monster that guards the gates of hell, many-headed. Like the hurricanes of the Atlantic, which get their name from the Arawak Indian *hurakan,* there are typhoons in the Pacific, baguios in the Philippines, and willy-willies off Australia. These most destructive of all winds are created over tropical waters—we still do not fully understand how or why—and may grow to occupy more than half a million square miles of whirling oversea tempestuous destructiveness.

How fast do the mightiest winds blow? Typhoons and hurricanes beget some of the fastest, which might blow up to 125 miles per hour. There are famous European winds—the mistral, foehn, and bora, which attain as great a velocity, but they blow in a more restricted area and thus are not as damaging as the vast overseas maelstroms. At the top of Mount Washington, New Hampshire, the record is 231 miles per hour.

Aubrey de Selincourt, introducing a handsome selection of sea pieces in *The Book of the Sea,* says, "We have become romantic about the sea, as about other elemental forces in nature and in ourselves. We even pretend, some of us, that we love it, though no true seaman would ever admit to such an absurdity. The ancient attitude to the sea was eminently practical. There the thing was, a familiar presence; it had to be crossed, sometimes for one reason or another—worse luck; and though the end of the trip might bring pleasure or profit, the trip itself was disagreeable and dangerous, a necessary nuisance."

The ancestral hatred not simply of life at sea but of the sea itself as a living thing, an all-wise enemy, was expressed by a character in a play by Eugene O'Neill that won a 1922 Pulitzer Prize, *Anna Christie*. I remember Greta Garbo—graceful, gawky, lovely—in *Anna Christie,* her first "talking" movie, in 1929. Old Chris, her father (George Martin), continually grumbled throughout the play against "dat ole davil sea," sometimes speaking of "her" as a woman, and at other times as a god: "Dat ole davil sea make dem sailor fellar crazy fools with her dirty tricks," and "Ay tank now it ain't no use fight with sea. No man dat live going to beat her, py yingo!" or "No! Dat ole davil sea, she ain't God!"

Garbo, as Anna Christie, expressed the other aspect of this hate-love dichotomy—not the feelings of the Jack-tar or lobscouser or *loup de mer* who goes to sea, but of the woman who waits ashore for her matelot's return. Looking out into the fog after she'd come to sea for the first time, Anna said, "It's like I'd come home after a long visit away some place . . . I feel clean, somehow—like you feel yust after you've took a bath. And I feel happy for once—yes, honest!—happier than I ever have been anywhere before!"

Anna, speaking for O'Neill, who, like Richard Dana, Jr., at the time of writing his great sea classic had actually spent only two years at sea, exclaimed, "Everything's so different from anything I ever come across before . . . Gee, I wouldn't have missed it for nothing. I never thought living on ships was so different from land. Gee, I'd yust love to work on it, honest I would, if I was a man. I don't wonder you always been a sailor."

Thus the zany, mad passion that will not let a person go, once he has experienced—or perhaps one should say been experienced by—the sea. *Anna Christie* gave Garbo a brand-new kind of fame. O'Neill had had the sense to insist upon a Scandinavian—for surely these descendants of the Vikings will always carry more of the sea in their veins than the rest of us more agricultural descendants. It is also interesting that at the time O'Neill wrote this and two of his other Pulitzer Prize plays, he was living most unhappily with his second wife, Agnes Kaufman—there is perhaps something about this tempestuous and uncertain relationship that is comparable to the sailor's affair with the sea; it begat much of the dramatist's finest work.

The utmost expression of seaitude, for the human terrestrial animal, was put into words by the Polish seaman Teodor Jozef Konrad Korzeniowski, who after twenty years of seafaring that took him over the Planet Water's windiest routes—he sailed twelve times around the Cape of Good Hope, twice around Cape Horn—turned author and, under the abbreviated name Joseph Conrad, wrote more than two dozen novels, short stories, and essays (more than half his works) about the sea. His friend André Gide said of him that no one ever lived life more fiercely and "no one has subjected life to as enduring, as aware, and as wise a transmutation into art." Conrad expressed the naked and alone experience that is a man's only honest approach to the sea: In *Heart of Darkness* he embodied the solitary approach of man to the oceanic immensity: "We live, as we dream—alone." But in *Typhoon,* he encompassed a vastly greater emotion that is perhaps the deepest passion man is capable of: "I received the instantaneous impression that the ship could not live for another hour in such a raging sea"; angrily, he went on to personify the sea as a living creature "that brings out the inner worth of a man, the edge of his temper and the fiber of his stuff, the quality of his resistance and the secret truth of his pretenses," then, finally, "the most amazing wonder of the deep is its unfathomable cruelty."

These are the words of a lover talking about, even rhapsodizing about, his great love. Few verses about human love ever achieve a comparable immense agony. Even Shakespeare's enigmatic and lovely sonnets to the mysterious dark lady, or maybe lad, and Solomon's song of love to a nubile maiden do not approach the depth of passion expressed by the great lovers of the sea, or, more exactly, of those greatly loved by the sea. Even when reading about it, one becomes involved in a deep vicarious-visceral experiencing of what the sea can do to a human being who dares to become deeply involved and infatuated with it. Without willing purposefully, participation in the greatest possible amour for a mere mortal, *the sea relation,* has always been an act of great human courage.

Conrad, again, expressed the final fearful feel, sound, and smell of this being taken by the sea as "the real thing come at last. It was something formidable and swift, like the sudden smashing of a vial of wrath. It seemed to explode all around the

ship with an overpowering concussion and a rush of great water
. . . A furious gale attacks a man like a personal enemy, tries to
grasp his limbs, fastens upon his mind, seeks to rout his very
spirit out of him."

"Man against nature" is a misused description of the peculiar
relationship between human beings and the forces of nature
that can actually be better expressed as "man *with* nature."
The vigor and virility of the encounter means fully as much to
a woman as to a man when she, too, experiences the paroxysmal
excitement of the strength of the sea. It begins, actually, in a
very small way, when we are quite young. I have seen lovely little girls proving the wonder of this kind of nature-thing in
mini-pattern when at a tiny age they start jumping rope while
their friends swing the jump rope. Today we've stretched the
rope into an invasion of space, where human endurance and experience take on the orgasmic encounter of the very cosmos
itself. Norman Cousins suggested in *Present Tense: An American Editor's Odyssey,* that poetess Marianne Moore should be
encapsulated and sent out into space as a member of a future
rocket crew, so that she can express, in poetic terms, how the
journey into space is, or should be, a sublime experience. "The
selection of astronauts ought not to be confined to men in the
military or in technology. Why not poets, philosophers, or theo-
logians who have demonstrated their capacity to think crea-
tively, and who have some convictions about the nature of
man?" Into space, as when we go to sea, the best journey is, of
course, if we are to be the complete and only experient, to be
made alone, "all, all alone," as was Coleridge's unfortunate
mariner.

Hurricanes are truly "against nature" in that they turn
"counter" about their maelstrom centers (the eye that is so deceptively peaceful) in contrast to the clockwise direction of the
ordinary wind currents, directed in great part by the earth's
turning. In the northern hemisphere, the *force centrifuge com-
posée* pushes everything to the *right,* and in the southern hemisphere to the *left.* Gaspard Gustave de Coriolis explained the
phenomenon in 1835, and it has been called after him ever
since. In an *empty* landscape, a snow-covered steppe, it is suggested that we would wander in the same way, drawn by the

mysterious great primal force of the Planet Water's turning. The invention/discovery of Jean Bernard Léon Foucault exemplifies both the fact that the earth turns and proof as to which direction; a golden ball hanging in the entranceway to the United Nations proves by slow pendulum motion the wonder of earth's west-to-east rotation (anti-clockwise) at somewhat over 1,000 miles per hour, thus creating the diurnal marvel of recurring dawns and twilights at approximate 12-hour intervals.

Tornadoes are more violent than hurricanes, but within extremely limited pinpoint areas, and there is perhaps no experience more unimaginable than to be seized by this whirlwind and carried outrageously far up into the sky. Waterspouts are simple tornadoes that have gone to sea. And surely there is no more extraordinary sight than this curious funnel, or *twister,* viewed from a safe distance. "The spout was dead to windward and bearing down upon us with fearful speed," James J. Wait described the waterspout overwhelming of a vessel in which he was sailing in the mid-Atlantic in the 1880's. "Each man almost involuntarily secured himself as best he might, and in an instant more the waterspout was upon us—with a roaring and bellowing as of a thousand demons, the cannonlike crash of breaking spars, the snapping of cordage, and the rending of timber. Then an irresistible rush of water poured down upon the deck, seemingly with the concussions of Niagara; it bore me back against the wheel casing and held me as in a vise, tore off my shirt and shoes and pressed with such a weight upon my chest that my eyeballs almost started from their sockets."

Seaman Wait recovered, but this probably was the greatest experience of his entire life—the strange joy-agony, adventure-misadventure relationship that operates when the sea takes its violent pleasure of a human being. I was too young to remember World War I, but let me somewhat transmogrify the Yank song into "How you goin' to keep them down on the farm, once they've been had by the sea?" Berlin will understand.

If you have ever seen a child's balloon or plastic blown-up seahorse go drifting out to sea, while its parents usually make up their minds, sensibly, to let the toy go rather than try to retrieve it, then you know this eternal reaching out of the sea for humans and other land creatures. Young boys in small plastic rafts are more liable nowadays than ever before—there are more plastic rafts—to drift off to sea and disappear forever.

But the sea prefers, apparently, to do things in grand-opera fashion. Nothing in the distant oceanic past could have been more dramatic than the storm that struck the Italian steamship *Michelangelo* in the mid-Atlantic during April, 1966. Passengers later said that tables, chairs, and smashed glass went flying around the public rooms, where they huddled, terrified by the sound of the continuous thunderous banging of the angry waves on the vessel's outsides. Captain Giuseppe Soletti called it "the most severe storm I've experienced in 41 years at sea." One passenger informed his companions that he was going back up to his stateroom on the boat deck. "I have got a front window, and I'm going up there to watch," he told them.

His stateroom was 70 feet above the sea, but as the ship pierced through a trough in the sea, a 50-foot wave struck, smashing windows along the boat deck—the most expensive staterooms on board—and drowning the passenger who'd gone up for his front-window view. He obviously already had a predestined terminal rendezvous with the sea, comparable to any classical encounter with the old sea deities in classical times, a genuine *appointment in suo mare*.

Safe in the New York harbor, another passenger exclaimed to reporters, "They were not waves, they were a moving mountain range," and added, "The next cabin I reserve will be a New Hampshire log cabin." I don't think so. This was the biggest happening in that passenger's life, and he'll inevitably go back to sea, to the sea that is always waiting for another one. Perhaps next time for him.

There is a close consistency in the circulations of the atmospheric winds and the oceans' currents. In a study of *The Ocean River*, the Gulf Stream, first of the oceans' vast pulmonary and venae cavae veins to be recognized as a part of the earth's great circulatory system of waters, Henry Chapin and F. G. Walton Smith suggested the possible relationship between "the prevalence or scarcity of the greatest of all our cyclonic storms and the polar fronts; but certainly there is such a relationship, which is gradually becoming more thoroughly explored. It is even possible that there may yet be charted indirect but consistent relationships between the fluctuations of the Gulf Stream and the incidence of hurricanes storming above its waters from the Caribbean. But these violent storms of late summer and fall roaring along our Atlantic coasts, and occasionally following the Ocean River clear to the English Channel, are important manifestations of the climate engine of the North Atlantic."

"Gulf Stream" is at least in part a misnomer (I prefer the combination Floribbean Current), for the entire ocean-river thing is the North Atlantic gyre. Off New England, the northward motion is a hundred miles wide, the equal of 700 Amazon rivers or 9,000 Mississippis, but extremely diffuse with almost innumerable unrecognizable branches. Chapin and Smith surmised that the Atlantic "on five separate occasions during a period between one and two billion years ago, spread itself across Europe and Asia and across a great part of northern America, and receded during the intervening times of mountain-building to become a much more restricted ocean than it is today."

David Ericson and Goesta Wollin remind us that "there is not a sizable area of any continent that has not at some time been beneath the sea. The sediments laid down during these floodings of large parts of the continents are the pages of the book in which paleontologists read the history of the development of life on our planet."

Ben Franklin made an excellent map in 1770 of the "Gulph Stream" (after a voyage to England on which he dropped string over the side of the vessel just as he'd once sent a string up into the heavens on a kite to "discover" the fact of electricity in the atmosphere) in order to help his colonial sailing compeers to make the best use of its flowing current. Alan Villiers, perhaps the finest student of the North Atlantic (and a leading authority and personal experient of all the planet's oceans) considers this Franklin anecdote to be spurious. In his *Wild Ocean,* he suggested that anybody who decided to sail the North Atlantic should have known all about the Gulf Stream and how to make use of its strength on eastward voyages and to avoid it when westing, surely at least a century *before* Franklin's famous voyage. Just listen to Villiers' 1957 sailor's yarn of this vast oceanic stream—"the subject of more speculation than any other movement of water anywhere in the world. Mariner, oceanographer and philosopher alike have added their laborious investigations into its behavior and idiosyncracies. More drift bottles, oceanographers' nets, scientific instruments and thermometers have been thrown into it than into any other current anywhere. It has been the subject of the most intensive and long-continued investigation ever lavished on a marine subject. To a greater extent, it is still shrouded in mystery."

The latest investigation was in mid-1969 by the *Ben Franklin*, 48-foot submarine on a 30-day, 1,500-mile *drift*, conducted by forty-seven-year-old Swiss oceanographer Jacques Piccard, son of the sky-high, sea-deep explorer Auguste Piccard. They found few fish ("Perhaps the stream's turbulence scares life away"), were attacked twice by swordfish, saw a 30-foot jellyfish, and Piccard reported "a small squid came and attached himself to the windowsill above my bed: we observed each other in complete tranquillity." The highlight of the journey was expressed by Piccard, with remarkable honesty: "The most spectacular thing we saw was the sun when we reopened the hatch."

The Gulf Stream is one of the five great surface gyres that are driven by the wind through the upper waters of the World Ocean—both this North Atlantic gyre and the one in the North Pacific move in a clockwise direction, directed by the Coriolis effect; the three Southern Hemisphere gyres, in the South Atlantic, the South Pacific and the Indian oceans, are driven counterclockwise. In *The Physical Geography of the Sea*, in 1855, hydrographer Matthew Maury was the first to call these the planet's arteries, comparing the circulation of the ocean waters to that of the human bloodstream.

Many of these surface ocean rivers—the Gulf, the Humboldt, the Benguela, the Kuroshio, the North Equatorial (9,000 miles long, this one)—are at least partway explored today. Meantime, we have learned that these might more properly be called the Planet Water's surface *veins*, since there are submarine undercurrent *arteries* flowing beneath them in counterdirections. The subterranean river beneath the Gulf Stream, moving southward in the North Atlantic, is an even mightier stream. Between these rivers of differing densities, salinity, and temperature occur internal waves that are more sizable than any ever seen between the sea's surface and the sky.

The Planet Water's deep arteries take their apparent primary force of motion at the polar latitudes, where the heavy sea water goes down, down, down to then invade equatorward and disturb the deepest bottoms of the seas along earth's more middle regions with motion. And the deep waters pump up—the expression is as enriching as the experience for sea life, upwellings—all over the mid-regions of the Planet Water. An opposite effect takes place, what one might call, with understanding, downgoes ("godowns" could be confused with an Oriental attic). Rachel Carson described the effect of upwelling on sea life: "Wherever it occurs, it is responsible for a profusion of life . . . Upwelling sets off the old, familiar biological chain: salts, diatoms, copepods, herring . . . the upwelling bringing up the nutrient salts from the deeper layers." Of downgoes, Ericson and Wollin noted that there are only two regions where important quantities of water sink from the surface to the abyss. "One of these is in the North Atlantic south of the southern tip of Greenland, the other is in the South Atlantic around Antarctica and, particularly, east of the Palmer Peninsula."

For the sea sightseer, it is unfortunate that one cannot view these super-Niagara reverse motions of water (the viewer would be instantaneously obliterated or swallowed up, or down, by the fluvial view). (There's also a similar lovely super-Niagara falls where the Hudson River Submarine Canyon escarps over the edge of the Atlantic deep.) But upwellings and downgoes are not the only oceanic phenomena not to be observed. There are two fantastic areas where ships have sometimes apparently been obliterated without trace. Some day, a logical explanation will be found, but for the present we must accept the sort of summation offered by John Godwin, the former Australian crime reporter in *This Baffling World*: first, of a North Atlantic Ocean "devil sea" where, "unlike their Japanese counterparts, American and British authorities have never officially admitted the existence of a 'Devil's Sea.' Nor are they ever likely to proclaim the area a 'Danger Zone.' But privately, both marine and aviation experts have confessed that they *may* be facing a phenomenon of environment rather than a chain of technical mishaps . . . in a portion of sea a rough square whose northern limits stretch between Bermuda and the Virginia coast, its southern boundary formed by the islands of

Cuba, Hispaniola and Puerto Rico. As far as researchers have been able to tally, some 60 ships and airplanes have sailed or flown into that 'void' and *have been swallowed up*." In the "Devil's Sea" off Japan, between 1950 and 1954, Godwin found that no fewer than nine ships vanished, "fair-sized coastal freighters with good engines and radio equipment." The area has been declared a danger zone, though nobody knows at all just what constitutes the danger. "There seems to be a definite parallel between that particular patch of the Pacific and the stretch of North Atlantic off the southeast coast of America." Godwin suggested: "However, the American 'sector' is unique as also a sky trap that swallows up airplanes as well as ships."

The loss of the U.S. nuclear submarine *Scorpion* during May, 1968, roughly 400 miles southwest of the island of São Miguel in the Azores, has of course already been too hastily attributed by alarmists to the "devil area" of the mysterious Bermuda Triangle. However, all indications are that its loss will ultimately be blamed on mechanical imperfections, as was the case of the *Thresher*, lost off Cape Cod in 1963; or the British submarine *Thetis*, lost in the Irish Sea in the same year; or the French submarine *Phoenix*, also lost in the same year off Indochina.

The loss of the submarine "begins" with some mechanical failure whereby the vessel begins to sink dangerously toward that point of no return (nuclear subs can go "safely" down only to about 1,500 feet), and, once past it, ultimately an implosion will occur, crushing vessel and crew. During May, 1968, when the *Scorpion* had not been heard from during a great Atlantic storm, veteran submariners suggested that first it could not send messages unless its 45-foot whip antenna could be raised above the ocean's surface, and also that any submarine running just below even the roughest of ocean *surface* seas would be in relatively calm waters.

There seems little reason to blame powerful submarine currents, for their flow would be, like the surface currents, of strong but relatively moderate velocity. Most oceanographers are still cautious in assaying the ocean-bottom currents. For example, Yale Professor Karl K. Turekian, in his *Oceans*, suggested that "observations of various kinds indicate the presence of currents on the bottom of some parts of the ocean that are strong enough to move sediments," which scarcely implies violent torrents likely to rip submarines to shreds: the pressure alone is sufficient to do this (the submarine implosion being the same sort of fearful experience, in reverse, as when your Midwestern home is suddenly "exploded" by the gigantic pressure of a tornado).

We know very little about the seas, actually. They are the vital bloodstream, obviously, of our planet. I like to think that our planet itself is "alive." Scientists—and poets too—are remarkably cautious about expressing themselves on this, and yet some form of "livingness" seems to appertain to every aspect of our curious spaceship that's so unlike anything else in the cosmos. Let me quote first the third-century B.C. geographer Salinus: "Our physicists assure us that the world is an animal which is formed of various members, that it is animated by breath and directed by intelligence. Now just as there is a vital force in our own bodies, so the depths of the sea are in a way the nostrils of the world: when the world breathes *in*, it lowers the level of the seas; when it breathes *out*, the sea levels rise again."

I'd hate to walk across the eyeball of a living giant, but I sense that maybe we all are doing exactly this, in Will and Ariel Durant's statement: "All the surface of the earth is a fluid form, and man moves upon it as insecurely as Peter walking on the waves to Christ." John Lear, assessing "the pulse of earth" for *Saturday Review* in 1969, came very close: "The pulsebeat of Planet Earth has not yet been counted; but a pulse *is* there: Several manifestations of it are regularly observed. A rhythmic throbbing in the magnetic shell enclosing the planet arises from the solar wind and has been detected by spaceships; within the magnetic sheath, earth's atmosphere expands and contracts with cyclic heating and cooling of the sun as day passes into night and into day again."

Most of this "living planet" lore is based upon *oceanic* investigation. And if the philosophers don't believe in a "living sea," the fact seems to be accepted generally by now that various forms of the more familiar kinds of life as we know it are assumed to have originated first in ancient seas, when amino acids learned how to link themselves into chains to form proteins. At some very early oceanic stage, the planet's seawater must have been a "cosmic soup" in which (this sounds very simply like what happens between mutually attracted ladies and gentlemen who encounter at any typical social gathering) "molecules presumably came together in increasing number and variety, sometimes merely colliding"—excuse it, please— "and separating, but at other times, *mirabile,* reacting with one another to produce combinations." In time, these chains of amino acid folks even learned to clothe themselves in membrane, and thus the first cells were born. Today's most elaborate societies of men, bees, or viruses may quite readily be explained as merely extensions and expansions of these ancestral cellular combinations of living civilizations. When any group goes out of balance with the rest, it is a "population explosion."

Research continually moves the date of life's probable origin on earth backward. During the fall of 1968 a Scripps Institution of Oceanography geologist, Dr. Albert E. J. Engel, seemed to have reached the ultimate birth time for the moment, when he announced the discovery of 3.5-billion-year-old fossil "remains" of the most primitive forms of life. His "ancestral remains" were not as large as Dr. Roy Chapman Andrews' fabulous dinosaur eggs, discovered in the Gobi Desert in 1923 by the "Missing Link" expedition. "We were looking at the first dinosaur eggs ever seen by a human being," Dr. Andrews later wrote modestly and fondly of them. But the dragon eggs had been laid by a relatively recent creature, some 70,000,000 years ago, in a bog or on dry land, whereas Dr. Engel's ancestral fossils were *fifty times older,* lived in the sea, and must represent creatures that were very close to the first offspring of the planet's first pregnancy—veritably vintage "in the beginning God created" vitality.

You can heft a dinosaur egg, if they'll let you, in the museum at Ulan Bator, Mongolia, or, less likely, at the American Museum of Natural History, in New York, and you can even think of the petrified little monster inside of it. But it is not as easy to get excited about Dr. Engel's ever so much more important and also ever so much older sea-creature fossil remains, because they're too microbic, too unimaginably tiny: the largest is a mere 39-millionths of an inch in diameter! What kind of grandparental family tree or ancestry is this? Greek mythology dealt with ancestral giants. Science gives us genuine mini-midgets.

You can observe these true ancestors of ours only by using a special microscope that magnifies 50,000 times! Nevertheless, Dr. Engel's tiny bits of, face it, our ancestral life, found in the South African Transvaal, are among the oldest chips of lumber likely ever to be wittled from our family tree of life. I hope that Scripps Institution will someday put them on exhibition for visitors to view through the appropriate microscopes required.

Where have we got since? This is a story of water, not of man, and so it is life in the sea that concerns us, rather than an attempt to run down and examine which ancient lines of micro-creatures may have ancestored mankind. But it is *all* a story of sea, all the way, since all of us simply live in the continuing land colony founded by our ancestors who came ashore so very long ago. All the way, our history remains a sea story, a water journal.

To begin with, most of the seas are *still* very empty of life. The Sahara Desert contains three enormous utter ergs that represent the utmost in terrestrial lack of living, areas of sandy emptiness. Even the camel caravans used to go around them. In the central ocean regions, as much as 90 percent of the ocean sea is barren, totally devoid of life, a sort of "wet desert." When you go to look at it (also searching an "oasis"—I cannot imagine what such a reverse might be like, especially if it were a *miraged* oasis over a wet desert, most mirages usually representing wet images over dry, ergic emptiness), you'll find it by the elemental and simple experience of color. For example, John Bardach, in his *Harvest of the Sea,* found that "water color is a good indicator of relative fertility. That, by and large, the bluer the sea the more barren it is has been known to fishermen from time immemorial. Carbon-14 measurements of photosynthesis have borne this out and have provided exact figures. Parts of the blue Mediterranean and the almost inky Sargasso Sea, for instance, had assimilation rates of around 0.05 g C/m^2 (per) day, whereas the corresponding figure for temperate and colder seas were ten times or more higher."

"The color of the sea is affected by clouds, waves and the altitude of the sun," Charles C. Cotter stated in *Physical Geography of the Oceans,* and added the suggestion that the "color" in shallow water is usually caused simply by the color of bottom sediments. For those who fly from New York City to various

West Indies islands this is especially evident. "In some regions," Dr. Cotter, a geographer at the Welsh College of Advanced Technology, Cardiff, found, "the color of the suspended material has a marked effect on the color of the sea. The Yellow Sea is a typical example. Here, the yellow mud brought to the sea by the great Hwang Ho River gives a vivid hue to parts of the Yellow Sea. The seawater off the mouths of the mighty Amazon is distinctive in color. The brown or reddish color to be seen in this vicinity is due to the lateritic mud which is brought to the sea by this river."

Professor Cotter detailed that "the olive-green color of polar seas is due to diatoms; the reddish color of the Red Sea and the Gulf of California, at certain seasons, to the presence of numerous red-colored dinoflagellates."

In the remaining 10 percent of the seas (nondesert) live the greatest proportion of the Planet Water's children. More than 80 percent of *all living creatures* on earth are at home in the sea. But for the comfortable American housewife managing her neat household, here is an added fact: "The space on the planet inhabited by drifting and swimming life exceeds that occupied by all other kinds of life in water and on land," R. E. Coker stated, in *This Great and Wide Sea.* "The great part of the organic world lives adrift as plankton."

We have only known about *plankton* for a bit more than a century. It is one of the pleasantest-sounding words that I've ever met. Victor Hensen of Kiel finally got around to naming plankton, in 1887 (from the Greek word meaning "wandering"). Cornell biologist La Mont C. Cole has warned that present pollution practices are threatening the lives of the planktonic diatoms that produce 70 percent of the Planet Water's oxygen by photosynthesis, "poisoning the marine diatoms and thus bringing disaster upon ourselves." Dr. Edward D. Goldberg, of the Scripps Institution of Oceanography, has estimated that the United States is responsible for around one-third to one-half of the contaminants thrown today into the air and into the sea.

Captain Jacques-Yves Cousteau writes about householders beneath the sea who seem (to me) exactly like householders in a human suburb-terrestrial environ: "I saw a pronounced squarish shape, angular objects alien to the sea: this must be some man-made thing. . . . Lying in the mud was an almost perfect three-by-five rectangle of white pebbles. An enclosure like that had to have an owner. Soon I spied him: dug into the bottom in one of the corners with only two large eyes showing was a pink-and-gray octopus. . . . I thought about this octopus 'ranch.' There were no pebbles within hundreds of yards of the stockade. Why such a heavy transportation job just to fence in a barren yard?" In the cuttlefish world, the octopus was apparently marking off the edge of his property, just as a human occupant of suburban real estate builds a fence. Both show the possibility of superconstruction of Stonehenges and Giza pyramids, made of gigantic rocks quarried and hauled incredible distances, usually by water, though we've not yet found any submarine octoputal pyramids or temples.

Freedom to move about is a most dangerous thing, surely, to the "propertied" mind. The drifting world of planktonic freedom represents the farthest out and the simplest escape of all. It is almost impossible for the limited human mind to grasp, perhaps mostly because of our tree and cave background. In the open seas, *there is no home*, no safety, no place to hide. It is as though a human automobile driver faced opposition traffic which might approach from any side—alongside, beneath, above, in front, or behind. All life at sea, the vast living tide, is a seeking after somebody else to beat up and devour. Unless one is a tiger shark, the pelagic depths are not attractive as a place of "freedom"—for even to visit them would be like being set forth on an eight-sided dinner plate awaiting one's devourer.

"Life below the surface is a savage and unrelenting struggle for existence," Dr. J. Gordon Cook, Fellow of the Royal Institute of Chemists, has stated in *The World of Water*. "With no lush vegetation on which to feed, the animals are obliged to eat each other. In this daring, slashing warfare of the underwater jungle the race is to the swift and the battle to the strong. Few animals on land can match the ferocious power of the hunting shark; few four-legged creatures could outpace the big blue marlin or the tuna as they speed through the water at sixty miles an hour or more.

"Life in the ocean is a carnivorous bureaucracy, built on a foundation of humble algae and rising through a hierarchy of increasing savagery towards the bosses—the sharks that attack almost any other living thing that swims across their path." Of the lack of privacy or hiding place, Dr. Cook found that all fish must be "for ever on the watch for food or enemies. So far as is known, they do not sleep, in the sense that land animals do. Fishes have no eyelids; they cannot close their eyes and rest, but must be constantly on the watch if they are to survive."

"Man has lost that sense of the full awfulness of the sea which aboriginally belongs to it. Consider the subtleness of the sea; how its most dreaded creatures glide under water, unapparent for the most part," Herman Melville ruminated in *Moby Dick*. "Consider, once more, the universal cannibalism of the sea, all whose creatures prey upon each other, carrying on eternal war since the world began."

Captain Cousteau reported that "the frightened pearl fish retreats inside the intestine of the sea cucumber (a kind of sea urchin). It does not enter the mouth. The pearl fish places its tail in the anus of the host and wiggles in backward. . . . The pearl fish must spend most of the day in the cucumber and go out at night to make its living."

The most cannibal sea of all is the Eastern Tropical Pacific. "This ocean is the *alive* ocean," Wesley Marx paeans the richness of its life in *The Frail Ocean*, "flaunting its fertility like the green parrot jungles of Central America. A key to this fertility lies in the constant winds that move the ocean in great criss-crossing currents: The Humboldt, the North Equatorial current, the South Equatorial current, the South Equatorial countercurrent, and the California current. Upwelling thrives amid this perpetual motion by replacing a depleted surface with cool, nutrient-rich waters from thousand-foot depths. (The nearness of the Equator is deceptive when one plunges a hand into this coolness.) The recharged waters sustain pastures of plankton, which, in turn, nourish swimming crabs, anchovy, anchovetas, sardines, and other small fish and crustacea. Sharks, sailfish, bonito, and mackerel all stalk the tiny predators of plankton. One hunter moves in schools as thick as buffalo herds, as swift as squadrons of waterfowl. Once spied by a school of sleek yellowfin tuna, the small fish may rush to the surface in a frantic attempt to escape their environment, only to be spied by seabirds that drop like white darts. Amid the

splashing frenzy, the Eastern Tropical Pacific once more cele-
brates its fertility. It is this fertility that attracts high-seas
fishing fleets and triggers one of the fiercest, most relentless battles for supremacy in man's predatory history."

The teeming sea life is classified into the floating plankton,
the swimming nekton, and the seafloor-creeping benthos. Our
first acquaintance is, of course, with the nekton fishes and mammals who leap above the surface. First of all, the flying fish:
Thor Heyerdahl, in his story of the epic journey of the raft
Kon-Tiki across the South Pacific, wrote, "We could see them
glittering like a rain of projectiles which shot from the water
and flew in a straight line till their power of flight was ex-
hausted and they vanished beneath the surface." The cook's
first duty each morning was to gather the flying fish, a half
dozen or more, that had landed on the raft during the night.

The favorite sea person of any seafaring human is, of course,
the dolphin, the great whale's small cousin, the cetacean who's
reputed to have so often rescued drowning men by pushing
them ashore. René Heurant wrote:

> Dolphin, timeless racer of the sea,
> O save me from the ocean's deeps.

Dolphins particularly enjoy traveling in schools or shoals. "A
porpoise does not merely show his fin," Wesley Marx said. "He
can vault clear of the ocean, all the time revolving in the air.
The spinner porpoise can do this in perfect accord with a thousand of his own kind, and the ocean suddenly resembles a stadium in which athletes are performing a thousand simultane-
ous somersaults." Captain Cousteau has described "a flying
phalanx of dolphins spreading before us to either rim of the
ocean. I tried to estimate how many there were. At a given minute, there were about a thousand out of the water on jumps
that averaged three seconds. For one in the air, there must have
been nineteen in the water. Perhaps twenty thousand dolphins
formed the living reef. The massive crescent of foam and flying
bodies, glistening in the sun, moved along the Hadramaut
Coast with no apparent destination, given up to some titanic
joy." Elsewhere, noting their smiling (fixed) lips and shining

eyes, he commented: "They are gregarious and, more than that, *social*. There are probably more porpoises in the sea than there are men on earth."

In an almost devotional book, *The Dolphin Smile*, about the charms of the boulevardier of the sea ("twenty-nine centuries of dolphin lore"), Eleanore Devine and Martha Clark said of him, "Wherever you see him—whether he's battering a shark to death, saving a man or tossing a ball—he'll be smiling. His co-workers smile back. And in marine-life exhibits from coast to coast, audiences turn beatific watching him. That his smile is structural makes it no less beguiling. It seems to say, 'I'm on your side, I like you.'" Ernest Hemingway had his old man in *The Old Man and the Sea* exclaim, "They are good. They play and make jokes and love one another. They are our brothers like the flying fish." And Melville said: "Their appearance is generally hailed with delight by the mariner. They are accounted a lucky omen. If you can withstand three cheers at beholding these vivacious fish, then heaven help ye."

A brief additional note on dolphins: Their horizontal "mammal" tail makes possible their "water walking," using it as, well, feet or ballet slippers. Dolphins "walk on their tails" on the surface of a pool, as proud as any vaudeville performers throughout history. I have been splashed by them at many carnivals and fairs, from their big canvas pools, and sensed their roguish pleasure in coming down with a great splash.

Of the so-called Seven Seas—the Arctic, North and South Atlantic and Pacific, Indian, and Southern—the richest in living creatures is the last, which is also called the Antarctic. This is the true Ocean Sea—and all the others are in fact merely arms of it which stretch northward to embrace the terrestrial continents. Here are the great marine-meadow sea-pastures of microscopic plankton, often served up as thick as soup or oatmeal, and browsed over by the earth's biggest animals, herds of giant blue whales who may grow up to a prodigious length of 100 feet and get to weigh up to 150 tons without watching or weight-worrying. They graze as amiably in contented family groups (pods) as though they were immense supercows (herds) gone to sea. Here is the extreme expanse and expression of true oceanitude, to be visited and observed by the human sightseer who wishes to get to know and acquire some feeling of the vast sea's total reality and omniscience.

I have not yet visited the Antarctic Ocean, but find its fascination overwhelming: here at the ends of the earth, "far to the south, in the 'roaring forties' and on beyond them in such waters as lie below Cape Horn, an almost ceaseless gale forever blows from West to East," Hawthorne Daniel and Francis Minot describe it. "Driving on around the world with no land mass to interrupt its progress, this almost never-ending gale builds up a steady sequence of great waves that are unmatched elsewhere in the world."

Here lives the king of all beasts, the mighty whale. Like ourselves, he is a mammal, but unlike the descendants of those creatures who emerged from the sea some 400,000,000 years ago to remain terrestrial, the ancestors of whales and porpoises returned to the deep some 50,000,000 years ago, giving up hind legs altogether and turning the fore pair into flippers, with their wagging tail spread out into propulsive flukes. Fish have vertical tails, as most of their swimming is from side to side. Sea *animals*, on the other hand, must frequently surface to breathe, and so their tails are horizontal, to provide swift vertical propulsion. In the case of the sperm whale, this of course becomes superpropulsion, for this giant cetacean regularly "sounds" to depths of 3,000 feet or more—enduring pressures up to 1,000 pounds to the square inch—remaining as long as an hour or more before resurfacing in a tremendous jet lunge. Captain Cousteau has described this living-fountain effect: "I turned and saw an eruption as large as the *Arc de Triomphe* a few hundred feet away and heard a loud, splashy boom." Just before, his companions had seen a 60-foot sperm whale leaping straight up into the air, its tail clearing the water by 15 feet. Cousteau suggested that the leap might be part of the sperm whale's daily feeding ordeal of descending into the deeps in search of giant squid. If the squid appeared to be winning, in one of these superencounters between the underwater supergiants (*Architeuthis princeps* sometimes has tentacles 27 feet long!), and the whale were running short of breath, he'd be all the more eager to burst surfaceward at jet speed. No wonder he spurts abovewater in such a tremendous water display!

In *The Cruise of the Cachalot,* Frank Bullen told how, hearing a violent commotion overside in the vicinity of Sumatra's chain of active volcanoes, he thought he might be about to witness the birth of a new one. Instead, focusing his night glasses on the troubled spot, he beheld "a very large sperm whale locked in deadly conflict with a cuttle-fish, or squid, almost as large as himself, whose interminable tentacles seemed to enlace the whole of his great body. The head of the whale especially seemed a perfect network of writhing arms—naturally, I suppose, for it appeared as if the whale had the tail part of the mollusc in his jaws, and, in a businesslike, methodical way, was sawing through it.

"By the side of the black columnar head of the whale appeared the head of the great squid, as awful an object as one could well imagine even in a fevered dream. . . . All around the combatants were numerous sharks, like jackals around a lion, ready to share in the feast."

Few of us will get to visit the Antarctic World Ocean. Instead, we can see an unbelievable "tame" whale in an increasing number of aquaria or the wonderful new make-believe whale (90 feet, 500 tons) diving from the roof of the Hall of Ocean Life at the American Museum of Natural History in New York City.

Whales, the splendiferous returned-to-water giant mammals who have found the seas the best environment and atmosphere in which to bring up their children, like elephants, are attractive to us partly or even especially because of their sheer immensity and the skilled delicacy with which they maneuver so massively about.

Americans continued to pursue whales for their oil until the 1920's. The discovery of petroleum a half-century earlier at last finished off this cruelest of all hunting industries. It is interesting that the last Norwegian whaleship went south in 1967–68. At the end of that voyage, they sold all their cargo of frozen whale *beef* (it has the consistency of bovine beef, but the taste of sardine—ugh, a difficult juxtaposition for conservative taste expectations) in England, but not a drop of their whale oil was disposed of.

For most of us the whaling industry ended in 1851, in the concluding passage of Herman Melville's *Moby Dick,* when "the great white one" sounded and carried Captain Ahab, wrapped afoul in the harpoon rope, below with him. Melville's whale book is surprisingly like Richard Wagner's god sagas. Both are magnificent, but must be taken with (1) an immense dose of sea salts or (2) the holy water of total acceptance. It is interesting that Melville wrote this finest classic of man versus whale after only four years of working aboard whalers and beachcombing (twice as long as the two-year apprenticeships of Dana and O'Neill before they wrote their sea masterpieces). "Both the romanticized travelogues with their blend of fact and fiction and the novels [of Melville] were the inspiration for all future American writing on the South Seas," Ernest S. Dodge, director of the Peabody Museum of Salem, Massachusetts, stated in his somewhat acerbic *New England and the South Seas.* "This peculiar type of fiction and fact blended so that it is almost impossible to separate one from the other." Noting that some of Melville's finest passages came from the original accounts of others, Dr. Dodge called special attention to the great final scene of Valhallahood "where the great white whale sends Ahab and the *Pequod* to the bottom; this came largely from the little book by Owen Chase of Nantucket on the sinking of the whaleship *Essex.*"

Narration at second hand has often given us the best means of vicariously experiencing. William Shakespeare, who probably *never* left England even for a brief weekend round trip across the British Channel, nevertheless made ever so many Continental and make-believe places more real for us than many "were-there" writers.

There are other ways of vicariously experiencing at second hand someone else's encounter with nature. For example, rather than personally enduring a great storm at sea from a slippery deck, we can visit the Tait Gallery and see *Snow Storm,* the great water color that J. M. W. Turner created, at the advanced age of sixty-six years, after having had himself bound, like Odysseus when he wished to hear the bewitching voices of the Sirens, "to the mast to observe the storm; I was lashed *for four hours,* and did not expect to escape, but I felt bound to record it if I did." This invited furious flagellation toward aesthetic interpretation of violence gives the viewer the remarkable chance not only to see a great masterpiece but also to become a part of the great storm at sea, while standing in the serenity of a picture gallery.

The orcas, or killer whales, are bloodthirsty distant cousins of whales and porpoises. Their special liking is the tongue of cousin whale. "Wolves of the sea that hunt in packs," Roy Chapman Andrews called them. "Armed with four rows of tremendous teeth, they will literally devour a whale alive." He told of personally observing a pack of killers attacking a gray whale, twice their size, when one killer "dashed up at full speed, forced its head into the whale's mouth by pressing against the lips, and ripped out great hunks of the soft, spongy tongue. Other killers were tearing at the throat and belly while the poor creature rolled in agony."

Wherever man has gone to sea, he has always encountered an ultimate enemy, the shark, one of ocean's oldest inhabitants. An early relative, the Cladoselache, "was in full command of the early oceans three hundred million years ago, a fearsome creature," Thomas Helm stated in *Shark*. "The shark occupies a unique position in the scheme of living things. He is neither fish nor mammal, but he possesses characteristics of both." The ruthlessness of the "family" is perhaps best expressed by what Helm said of shark childbirth: the newly born shark, a miniature edition of his parents, complete with a full set of teeth and the ability to fend for himself from the moment he enters the sea, "had best keep a sharp lookout right from the beginning, for if his own mother is hungry, she is liable to make a meal of her newly born brood!"

Bony fishes probably originated in freshwater and, like sea mammals, later returned to the oceans. "During different stages of their lives, shad, salmon, eel and many other fishes live in fresh and in salt waters," R. E. Coker says. About animals of the field and wildwood, we have a considerable literature, particularly for children, based upon the anthropomorphic fiction that woodchucks, skunks, and rabbits think and talk like humans. Thornton Burgess helped to make my early youth a joyful time, when I used to pretend that I was Farmer Brown's boy, but just as often that I was maybe Jimmy Skunk, who talked like a man. A quite opposite and ever so much more wonderful miracle was accomplished in *The Once and Future King*, by T. H. White, when Merlin transported the future

King Arthur into the person of a small perch, as part of his education in the wonders of the world in which we all live. This bit of magical ichthyomorphism, wherein the Wart—a nickname "more or less rhymed with Art, short for his real name" —gradually learned to *think like a fish,* came true as Wart discovered that "it was no good trying to swim like a human being, for it made him go corkscrew and much too slowly." And so, with the guidance of Merlin, who came along as a tench, he learned the true *fishy* ways of self-navigation.

Sea life may be observed at its most exotic along the Great Barrier Reef ("nature's first showcase of the wonders of ocean life," Australians boast proudly), stretching some 1,250 miles along the northeast coast of Australia. This is a 30,000,000-year-old reef created by the greatest homebuilders on earth—supertrillions of tiny living coral polyps. Their former skyscraper homes are now inhabited by a new teeming population of rainbow-hued fishes and other strange and mysteriously beautiful forms of sea life. The 80,000 square miles of coral continent contain more than 300 varieties of life contrived in the most weird and delicate hues, shapes, and sizes. If Australia is too far overseas for a rapt visit, there is the fabulous Padre Island National Seashore Reef off Texas. Last winter, having never yet seen a coral reef close up, I flew 4,000 miles for a visit to Buccoo Reef, off the northwest corner of Tobago, in the West Indies. After we'd snorkled and ogled our way about among the most beautiful dress-ball creatures one could ever imagine, we were taken to swim in a ground-coral bay nearby called Nylon Pool. I should like a bed made of the stuff. The next day, flying back to New York from Trinidad, we flew low over this bay, a great mass of translucent greenish hue as though an immense submarine emerald stone were glowing somewhere far beneath the surface.

Comparable to coral reefs for wonderment, but quite different in terms of security—niches where one might hide (if an electric eel is not waiting there to infra-ray a visitor for dinner) —is the floating brownish-green fairyland of the Sargasso Sea, a 10,000,000-ton spinning wheel of Sargassum weed roughly the size of the United States that floats eternally in the mid-North Atlantic Ocean. If any of its inhabitants of billions and billions of tiny creatures lets go its careful hold on the weed, it inevitably plunges very slowly, four miles down to the ocean floor below. That's being really dead—and we "secure" humans with a so-called solid floor beneath our feet discuss terrestrial insecurities! Columbus, and his daring successors, believed that a ship caught in this massive mess of floating weeds would be held in a death grip until it rotted and sank. In 1969 man's pollution was reported to have reached the Sargasso: It's now coated with oil and tar.

The Sargasso Sea turns clockwise, to the right, spun by the Gulf Stream and the prevailing westerly trade winds. One would have to fly terribly high, and terribly slowly, to *see* this sort of gigantic geomorphic twirling. The first American spaceman to circle the globe as an astronaut, Alan B. Shephard, Jr., described the tropical view of coral-reef-wreathed islands in *We Seven*. On his first journey around the Planet Water, he says, "I shifted to an open area and identified Andro Island and Bimini. The colors around these ocean islands were brilliantly clear, and I could see sharp variations between the blue of deep water and the light green of the shoal areas near the reefs. It was really stunning!"

Neither Jules Verne nor Edgar Allan Poe probably ever saw the famous maelstrom, that giant whirlpool of the Moskenstrom which twirls so dangerously between the islands of Moskenaes and Mosken in the Lofoten Islands off Norway's west coast, but their ghastly descriptions of being swept down into the vortex are nevertheless terrifying. The Garofalo whirlpool in the Strait of Messina, Sicily, is today's reality of the famous mythical Charybdis, opposite that other monster Scylla, offering the doomed sailor a quick road "out" to the bottom of the sea. (The with-it reader will suffer this journey with Aeneas as much as he endures the other one with Poe's unlabeled companion.)

Away down there, at the end of the maelstrom funnel, within Davy Jones' dread locker, at what Milton called "the bottom of the monstrous world," is the truly unkown part of our globe. It is estimated that only about 3 percent of the bottom of the world's oceans has ever been even partially surveyed. "Back in the 1920's," Dr. Francis P. Shepard, of the Scripps Institution of Oceanography, commented in 1969, "when I was a student, it was generally believed by geologists that most of the sea floor was monotonously flat. The development of echo-sounding and the resultant profiles now available have relegated this 'monotonous oceanic plain' to the limbo of old wives tales. We now know that the ocean floor has just as rugged mountains and valleys as are found on the land. An inverted Mount Everest could be dropped into the Mariana or Tonga Trench and still leave water above the mountain's base. The mile-deep Grand Canyon is an awesome spectacle, but a canyon on the sea floor in the Bahamas has been found to be cut *three times as deep* below its bordering flat islands." (Challenger Deep: 35,800 feet.)

The most dramatic submarine fact is the 40,000-mile-long mountain range that extends southward down the mid-Atlantic Ocean from Iceland, eastward around the "bottom" tip of Africa across the Indian Ocean, then past southern Australia, next northeastward to become the Pacific Rise, thence northward to come ultimately ashore in North America at the southernmost tip of Baja California alongside the Sea of Cortez.

When Richard Hakluyt's early maps and great book *Voyages* were published in London, the philosopher Francis Bacon must have studied them closely, for in 1620 he was the first to suggest that Europe, Africa, and the continents of the New World may once have been joined together as a common land body. In 1920 German geologist Alfred Wegener formally proposed that the origin of all the continental land masses was a single original earth island (on the Planet Water), which he named Pangea (Greek, *pan*—all *ge*—earth), located in the southern hemisphere and surrounded by the universal ocean, the Panthalassa.

In time, Wegener reasoned, Pangea broke up into two continents, Laurasia in the north and Gondwanaland in the south. Later these in turn "drifted" apart to form today's relatively scattered continents. During the past half-century, Dr. Wegener's theory was at first widely scorned; but recently, many geographers have begun expressing varying degrees of total agreement. N. J. Berrill, in *Inherit the Earth,* summed up that "the continental masses have not been *drifting* apart, but have been and *are being pushed* apart by the continuous formation of new crust in between. The Atlantic Ocean widens as mantle material continues to well up through the mid-Atlantic ridge, while the western edge of the American continents pushes hard against the eastern margin of the Pacific Ocean floor." Many

marine geologists have gone to the opposite extreme of the
1920's "monotonous oceanic plain" theory of the ocean bottom
to now suggest that ocean basins may be the most geologically
active regions of the planet's surface.

In April, 1967, a University of Toronto physicist, Dr. J.
Tuzo Wilson, suggested that the continents possibly drifted
back together a half-billion years ago and, when they again
drifted apart shortly thereafter, Europe carried away northern
Ireland, Scotland, and half of Norway, but North America in
exchange meantime carried away most of New England, which
had previously been a solid part of Europe. In August, 1967,
Dr. Patrick M. Hurley, a Massachusetts Institute of Technology
geology professor, said that work at M.I.T. and at the University of São Paulo, Brazil, had apparently proved the direct cor-
relation of the geological terrain of South America and West
Africa. So maybe there once was an Ameurasiafricstraliantarc-
tica!

Suddenly the scientific world has discovered the new frontier
of the undersea great unknown. Today more than fifty American colleges and universities have established doctoral programs in oceanography and marine sciences. Marine geology
encompasses the study of sea-floor topography, marine sediments, and wholly unknown formations beneath the ocean
bottom. The New York Times editorialized: "Submarine colo-
nialism is not yet a major international issue, but it could become one in the 1970's. The term refers to a possible race
among nations to appropriate the sea bed—and the riches lying
under it." The Times was particularly struck with a $1.5 bil-
lion supposed trove of treasure minerals under the Red Sea that
a Californian, John E. Crawford, of Crawford Marine Specialists, had already announced he was investigating. John L.
Mero, author of The Mineral Resources of the Sea and called
"the chief apostle of ocean mining," is quoted by August Gribbon in Sea Horizons: Man's Latest Discoveries in the World
Ocean: "We can use the modern equipment now available,
adapt it to the sea, and mine profitably. More profitably than
we can on land, in some instances." Elsewhere, Gribbon cautiously noted that when the eminent oceanographer-adminis-
trators of marine institutions talk privately about the future,

"they are the first to concede that major exploration of the seas is not years but perhaps generations away. This is so in part because the rich, technologically advanced nations do not now need much more from the ocean than they are getting. There is no popular demand for the fragmented fishing industry to shape up, for the mining firms to pluck all those manganese nodules from the sea floor, for the Weather Bureau to start manipulating its curly patterns of highs and lows." What is needed, he suggested, to give industrial oceanography (and he quoted an unnamed specialist) is "visible international competition. If it weren't for the space race, remember, a manned landing on the moon would still be many years off."

Gribbon knew whereof he suggested. More than two-thirds of all university research funds today come from the Atomic Energy Commission, the National Aeronautics and Space Administration, and the Department of Defense. If somehow the oceanographers could prove/scare the Congressional fund-its with the idea/fear that Russia is about to "take over" the bottom of the sea if we don't get there first with American investigative know-how and "usitis," why, the new oceanic research could move instantly into high gear, with immense and endless federal funds made available forever.

In any case, we are barely entered into a wonderful new age of subocean discovery. John Bardach signaled the arrival of modern echo sounding as being on the same high level as the first telephonic exchange between Dr. Alexander Graham Bell and his associate: "The invention in 1911 of echo sounding, attributed to the American physicist Reginald Fessenden, is like the step from the airplane of the Wright brothers to the modern jetliner. The weight could descend at 100 fathoms (600 feet) a minute; a sound pulse travels at a speed of about 700 fathoms (4,200 feet) a second. . . . Obviously, since echo sounders allow for a running profile of the sea bottom, and since radio direction finders and gyrocompasses allow for very accurate triangulation of a ship's position, the making of exact maps of the sea floor is now relatively easy and can proceed at some speed."

As in a living theater, a sightseer aboard ship can "view" the ocean's bottom topography, its towering cordilleras and gaping in-between chasms, by watching the profile of the marine side as it is slowly portrayed on a revolving scroll by the stylus, recording the information received from the echo sounder, as his ship passes swiftly over the unknown depths.

There are also an increasing number of devices for taking one down for on-the-scene investigation. The U.S. Navy's Hikino diving craft is intended to go down ultimately to 8,000 feet. Lockheed's Deep Quest will penetrate to the same depths. Alvin, operated for the Navy out of Woods Hole Oceanographic Institution, can go down 6,000 feet and has immense claws for making grabs at ocean-bottom samples. Ocean Systems' Perry-Link Deep Diver is designed for an operating depth of 1,350 feet, a lock-out depth of 1,250. At present, the use of these devices will be limited to scientists. Next will come the mining specialists, in search of riches awaiting bottom-surface extraction. Only then will the way open up at last to sight-seeing vessels carrying students and scholars of undersea investigation, amateur explorers who will go for the pleasure of knowing, just as today they circle the globe in order to view the wonders to be seen above sea level.

Temperature at the bottom of the seas is largely only a little above zero, heated in part by adiabatic warming, the effect of the great pressure at deep levels. Another effect of the compression of water in the seas affects the general sea level: if the waters were not compressible, the oceans would be 93 feet higher than at present. At the bottom of the Norwegian Sea, more than two miles down, live frigid fish in water at a temperature *below* the freezing point of freshwater. In contrast, the bottom of the Red Sea contains four deep rifts from which torrid heat (up to 135 degrees Fahrenheit) erupts, making the local waters saltier and at the same time more acidic, but also causing, apparently, the creation of fantastic sea-bottom riches in minerals, a vast profusion of rare—gold and silver—and base metals.

Heat flow from the ocean floor has been found to be greater than that rising from the continents, all owing not to a general cooling of the molten center of the globe but to the constant heat-producing effects of inner-planetary radioactivity. Areas of higher temperature result perhaps from the effect of immense convection currents within the earth's mantle—that mysterious middle region between earth crust and earth core—rumbling and tumbling over and over like the slow roiling and boiling of a kettle of simmering soup. It has been suggested that this convective action is responsible for raising all of the planet's mountains (on land and in the sea), and even for the shifting of continents.

We may expect to learn much more about the mysterious mantle during the 1970's, notably from the borings of the *Glomar Challenger* beneath ocean floors, which are beginning to prick beneath the top edge.

Much of the Planet Water's surface variety of rich elements may originally have come up out of the mantle—perhaps the water vapor that ultimately liquefied to become the oceans; the minerals which we use in all our industries and fabrications; and, finally—richest loot of all—the choicest stone, the diamond, and the rarest metal, gold, which originate deep within the planet's mantle. It is down there that pioneers of the future will someday find hoards of unbelievable riches that will outshine all the treasure lodes of the past.

Is the United States about to undertake an elaborate underseas research program? A special report to the federal government by Ocean Science and Engineering, Inc., in December, 1968, stated a strong negative, that there is neither need for the suboceanic materials *yet* nor hope of sufficient recovery of undersea minerals to warrant governmental investigation at this time. The treasure *is* there, within the seas' waters—"All the rivers run into the sea," Koheleth stated, in the Book of *Ecclesiastes* in the richness of Biblical poetic prophetic thought, "yet the sea is not full." Yes, it *is* all there. Only nobody has yet thought up how to extract the seas' riches. It reminds one of the disastrous British "South Sea Bubble" episode, when so many cautious Englishmen invested their life savings in a nebulous promise of riches to be gained by trading with Spanish Latin America. The riches certainly *were* there, but the commerce just never managed to get going. Today (as I write this) numerous investment firms with highly reputable aims are collecting funds for future undersea exploration and acquisition. *Life* magazine, in a special feature, "Into the Sea," reported "a host of middlemen interested in making a profit. There are some 20 U.S. Governmental agencies alone that deal with the sea, and hundreds of companies with investments of millions of dollars."

In 1968, a "World Peace Through Law" conference of some 2,000 lawyers urged that the United Nations "assume jurisdiction and control" over the huge mineral resources within the oceans and beneath them, in order to furnish the financially beleaguered U.N. with its own "self-engendered" future independent income "to use for the benefit of all mankind and all nations." As splendid as this suggestion by a trade of men who usually spend most of their time looking out for the special interests of their private clients may seem, one immediately questions what would happen if that treasure trove worth billions beneath the Red Sea, already mentioned, were to be claimed by the United Nations. The adjacent nations would be the first objectors: Let's see, United Arab Republic, Ethiopia, Israel, Sudan, Yemen, who else lines up alongside the Red Sea? All the hungry neighbors in that part of the world who have needy children of their own not yet provided for. Which nation would give up its claim to a U.N. global "need" and supremacy?

More possible of fulfillment is the ever alert Sierra Club's insistence, in August, 1967, that we Americans "must not wait, as we did with our land frontiers, until the undersea wilderness is almost gone, before we decide to save some of it in parks and other reserves." Sierra persuaded numerous national legislators to propose laws establishing "a national system of marine sanctuaries" under selected areas of the nation's publicly owned coastal waters.

December, 1968, had brought a negative report regarding governmental expenditures undersea. In January, 1969, another, quite opposite report was published by the Commission on Marine Science, Engineering and Resources, accompanied by a handsome 305-page picture book and a whopping recommendation by the commission that the government should establish a new federal service, to be called the National Oceanic and Atmospheric Agency (NOAA), which by 1980 would be expending $2 billion annually on a wide diversity of oceanographic pursuits. The New York *Times,* which had ignored the earlier (negative) National Council on Marine Resources and

Engineering (NCOMRED) report, waxed enthusiastic over the NOAA dream project (positive), hailing such startling imaginary projections as, for example, that " 'seasteading' will replace yesterday's homesteading, and underwater tourism will compete with foreign travel as a conventional source of recreation." However, the newspaper cautiously concluded that "much more must be learned about the oceans, and unraveling the many mysteries still hidden in the deep will be neither easily nor quickly done."

Willard Bascom, a man who never saw the sea until he was twenty-nine years old and then went on to become an in-the-waves experient (he has since directed the Mohole Project and is now head of Ocean Science and Engineering, Inc.), noted sadly a few years ago that "there is danger the study of waves will fall entirely into the hands of men who have never seen the sea." When one simply *reads* some of the governmental reports out of Washington, D.C., committees, most of whose members have no apparent personal oceanic interest—poetic, scientific, or practical—beyond the habitual administrative dance that "preliminates" setting up another centralized Washington operation, one sees the ocean future: the undersea landscape disappearing just as the terrestrial landscape was and continues to be inundated and polluted. The Sierra's mild plea for "a few undersea wilderness areas" doesn't appear at all far-fetched. It's very much for real, and most urgent.

Perhaps what is most unfortunate about our big-name committees, national reports, federal agencies, investigations, instant surveys, and in-depth studies (few take more than a year or two) is that they all get so far away from the *real thing*. Reports, reports, reports—there will surely be dozens more of them during the 1970's, each one more importunate and seemingly more purposeful than the previous, and often created by men who, as Bascom foretold, have never even *seen* the sea. And so, just as we have already lost touch with the land by becoming urbanites residing and working within sterile cities made of steel, concrete, and glass, and breathing polluted non-atmosphere, we are now all too obviously about to destroy the ultimate umbilical connection with that other, more ancient heritage of mankind, the sea. Wesley Marx assessed in a snail shell what is so often wrong with our ocean "studies": "Heat, noise, sewage, DDT, breakwaters, harpoon guns, and dams can disrupt the oceans' processes and, in turn, our own marine ambitions. This careless corruption springs from an appreciation out of balance. Although we value the ocean as a resource, we appreciate it very little as an environment."

One need not read very far through the thousands of pages of oceanographic reports—private, governmental, and international—to discover that the prospect is very slim for a *real* preservation of the seas. In 1969 the United Nations began a study, which could well continue for the next decade, on how its 126 member states may set up jurisdiction over the Planet Water's seabeds. Its committees will "observe," but it is unlikely that they will ever have the power to *enforce* strict regulations to prevent the desecration and depletion of oceanic resources beyond the danger point of no return. Political humanity must recover the viewpoint of the poets. Francis Thompson's "secret world of wonders in thyself" is in danger of becoming wonders to be unraveled by a special new kind of ruinous submarine enterprise resembling the total destruction of the planet's land areas by deforestation and strip-surface mining.

The experts are just beginning to speak out, to express how near we are to the oceanic end. In *Ramparts*, September, 1969, Dr. Paul Ehrlich, leading world ecologist, foretold the *death of the oceans:* In this eco-catastrophe, "the end of the ocean came *late in the summer of 1979,* and it came even more rapidly than the biologists had expected!" (T. S. Eliot: "This is the way the world ends/Not with a bang but a whimper." Good night, sweet waters! Good night, sweet Princess Planet Water!)

To enter the sea, to know the sea—Jacques-Yves Cousteau has quietly dimensioned this new unknown world that is just now beginning to open up to us: "From the surface of the ocean to a depth of 40 meters (131 feet), there are 50 million cubic kilometers of 'safe' water awaiting the aqualung diver. This is the sea's most *living* layer—where nearly all the plant life is produced by photosynthesis. Consider a comparison: On land, in our own element, the volume of space actually inhabited is a layer extending from a few feet underground to the tops of the highest trees. This adds up to about 4 million cubic kilometers—hardly more than a quarter of the sunny and crowded upper layer of the sea accessible to millions of divers!"

This is the most up-to-date, immediate, twentieth-century poetry (Cousteau wrote it in 1966), as apt to our time as Byron's descriptions are also still apt—he used to body-surf joyously in the North Sea, which he considered secure from man's depredations ("Man marks the earth with ruin—his control stops with the shore"; if the good lord could have been at Santa Barbara, California, in 1968–69, he'd have written a different, very angry poem about man's invasion of the sea, to be sure).

Each one of us has a personal and quite *private* relationship with the sea when we go out into it. None of the Washington reports gives one any feeling of what the sea is really like to the bureaucratic reporters, so that one suspects they may be dealing perhaps with some "make-believe" ocean. Unfortunately, this could prove to be the case: when the "harvesting" is done, there may be no fish left; and when the submarine "mining" is accomplished, there may be only a divested undersea Appalachia left. The concept is distinctly *not* funny, and, alas, highly probable.

So lovely and richly beautiful a thing she is! But when these men talk of mining her, it is as though a man were to melt down a beautiful woman for the chemicals in her body.

We return to the sea so casually, so easily! On the Planet Water, this *is* the most evident fact. Antipater said it, in 319 B.C.: "Every sea is a sea"; or, more exactly, Horace (Quintus Horatius Flaccus) in 30 B.C.: "The hungry sea is fatal to sailors." Aquanauts, oceanographers, aqualungers, surfers, swimmers, dippers, waders—the fatal, grabby sea does take us all, in its own way, and in each our own way, too. Themistocles made a statement which has the sound of the unoceanic Washington reports: "He who commands the sea has command of everything." I rather think that when the final time comes around to assess things, it will turn out that the sea it is which commands everything. And you. And me. And all of those who go down into it.

III The Battle Royal: Sea, Land, and Air

Wª HAT and where is the greatest sight to be seen
on the face of the Planet Water? Sightseers always must deal in
superlative wonders. To begin, the greatest sight is surely not
the Grand Canyon, a splendid though dreadfully dried-out historic monument to ages past; not even the cosmos-reaching skyscrapers of New York City, though they reveal somewhat the
stark wonder of man's persistent pursuit of verticality from the
Tower of Babel to the Empire State Building, along with his
insistently compressed hiving instinct, with most urbanites
stuck within inner windowless closet-offices; not the great Egyptian pyramid of Khufu, though this will surely remain for all
time the most monumental combined proof of man's belief in
the never-ending afterlife and at the same time utmost evidence
of megalomania run berserk; not the modest New England hillside strawberry patch whence Dr. Robert Goddard's first
"space" rocket flew all of 40 feet skyward; not the gigantic
launch pads of Cape Kennedy, whence all of us have begun to
rocket vicariously into space via the TV crazyboxes in our
living rooms every time a U.S. space rocket is launched.

One could name endless arrays of "most tantalizing sites to
behold" for each man's different complex reasoning. However,
without question, the most remarkable view for all of us earthlings is to be experienced at one of those great dramatic arena
points where the three great elemental forces of our planet's
surface come together most brutally in perpetual battle royal—
the hydrosphere of waters, the lithosphere of solid earth, and

the overmantling atmosphere of air. Seascape, skyscape, land-scape—inevitably the human viewer carries an inherited spirit-ual concept that was beautifully expressed in the very first chapter of Genesis, in which his personalized God, having called the spatial firmament "heaven" and the dry land "earth" and the gathering together of the waters the "seas," "He saw that it *was* good."

As we look about us, our world is full of violence and mur-derous competition, of ruthless jungle warfare and expected cannibalism, with survival of the fittest the apparently inevita-ble answer to each changing battle situation. But nowhere is the warfare more cruel or final or never-ending than among the three great fundamental elements of sea, land, and sky. In the tactical motions on any seashore (or land edge, if you like), or hilltop or wavetop, it is amazing that the battle royal continues so endlessly, with ever renewed vigor, as it has for some 3,000,000,000 years now. The ascendancy seesaws back and forth, in such fashion that we can today have only the barest idea of how it has been won and lost down through the billennia: The tops of all the highest mountains reveal, in their contained skeletal remains of sea-bottom creatures, that they were once losers, floored at the bottom of ancient enemy seas. Who won which of those battles so long ago, those long-continued wars that still go on? The sea, or the land, or the sky?

The faintest traces of what may have happened is revealed in various indications of former seashores, where land and ocean each brought up its most powerful forces to drive the other back. Each had all manner of special surprise components—for example, the masses of ice that the oceans used in a great many of the wars, to force the land surfaces downward (some of them are still only barely recovering from the last ice-age battle, and, of course, Greenland and Antarctica's continents [or islands?] are still far beneath the water-victor overlordship of immense ice caps); or the land's use of fifth-column exploding submarine volcanoes which occasionally create new islands, new *lands* in the midst of the hostile watery seas.

Polynesian babies are said to learn to swim before they learn to walk. They grow up to experience what is perhaps man's most natural lifelong habitual enjoyment of the sea. Urban babies grow up at an ever-increasing distance from both sea and land, in their strange city environments. *The Water-Babies* was the Reverend Charles Kingsley's 1873 fairy tale of a dirty little London chimney sweep, a nineteenth-century polluted city dweller with asphyxiation problems similar to our own: "He cried when he had to climb the dark flues, rubbing his poor knees and elbows raw; and when the soot got into his eyes, which it did every day in the week. His name was Tom, he could not read nor write, and did not care to do either; and he never washed himself, for there was no water up the court where he lived." At last poor Tom fell into a stream—"I will be a fish; I will swim in the water; I must be clean, I must be clean"—and either was drowned ("They found a black thing in the water and said it was Tom's body, and that he had been drowned; but Tom was quite alive, and cleaner, and merrier than he ever had been") or else was taken over by the water fairies, grew a fine set of external gills, and discovered the joys of underwater living exactly a century before Cousteau's experients began living tentatively underseas. Perhaps Cousteau's underwater babies will also someday grow external gills.

We should return our dead immediately to the sea. It would save all the questions about graveyards taking up too much space on land, or that other momentous decision whether to cremate or to seal a body in an eternally impermeable concrete mini-imitation of Pharaoh Khufu's masterpiece. If all our ancestors, departed friends—and enemies, too—were to be buried at sea, we could dutifully honor all of them at the same time, every time we went to visit the seashore.

As the accepted place of our origin, the seas seem the most *natural* place also for our final personal physical destination. It has surely a greater drawing power on each one of us than any other planetary phenomenon, a spiritual/physical/sexual thing between people and the immensity of oceans that is comparable, for example, to the fact of gravity, which Isaac Newton first proved into natural law: Every particle of matter is attracted to and attracts every other, no matter what its size. The sea is, of course, previous in fact and sentiment to any ancient land gods or goddesses, and yet it would be a sort of supreme irreverence to try to "humanize" it or, for that matter, to attempt to "deify" the sea and worship it as a kind of male or female deity.

It is the only entity on earth that is somehow both, and more at the same time, or maybe simply different.

Men have both suffered and enjoyed the experiencing of the places where sea, land, and sky come and overcome together in violent ecstasy and are apparently at war: the extremes of human capacity are amazing. One man is wrecked, as a member of the crew of a storm-wracked ship, on a shore where another man, in another age, comes riding in to shore joyously on a surfboard, experiencing one of the greatest of human exultations. Both are, curiously, experients of a direct physical-attraction "thing" between them, personally, and the great, immense but individually related sea. To explain the "personal" interrelationship between the individual human being and the immense personality of the probably similar "individual" sea would be as impossible as to try to propose or suggest individual relationships in the gravitational attracting orbits and relationships between planets and their moons, or the sun and its hovering, affectionate (?) planets. In an early inkling of gravitational guesswork, Johannes Kepler suggested there was "some kind of magnetic attraction between the moon and the earth's waters." There is also some kind of magical attraction between the waters and many individual human seamen and swimmers.

In 1945, Willard Bascom joined a World War II "Waves Project" and was sent to the Pacific Coast with a field party whose mission was to drive Dukws right out into an area of 30-foot-high pitching and plunging waves. "Since I had never seen a wave before, much less the Pacific Ocean, I did not quit on the spot. Thirty-foot breakers sounded like a reasonable size for an ocean as large as the Pacific," he wrote in 1964 in *Waves and Beaches—The Dynamics of the Ocean Surface*. Of surf breaking on a beach, he said, "Waves have many stages. . . . Born as ripples, they grow into whitecaps, chop, wind waves, and finally into fully developed storm seas. All this seems to be merely preparation for the final and most exciting step: The crest tumbles forward, and the momentum carries the broken water onward until the wave's last remaining energy is expended in a gentle swash that rushes up the sandy beach face and sinks from sight. The wave is gone! This zone where waves give up their energy and where systematic water motions give way to violent turbulence is the surf. It is the most exciting part of the ocean. All of the energy so carefully gleaned from the winds of the distant storm and hoarded for a thousand miles of ocean-crossing is gone, expended in a few wild moments. Because the energy is released so rapidly, the energy density in the surf is actually much higher than in the storm which originally created the waves."

Scientist Bascom, poet as well, confessed, as all sea infatuates must, that his pleasantest hours "have been spent in watching waves and examining beaches, trying to understand them. The inner peace that comes with the quiet contemplation of a beach on a still, calm morning, or the feeling of exhilaration that comes from riding a great wave in a small boat, is more reward than most men ever know. Fortunately, the beaches of the world are cleaned every night by the tide. A fresh look always awaits the student, and every wave is a masterpiece of originality. It will ever be so."

Jack London, a seaman from the age of nineteen, wrote a wondering, wonderful description of the melding of man and wave in the act of surfing, in *Cruise of the Snark,* while on a visit to Waikiki. "Half a mile out, where is the reef, the white-headed combers thrust suddenly skyward out of the placid turquoise-blue and come rolling in to shore. One after another they come, a mile long, with smoking crests. . . . And suddenly, out there where a big smoker lifts skyward, rising like a sea-god from out of the welter of spume and churning white, on the giddy, toppling, overhanging and downfalling, precarious crest appears the dark head of a man. Swiftly he rises through the rushing white. His black shoulders, his chest, his loins, his limbs—all is abruptly projected on one's vision. Where but the moment before was only the wide desolation and invincible roar, is now a man, erect, full-statured, not struggling frantically in that wild movement, not buried and crushed and buffeted by those mighty monsters, but standing above them all, calm and superb, poised on the giddy summit, his feet buried in the churning foam, the salt smoke rising to his knees, and all the rest of him in the free air and flashing sunlight, and he is flying through the air, flying forward, flying fast as the surge on which he stands."

On the leeward side of Oahu Island, Hawaii, is a place of mountainous waves, the Banzai, Pipeline, and other surf beaches. Here surfer Paul Allen once said that when he is locked in the curl of a superwave, "Then you are really plugged into life: it is all light green and crystal and shining, like a cathedral, everything all at once, back to the womb." The shore-bound sightseer, equipped with binoculars, can get some faint sense of what the surfer is experiencing, too, a distant, vicarious aquabatic thrill that is rather like peering at Nureyev in mid-leap, or at Cordobes in mid-bullfight, or at Bjocrn Wirkola sailing more than 300 feet through the air on his skis at Garmisch-Partenkirchen. But the surfer and the ski jumper are especially exciting to behold because they are moving, daringly, in the very no-man's-land of the battle-royal frontier between sky and water, snow and land. And it is the body surfer, finally, whose body becomes a part of the wave, who truly and totally experiences the surf, that ancient surging of the Planet Water's seas inspired by sun and moon, which Gilbert Klingel has summed up so tersely: "All living, when looked upon in a large sense, is a tide." And when we are in the surf at the edge of the sea, we readily become what we once were and perhaps still are, once more a part of the living sea.

The part of a sandy beach above the high-tide level is so bone-dry, so desert-lifeless, that it is easy for us to think of the high-low tide margin as also without life: when we are enjoying the typical beach, it can appear to be a hygienic spa dissociated from the crowded activities of living, vital areas.

Even while we lie on the sand, lazily watching the waves come in, we quickly learn that this "dead" assumption is not true. For little bevies of sandpipers (or sanderlings, which are said to differ from sandpipers in that they have no hind toe) come dancing along the beach, nibbling some sort of goodies infinitesimally small, meantime barely avoiding getting wet by the insliding leftovers of the broken waves. It is, of course, our lack of microscopic vision for small wonders that is missing, else we could *see* and know that this "dead" and hygienic area is no such thing, but in fact one of the busiest, happiest, liveliest water places on earth. In *The Edge of the Sea*, Rachel Carson casually brought to life this intertidal zone, "the minuscule world of the sand grains, the world of inconceivably minute beings, which swim through the liquid film around a grain of sand as fish would swim through the ocean covering the sphere of the earth . . . a world in which one micro-droplet of water separating one grain of sand from another is like a vast, dark sea."

The ocean likes to play Gargantuan fun-and-war games—tricks upon and with its sandy shores, sometimes piling them high with gigantic dunes and at other times carrying entire beaches off to sea. Men since the beginning of seaside residence have persistently insisted on building summer cottages far too near to the edge (ignoring the Biblical parable of a "foolish man" building a house on sand), then shouting angrily about "property losses" when the ocean, in a typically rollicksome mood of midwinter storms, suddenly carries sand off to sea, with, of course, all the summer houses built on it. Many jetties have been built along the North Atlantic Coast—in 1960, Congress authorized an 83-mile, $38,000,000 "restoration" of Long Island beachfront oceanic "removals" from Fire Island Inlet to Montauk Point. By February, 1969, with hundreds of millions of dollars' worth of sandfill fed onto beaches behind the handsome new jetties, most of it to be later carried off by the hungry ocean, it began to look as though the U.S. Corps of Engineers and the county supervisors were engaged in a project to "feed" sand, endless tons of it, to the hungry North Atlantic Ocean: a great big fun-and-games treat for the ocean, almost comparable to the fun the North Pacific has, in wrecking huge lumber barges along its North American East Coast. "It's the most futile feeling in the world," Mayor Theodore O. Hulse of Westhampton Beach told reporters, "just to stand here and watch these homes go into the ocean." Mayor Robert L. Sharp, of Ocean City, New Jersey, mourned: "A total of $4,500,000 spent in 25 years, and we have no beach." The Atlantic Ocean played along the seaboard beaches long before we learned to—their sands so absorbent on which the ocean could take out its angry tantrums and violent gavottes during the winter-month northeasters when the winds reach near-hurricane force and rains come down torrentially. Here is an aqueous Aceldama of the great battle royal among the three elemental powers, sea, land, and air—by giving a little (sand), the land seems to win, since the beach is still there, much depleted, come spring. But the players on the local human team, with their houses, obviously think the land should and must win *all* the battles, a silly impossibility. D. W. Bennett, conservation director of an organization dedicated to reasonable treaties between man and water, the American Littoral Society, recently repeated the stance of this group toward human invasion of the "militarized" zones between sea and land: "The solution is to discourage all construction in the oceanic flood plain and to treat the beaches as places that people can use when the ocean doesn't need them. Man has been notably unsuccessful at getting the ocean to behave itself along the shore; natural beaches have done the job better than any manmade structures."

During World War II, many of us first began discovering gobs of oil on our feet quite often at the beach. Among man's worst defilements on the oceans and at seaside has been the befouling of ocean waters with oil slicks. Both 1968 and 1969 were record years for beach oil-smearing, notably because of the breakup of the supergiant oil tanker *Torrey Canyon* on Pollard Rock, thus tarring the Cornwall, Brittany, and Normandy coasts and beaches, and the leaks sprung in an undersea oil well off Santa Barbara, California. Press accounts of the California fiasco mentioned that the leaking oil well was "the first of hundreds of wells contemplated in the Santa Barbara Channel," and there are announcements of supertankers to come that will be even larger than the *Torrey Canyon*.

One of the pleasantest chronicles of a year-round solitary residence on a beach is Henry Beston's *The Outermost House*, in which he described his life on the Great Beach of Cape Cod in 1926–27. You can still see the tiny house today, since it's been monumentalized within the National Cape Cod Seashore. Nearly a half-century ago, this man wrote feelingly of "a new danger that now threatens the birds at sea. An irreducible residue of crude oil, called by refiners 'slop,' remains in stills after oil distillation, and this is pumped into southbound tankers and emptied far offshore. This wretched pollution floats over large areas, and the birds alight in it and get it on their feathers. They inevitably die. I am glad to be able to write that the situation is better than it was. . . . Let us hope that all such pollution will presently end."

At the time of the Santa Barbara Channel oil-smearing, an

oil official reportedly told the Senate Subcommittee on Air and Water Pollution, "I'm amazed at the publicity for the loss of a few birds." A year later, when a Hudson River nuclear power plant caused "massive fish kills," a pollution official said there had been "much too much emphasis on fish kills." Beachcomber Beston would find the 1970's far worse than the 1920's. In March, 1970, nearly a half century after Beston's report of petroleum slop, the U.S. Secretary of the Interior was said to be "planning" to put a stop to the dumping of oil-polluted ballast from tankers at sea! But *when?*

The twice-daily tides of the seas, during each lunar day of 24 hours, 54 minutes, are a most intimate *visual* experience of the gravitational pull of sun and moon on our planet and especially on the planet's surface waters (the land surface is pulled upward, too, of course, by the circling moon). Adults who like surfing usually prefer to swim at high tide, whereas families with young children prefer the time of low tide, when there are often many wide, shallow pools for the children to wade and play in. The incoming tide is the best time for building sand castles (and defending them, of course, against the advancing waves of the sea enemy). It is useful to realize that there is a daily recession of time of tide, since the moon's lunar-month circling of the earth-moon "center" takes 27 days, 7¾ hours, of about 6 hours a week, so that by the end of the first week of a fortnight's vacation at the seashore low tide will be occurring at the same time as high tide at the beginning of the week.

Any tidal beach is a miracle to behold. American visitors to Europe are constantly discovering with surprise that the Mediterranean is practically tideless, and so consequently there's no surfing to be enjoyed there. The same is true, of course, of the Caribbean islands. Fortunately, the Mediterranean offers the antiquarian the chance to dive for classical tidbits of statuary or wine jars ("For one jar full of wine the exporters obtain a slave," Diodorus Siculus, a Sicilian historian of the time of Julius Caesar, reported), and the West Indies islands also give the chance to dive among coral reefs and discover that living coral is actually green and only when it dies and dries out is the dead red skeleton revealed. But at the equatorial zone, one inevitably misses the tides, as one also misses the changing of the seasons. The human sightseer exists as a genus for the very reason that he is constantly in search of remarkable differences. The Planet Water's greatest watery extremes are the dynamic supertides that "happen" in only a few very special places.

One of the most spectacular tidal viewing sites is the Bay of Fundy, which averages 35 miles wide, is 180 miles long, and has a fantastic tidal range of up to 53 feet. All of 100,000,000 tons of water rush in and out of the narrowed configuration of the immense bay daily. There's a viewing platform at Moncton, New Brunswick, where the twice-daily tumbling, foaming advance of the great sea tide inlandward may be observed. At Petitcodiac Point, the local pigs have learned to behave like giant sandpipers on the beach between incoming tides, for they comfortably root about in the riverbed, then scurry up at the very last minute, barely in time to escape the inrushing waters. The Saint John River passes between the twin cities of Lancaster and Saint John on its way through a 450-foot gorge into the Bay of Fundy, and there twice a day the unnatural vision of Reversing Falls Rapids is created, tumbling wrongway upstream. President Franklin D. Roosevelt, fascinated by the massive force of the Fundy tides from his lifelong observation of them at his summer home on Campobello Island, started the Passamaquoddy Project to harness them for hydroelectric power. Alas, an American President proved as powerless as King Canute, in commanding the tides to "obey." The scheme fell apart, but visitors still recognize that one of these days FDR's dream dam will inevitably become reality, supplying power to a vast part of eastern North America (it should be called, such a superdam, respectfully, the God Dam). On the North American Pacific Coast is the second highest tide, from 24 to 27 feet at the head of the Gulf of California/Sea of Cortez (to be best viewed at Santa Clara Cape.) The hydroelectric "tidal dam" is already operating, a huge *usine maremotice,* a tide motor in the Rance estuary near Saint-Malo, France—a $100,000,000 "reversible" power unit that began operating in 1966.

A tidal bore is a supertide that happens when most of the tide enters a river as a single great wave with a high front. The largest and greatest known is that of Tsientang River in China, which advances upriver from Hangchow Bay in a 10-foot-high wave that reaches a height of 25 feet during spring tides of the full and new moon. The bore of the Amazon River travels 200 miles upstream, so far that as many as five different tides send their superwaves upriver at the same time. Both of these sometimes resemble a mobile waterfall moving rapidly upstream. The Hangchow boatmen casually pull their boats ashore minutes before the bore arrives, as casually alert as the Petitcodiac pigs, and as casually refloat them shortly thereafter in the higher water level.

At Inch'on, Korea, the tides rise and fall up to 33 feet, which makes unloading of cargo a feat to behold. At Awaji, Japan, there's a mile-wide strait connecting the Pacific Ocean and the Inland Sea, through which the Pacific waters rush frantically at high tide. Visitors may either take part in this sudden high-rise spurt aboard a sight-seeing vessel or else passively observe the wild whirlpools in action from a safe observation platform ashore.

The sheer contrast of towering high-forested land soaring far above long fingers of penetrating ocean fjords may best be observed in the far north or far south regions of the globe, for all of these deep ocean bays were dredged out of the granite cliffs by the sharp claws of the Planet Water's generations of polar-ice glaciers, when the great sheets of the latest ice-cap age began to retreat some 12,000 years ago—out of Norway, west Scotland, Iceland, Greenland, along Alaska's Inland Waterway, British Columbia, and, away down southpoleward, in South Island, New Zealand's fjord country, along the famous Milford Sound Footpath (sometimes described by overseas visitors as the loveliest walk in the world; it *is* at the end of the world).

Thalassotherapy—the curative action of sea bathing and the effect of breathing the healthful bromide- and iodide-laden atmosphere just above the ocean's surfaces—also creates a wondrous scenic enhancement toward improved mental health. Jean Chatelain, director of the museums of France, once expressed this thalassophilosophy when asked what art treasures he'd care to take along to a desert island: "Nothing: I think one ought, on a desert island beach, to feast on the magnificent rising and setting of the sun and perhaps the seashells and birds; but if this is not enough, I will make sand castles."

M. Chatelain mentioned enjoying the seashells, but did not specifically suggest listening to them. The smallest child is told to hold the lips of the shell to his ear, that he will then maybe hear the very *sound* of the sea. (A man who described himself as a "born loser" in our too busy urban society complained, "Even when I put a seashell to my ear, I got a busy signal.") Poet Eugene Lee-Hamilton has explained that we are indeed listening to the sea, but to the surprising sound of its waters many millions of years ago when we once lived in it, since the sound is, in fact, the sea *within* us:

> The hollow sea-shell held against the ear
> Proclaims its stormy parent, and we hear
> The faint, far murmur of the breaking flood.
> We hear the sea. The Sea? It is the blood
> In our own veins, impetuous and near.

And it is also, simply, the gathered-in sound of things around us, reflected inward to our ear out of the shell's audial mirror.

When we visit the beachside, it is unfortunate that we must usually "face" only to either east or west, since beaches usually edge continents, and thus we must accept either sunrises or sunsets. I am greedy to the extent of wishing for both. I want to get up with the sight of the dawn coming up over the sea; but that same evening I should also like to be able to observe the sunset take place down over the face of the sea, and, especially, I want to see that rare sight, the *green flash* that takes place under the right circumstances when the sun sets into (over) the ocean. I want also to listen for the faint "sizzle" that was once said to occur when the sun goes down into the sea: in the Middle Ages, *every* careful scientist-observer claimed that he had actually *heard* it.

The seaside is a great place also for studying the stars. Abraham Lincoln is reported to have often gone up to the battlements of the Smithsonian Institution, during his Presidency, to observe the motion of the stars. The open sky over the sea is a much clearer place out/up into which to look to discover for oneself how far is *up*, and also how high is *out*. In December, 1966, a United Nations Committee on Outer Space was not able to define just what "outer space" may be! A delightful cartoon by Jaf showed a little boy and girl beneath galaxies of stars, with one asking, "And where do you come from?" as we may all ask each other, at the beach, whenever we look upward/ outward at night.

Shoreside is a place for viewing moonbeams, and also for examining rainbows and that rare other occurrence—moonbows—as well as that still rarer other seaside phenomenon (common to foggy areas like Monhegan Island in the Bay of Maine northward to the Grand Banks of Newfoundland), fogbows.

One cannot help thinking that man's oldest night science, astronomy, must have begun on a Greek beach. Daylight skywatching on the beach is also wonderful, for the cloud formations to be studied: great pilgrimages and caravans of camels, hippomonstrosities, and various other unidentifiable monsters that could have just risen living out of the living sea, from just over and beyond the horizon. And some simply look like huge icebergs floating in the sea of the sky, as though they'd quietly risen from the Oceanic Labrador Current, shifting quite naturally upward into the air currents of the sky above. Such gigantic sky-wide displays, and all made of such simple, primitive elements as a little dust surrounded by a modicum of water vapor!

A storm is especially exciting over the beach (when it is arriving, beach umbrellas, blankets, and chairs are hastily folded up, and lunch baskets tucked under arms and carried precipitately back to the car). "Primitive peoples explained weather simply," Commander David C. Holmes, USN, and Marvin Pitkin explained, in *On the Wings of the Wind.* "It was a form of punishment or reward visited upon them by the deities. Good weather came from benevolent, happy gods; storm and drought meant that these overlords were angry. The beating of drums and the offering of sacrifices were the best way of appeasing their wrath and changing the weather."

After a spell of foggy, overcast beach weather, many vacationists join in rites guaranteed to clear the skies quickly. Sometimes they do. Meantime, the *Wings* authors have described the massive unities present in the atmosphere that are on a planet-wide scale immense enough to make battle royal on an equal power basis with the sea and the land: "The air over us is divided into huge *air masses*—continents of air drifting with the

winds of earth. These air masses have vastly differing characteristics and, as they drift over our part of the world, they vary our
weather and cover us with alternate umbrellas of rain, snow, or
sunshine."

"Now" is such an evanescent thing that the great storm
which we experience personally beside the sea is soon a part of
our memory, no longer much more personal than, say, the vicarious memory of Demosthenes practicing his rhetoric at seaside against the wild waves' voices. To put small pebbles in
one's mouth and then try shouting against the sound of the
waves isn't a helpful way to learn to declaim, because the waves'
sound comes and goes; but so does the interrupting outcry of
individuals in an audience or a mob, so perhaps this *is* an excellent means of preparing for public speaking. But in memory,
the "real" personal experience and the experience remembered
from having read about it are soon melded into part of the
same common memory web. The "now" that we live in moves
steadily forward as the ever living "present moment," while all
else quickly disappears, gone down either into the wastebasket
of total oblivion or into the half-shadow of something called
memory. Places revisited, whether historical and read about or
actually and personally experienced, are all part of some mysterious past that is at least part fiction on a grand scale, though
known respectfully as "history" (made up by others) or recol-
lection (our own personal made-up history-fiction). Herodotus,
known respectfully as the Father of History, could equally be
called (with all respect, too) the Father of Fable. Each of us is
similarly part fabulist and part historian, when remembering
our own past personal and vicarious experiences.

And each of us, on the beach, is washed clean and new, as is
the beach itself, the very latest form of life that has come out
of that mysterious space/cosmos/emptiness up/out there in the
mysterious everythingness overhead. In a recently compiled immense potpourri of seaside information, *Beaches—Their Lives,
Legends and Lore*, Robert and Seon Manley asked the visitor to
"take a look at any beach; it appears old and changeless, but
every day it is in the process of being reborn. It changes with
the mercurial swiftness of adolescence; with one wave the beach
is cleared of the sand castle of childhood; with one winter storm
its new maturity can be eroded." But the Manleys could have

added that the visitor at the beach can also reexamine himself as someone new. For it is a surprisingly free area of renewal where one can almost forget the past and hopefully contemplate the future. Overhead at night one may see falling stars, the cosmic dust of dead meteoritic material burning out in our atmosphere (15,000 tons of solid matter falling from outer space per day) or, on clocklike schedule, the repassing of rockets in orbit that man has set in the sky to extend our examination and understanding of the outer atmosphere. The New York *Times* carries a daily timetable of visible rockets, appropriately adjacent to the listings of ship arrivals and tidal information.

The most important thing at the beach for all of us is not the big celestial-cosmological show overhead (even though it is sufficiently impressive to make a pantheist out of the most dedicated atheist or even agnostic among us). My special seashore bag has always been the seashells underfoot. Not a dedicated and educated conchologist (which I understand to be a knowledgeable shell collector, though it also applies to the Bahamians who eat conch for breakfast, lunch, and dinner—in soup, salad, and entrée daily), and not knowing by name *who* used to live in them, I *do* nevertheless enjoy gathering them. The former householders are long departed, and the broken bits of shell now will make especially excellent pocket twiddies, what the Greeks call *komboloi*, "worry beads," and the American Indians made into wampum, money or compiled tribal history: something to give especial digital pleasure and oceanic memories to the twiddler when he is far from the seashore. Finger feelies or digital diddlies may also be chestnuts, rabbit feet, or numerous other what-alls, carried as good-luck charms; but my pleasure in them has always had purely to do with the constant evocation of sense of touch and, especially, the evocative, emissive power of bits of *sea*shell. They should be called "jolly beads," not "worry beads." This is important, in our age when so much of our so-called activity consists of passive bystander-spectatorhood, wherein we are not part of the active, creative spectacle: "To Grandma's house we go," one can enunciate, twiddling a tidbit of seashell and imagining oneself to be a mollusk descendant on the way to Grandma Mermaid's undersea palace.

Prayer beads are a precious spiritual commodity among the pious of many sects. Among Muslims, black coral is held to be especially sacred. Captain Jacques-Yves Cousteau reported that at Djeddah, Saudi Arabia, the local dock workers asked for the chance to hold pieces of black coral, which they then pressed against their hearts and foreheads. He gave a holy *morceau* of the precious black coral to the great artist Pablo Picasso, and when he visited him a year later at his villa at Cannes, "Pic" was still carrying it in his pocket. "As he drew it out, I saw," Cousteau remarked, "that the polish had been further heightened by the caresses of the most creative hand in the world." Each of us does this to the pocket pieces we carry, in our own equally secretive, creative way.

In Honolulu, a new firm, Maui Divers of Hawaii, set out at the end of 1969 to sell pink coral (valued at $500 to $600 a pound) made into jewelry. Does "pink" coral have the holiness of the black? If so, it's of course worth a half-thou a pound. What a truly *crazy* planet this is.

If "Full fathom five thy father lies;/Of his bones are coral made. . . ./Nothing of him that doth fade/But doth suffer a sea-change/Into something rich and strange," then maybe good old dad turned into a water baby? Is rubbing a bit of coral therefore a sort of ancestor worship (or father befuddling)? It is interesting that Shakespeare gave these lines to Ariel shortly after Sir George Somers' famous shipwreck-discovery of Bermuda in the late summer of 1609.

In *Ring of Bright Water*, Gavin Maxwell gave a beautiful picture of the treasure trove of seashells to be discovered along the shores of his beloved Camusfeàrna, in northern Scotland, but I found far more fascinating his investigation of "every weird piece of flotsam or jetsam and considering what useful purpose it might be made to serve." He summed up the richnesses to be expected out of the seas' bounty: "If one waits long enough practically every imaginable household object will sooner or later turn up on the beaches. . . . Beachcombing retains for me now the same fascination and eager expectancy that it held then. After a westerly or south-westerly gale one may find almost anything."

One goes to beaches either in great crowds, both awful and awesome, armed with transistor radios and overheard conversations, or else for genuine privacy, which so many people are afraid of. However, if you manage to go at off-hours to even the usually most crowded beaches, there is still some splendid privacy to be discovered and enjoyed there. We very much need *both* kinds of beach experience—the extremes of many people joyfully released all together beneath the sun and beside the sea, and the private, very personal pleasure of giving oneself up to the solitary joy of being enjoyed by the ocean. The greatest danger today, and a very real one, on a par with the pollution problem (in 1968, a Water Pollution agency of the U.S. Department of the Interior announced the invention of a new underwater "bubble" curtain to block polluted wastes offshore from beaches; this could hold off from man's pleasure beaches the pollution, 90 percent U.S.-contributed, that man has poisoned the sea with) is the steady increase of legal moves by private property owners to *close off* "their" beaches that had always previously been assumed to be open to public use. GET OUT OF MY SAND: DISPUTES FLARE OVER PUBLIC USE OF BEACHES, the *Wall Street Journal* headlined the "Keep Out" meanness, in January, 1969. Of some 12,000 miles of general shoreline in the United States (that includes Hawaii and Alaska), only about 1,000—or a little more than 8 percent—are state- or federal-owned and therefore protected for universal public use. The rest has always been up for grabs, very much so, and been going-going-gone far too fast into KEEP OFF private possession of the worst sort. When a man buys property, he *should* realize that he is only holding it in trust, this oceanside paradise, for others also to enjoy. Few property owners ever get to recognize and *enjoy* the generous invitation that is an integral part of their conditional and temporary "ownership"-occupancy. Instead of inviting every stranger to be a guest and enjoy the view of the surf, the sound of the waves, they usually ruin their own pleasure by forever "standing guard" against the outsider. Or perhaps that *is* the oceanside property owner's true pleasure, to be able to deny to someone else the joy of it.

The shorefront landowner cannot spread out, like an immense cabbage leaf, to cover his property. But why doesn't he ever joyfully *share it*? "Welcome," in this situation, is as weird an invitation as the U.S. Army's "Greetings" extended to the new draftee. Privacy? After poet Maxwell wrote his north Scotland saga, his hiding place was incessantly invaded thereafter by countless insistent readers who'd loved his story and considered that they therefore had a *right* to go check the local seashore. Privacy we all need, but where is the drawing line? There are so few places where inlanders can simply go to the seashore and have relative aloneness with the sea. Today somebody else usually owns it.

Of all the fearful and wonderful things that the sea can drive up on the beach, the most woebegone are human refugees from shipwreck. The best stories I know of this castaway clash are all pure fiction, for example, Dickens' description of the wicked Steerforth shipwrecked and drowned as punishment for having long before coaxed the good Little Em'ly to run away with him. Her honorable, licit lover, Ham (as meek a man as Dobbin, the decent gent who loved Becky Sharp so rewardlessly in *Vanity Fair*), loved Little Em'ly in *David Copperfield*: meek Ham was rewarded with death, alongside the wicked Steerforth, by drowning. Ham is, I guess, representative of all of us who hang about a seashore at stormtime and shouldn't. By all *moral* projection, Ham should have won Little Em'ly. Another piece of fine fictioneering is Robinson Crusoe's arrival through the surf to safety, brief solitude, and later the delightful life of an English gentleman on an isolated island—with a lifetime indentured manservant, Friday. The claim has always been put forward that Tobago is Robinson Crusoe's Island, yet every bit of evidence indicates that Defoe was rewriting, ever so magically, the story of Alexander Selkirk, the Scottish mariner who in 1704 was put ashore (not marooned: he had asked for it) on Mas a Tierra, off Chile, in the Pacific Ocean, where he spent four years and four months before he was picked up by Captain Woodes Rogers, became mate of the vessel, and later rose to his own command.

Dickens and Defoe are both as suspect as exact historians as was Herodotus, because they too are such excellent fiction writers. *Did they experience it themselves?* No! The answer presumably is that this is fiction and should be recognized as romanticized make-believe. In similar fashion, Melville's giving stark life to Owen Chase's rather sparse narrative of the sinking of the whaleship *Essex,* in the final traumatic death-scene episode of *Moby Dick,* is questionable in its reality. Reality is often so dull, until the fabulist and inspired fictioneer get to work on it and give life to what ordinary mortals cannot express with sufficient richness to grab us, though anyone at all may make notes or keep diaries on what has happened to him. Hopefully, the diary then falls into the right fictioneer's hands!

Dickens: "The tremendous sea itself, when I could find sufficient pause to look at it, in the agitation of the blinding wind, the flying stones and sand, and the awful noise, confounded one. As the high watery walls came rolling in, and, at their highest, tumbled into surf, they looked as if the least would engulf the town. As the receding wave swept back with a hoarse roar, it seemed to scoop out deep caves in the beach, as if its purpose were to undermine the earth. When some white-headed billows thundered on, and dashed themselves to pieces before they reached the land, every fragment of the late whole seemed possessed by the full might of its wrath, rushing to be gathered to the composition of another monster. . . . The height to which the breakers rose, and, looking over one another, bore one another down, and rolled in, in interminable hosts, was most appalling" (*David Copperfield*).

How does one come ashore from this? Daniel Defoe: "A raging wave, mountain-like, came rolling astern of us. It took us with such a fury that it overset the boat at once: we were all swallowed up in a moment. Though I swam very well, yet I could not deliver myself from the waves so as to draw breath, till that wave having driven me, or rather, carried me a vast way on towards the shore, and having spent itself, went back, and left me upon the land almost dry, but half-dead with the water I took in" (*Robinson Crusoe*).

Sandy beaches are usually best for bathing, whether one is wading only up to the knees or plunging through the waves. Most beach bathers have always believed that something dangerous called "undertow" can suck them out to a watery death in time of storm. But Francis P. Shepard tells us that "in some of our early studies of shore processes at Scripps Institution we helped dispel the old myth about the dangers of undertow. . . . The really dangerous currents, which cause so many drownings, move seaward at the surface to an even greater degree than they do along the bottom." He also explained that the water carried in by the waves must return somehow, and usually does by an offshore movement called a rip current or riptide or sea puss. "The best means of escape," he advises, "is to swim parallel to the shore until free of the current on one side or the other, where the water is shoaler and where the current is either slack or moving toward the beach." Outward-bound surfboard riders often use a strong sea puss to ride *out* through the breakers.

Oceanside bays and marshes are today, as they have perhaps always been, the birthplace of many sea creatures, but they are also the magical in-between ground where our ancestors at some point made the decision to leave the sea and come ashore to live. Bewailing our vanishing shoreline, Alfred Bester described this in-between territory wherein "the outward flow of the river is strong enough to offset the inward thrust of the ocean tides. Consequently, the marshes of the estuary are neither salt nor fresh, but brackish. They provide a haven and nursery for fish fry, baby shrimp, and shellfish. The salt-water predators don't like the fresh water in the bay and won't come in after their prey. The fresh-water predators don't like the salt water and won't come down the river. On the other hand, the swarming marshes are an ideal feeding ground for wildfowl."

I like best to visit the bays and marshes at nighttime and at low tide, when life is busiest and the aroma of the brackish fresh-salt water is most pungent. One must carry a flashlight, and look sharply, in order to see the hermit crabs dashing about with their trailer homes over their heads; it becomes a game to see which snail shell has an inhabitant. Old horeshoe crabs lumber about with senatorial dignity and are not as terrified as in daylight. I am always respectful of these senior persons, as it has been suggested that they may be in the direct line of our vertebrate ancestry ever so far back to the Arthropods. A shallow bay, with low tide rippling over the seaweed and pebbles, and a few of these old gentlemen and ladies moving sedately about (they pick up soft marine worms in their nippers and tuck them into their mouths, not altogether unlike our own table approach to certain raw cocktail snacks), is the place also to contemplate that first great migration of life from sea to land, which must have taken place in some such shallow, brackish place as this.

Less than a hundred miles north of New York City, wholly

neglected and rarely mentioned in tourist literature, are the Gilboa fossil tree fern stumps, remains of the oldest-known petrified forest on earth, which once grew beside a shallow sea in the Middle Devonian Period some 370,000,000 years ago. The seashore and site of the forest happened to be at Gilboa. A little more than a century ago, in 1860, a flash flood in the valley of Schoharie Creek exposed these strange, utterly unknown chunks of defunct lumber that looked (and still look) like immense petrified elephants' feet. These were among the first living creatures to make up their minds to leave the sea and take up existence on the bare land surface.

There's a reconstruction of the discovery site in the New York State Museum, at Albany, but the half-dozen stumps standing in a lonely wood in Gilboa are far more impressive, all by themselves. One can with imagination enjoy their waddling ashore. In their prime, they once stood some 40 feet tall. A big pussycat was sitting on one on the day of my visit, and she rose to greet me, later disappearing, perhaps back into one of the fossil tree stumps. In fact, I wondered if she were not perhaps a modern reincarnated spirit of the earliest quadruped amphibian that came ashore to live beneath the giant new tree ferns. Greetings, *Diplovertebron,* though the modern spirit purred and the original was silent. Silent also were the immense dragonflies, cockroaches, scorpions, spiders, millipedes, and other insects who came out of the primitive seas to crawl, creep, or fly above the marshy, boggy swamps, and the innumerable new breed of seaside tree ferns. A few million years more, and the gigantic reptiles would arrive to replace the amphibians, and presently the strange new creatures called mammals, who hatched their eggs instead of leaving them hapless in the sea or carelessly buried in sand, and then nursed the younglings with warm milk (they were warm-blooded, too) and introduced to livingkind the strange, new warmth of motherliness to which we mammals still cling. Fatherliness must always have been present, as still evidenced by the fatherly elegance of the ancient horseshoe crabs who still stomp about in patriarchal dignity. Ginkgo trees arrived 100,000,000 or so years after the Gilboa breed, and this remarkable fossil breed of trees is still with us; when I stand beneath a ginkgo in Stuyvesant Town—in the heart of New York City's crowded Manhattan—and look up at these handsome, ancient trees, it is quite easy to imagine a dinosaur scratching the immense side of his hide against it, or eating it as a modern muley cow will devour grass.

We go to the sandy beaches in order to plunge into the sea, and to the marshy bays to study life at the sea's verge, but there is a third area where the most titanic battles of sea, land, and air take place—where there are high cliffs that face the seas head-on and take the brunt of mighty storms. This area contains the best places from which to contemplate the never-ending wars. The outermost western American coasts, where the granite cliffs are not merely holding off the attacks of the sea's waves but are actually taking the battle to the enemy, are the most dramatic scene of this elemental conflict between irresistible water force and immovable granite object. The great cliffs hold off the sea's attacking waves—whose force can reach up to three tons per square foot, and whose fearful sound has been reported, at Tierra del Fuego, Chile's southernmost tip of South America, as booming more than 20 miles inland. Rachel Carson once described this furious onset in the area that oceanographers refer to as the "seamill": "On a rocky shore this grinding and polishing of rocks and fragments of rocks goes on incessantly and audibly, for the breakers on such a coast have a different sound from those that have only sand to work with—a deep-toned mutter and rumble not easily forgotten."

Along the 90-mile stretch of California coast from the Monterey Peninsula to Los Angeles, one may drive southward upon the sharp edges of the Santa Lucia mountain cliffs where they steeply overhang the Pacific Ocean, sometimes almost seeming about to tumble over. "On no other part of the coast do earth and water come so dramatically together," Calvin Kentfield has said, "and at no other place does the traveler feel so strongly that he is at the limit of his human world—hanging on by his fingernails."

One cannot excerpt "simply" from the works of Robinson Jeffers. Ralph Waldo Emerson is unreadable "in bulk," but his nuggets of wisdom on innumerable subjects are forever the best. Jeffers has best poeticized Big Sur: "Here where the surf has come incredible ways out of the splendid west, over the deeps." And: "The tides are in our veins, we still mirror the stars, life is in your child, but there is in me older and harder than life and more impartial, the eye that watched before there was an ocean."

All right, one mustn't start picking at it—you need great *belts* of Jeffers, as of Randall Jarrell: neither will get neatly excerpted into neat, Emersonian concentrated ingots. There are all kinds of different richnesses. Jeffers was horrified—almost beyond expression—at the changes happening, chiefly manmade, to the Pacific shore. Perhaps the worst experience, for a reader, is to examine the work of a sincere poet describing the work of man the polluter. Jeffers (Jarrell also), even as you and I, should have lived in better, less cancerous days!

The 17-mile circuit of Monterey Peninsula is a microcosm of the best in ocean-land battle viewing. When Robert Louis Stevenson was living there, in 1879, and garnering much of its wondrous scenery to later furbish out *Treasure Island*, he described this shoreland of ancient cypresses and offshore colonies of sea lions as "the finest meeting place of land and water."

The Washington-Oregon seacoast is a vivid northward continuation of the violent war zone. Across the continent, Acadia National Park, on Maine's Cadillac Mountain, has low seaside cliffs where visitors may view the Atlantic Ocean flailing the retreating North American coast at Thunder Hole and Anemone Cave—and being resisted by the land with pertinacious Yankee granitic fury. Charlton Ogburn, Jr., spoke with an unexpected tenderness of the terrible effect this constant buffeting has on the land. In *The Winter Beach,* he said: "The sea never ceases its attack on the rocky shores, never for a moment through untold centuries, through millennia. It has two chief methods for cutting them back. One is by the explosive force of the waves as they are slammed together against an air pocket in a crevice or under an overhanging ledge. The other is by using the rocks thus dislodged to batter and grind one another and the exposed bedrock. On such a coast as Maine's, if the sea is running, you can hear the continual dull knocking and scraping of rocks on rocks—an ominous sound if you have the interests of the land at heart and of the trees at the edge of the cliff."

One summer, I spent a week of contemplation and cliff climbing on Monhegan, which is, in a small, tight-up, and puritanical American sort of way, our holy isle, the Occidental equivalent, say, of what Ceylon is for ever so many Muslim,

Hindus, Buddhists, and Christians (where there is even a foot-print of Buddha or maybe Adam, plainly visible on a sacred mountain peak). Instead of posh parades of elephants bearing holy relics, at Monhegan—out in the Bay of Maine—one can just live simply, after foggy nightfall, by lamplight (there's no electricity) and spend the daylight hours climbing the cliffs that border the sea.

Here there are no automobiles (only a half-dozen trucks that operate only along the one roadway between dock and hotels and guest homes), no bustle, no sidewalks, no crowds. The great cliffs on the outer side of the island were hailed by the Sierra Club as "about as close an approximation of true wilder-ness as is likely to be found along the coast of Maine." From the cliffs, examining and listening to the ever-changing sea, one is assuaged as Euripides must have been, nearly two and a half millennia ago, when he said: "The sea doth wash away all human ills." But I found Job was also with me, after all that painful climbing of cliffs, with his wisdom: "Speak to the earth, and it shall teach thee."

At such a place one contemplates the sea partly in worship and partly in sheer confrontation. A New York photographer showed a comfortable summer audience slides of a wild winter scene: a nor'easter storm whose spray and spume were roaring over the top of 160-foot Black Head, the highest cliff on the island. When Charlton Ogburn visited Port Clyde (the land-ward end of the year-round ferry service) on his icy tour of win-ter beaches, he picked up a chunk of granite—the stuff of continents—and a comparable wedge of basalt, the underlying heavier magma. Here one is surely very close to the aboriginal beginning of all earthly things. My son and I toured the intri-cate network of clifftop trails, carefully avoiding the wet sea-weed as the island literature ominously advises. While we were there, another man and teen-aged son were both drowned. The Monhegan Associates booklet warns: "Never walk on rocks covered with seaweed; combers come without warning"—a vivid example of how this great force in our lives, the sea, when given the sly chance to take one of us, often cannot resist the amorous impulse. The body is, of course, almost always re-turned: it is the spirit, obviously, that is found so desirable.

At many a high point along the edges of the continents there are special command posts where the war against the sea is waged most extravagantly. Such a place is Land's End, in British Cornwall, which has the added wonder of continuous occupancy ever since earliest human times by seafaring men. Along the sharp coasts, steep cliffs stand up to and hold off the perpetual North Atlantic poundings; inland, there are immense megalithic temple ruins, at Stonehenge and Avebury (nobody knows how the huge stones were rafted overwater from the quarries 190 miles away, with plenty of—Serfs Up—slave labor), and the old tin mines that once provided the metal to early sea visitors from the easternmost Mediterranean, who carried the treasured tin back to Anatolia and Greece and Phoenicia, where it could be cleverly joined with locally mined copper to create bronze tools and statues that are still beautiful today. The fantastically courageous early Mediterranean mariners, after braving the eastward-inflowing waters at the Pillars of Hercules, as they edged out into the extreme Atlantic, must surely have known as they drew near to the cliffs of Cornwall that they were approaching the terrible platter edge of the flat earth, over which the unwary could so quickly and easily tumble into the infinity of oblivion. What truly brave, and avaricious, men! Since they came from the tideless Mediterranean, one wonders with what dread they must also have observed for the first time the teeming, heaving tides in the open North Atlantic—stirred up, obviously, by tail waggings of the most ferocious, colossal sea monsters (hungering, they must have also supposed, for sun-toasted golden Greek seamen as a pleasant change-off from codfish, herring, and other cold-blooded prey).

Along Long Island's Old Montauk Highway, there's a brief corniche atop the gravel cliffs that may remind the wider traveler of cliff-hanger roads in Monaco or along the Italian Riviera, but here one sees no Rivieran sun-seekers in sheer bikinis on an unbeach (there are no "true" sandy beaches in southern Europe, as Americans know them, mostly because of the Mediterranean lack of tide, and too many northern European beaches are of rough, coarse shale); rather, one views a vast mass of patient human surfers on boards, waiting-waiting-waiting for waves. Not far beyond this usually undramatic beach (which someday I hope to see while a great, surging Atlantic storm is bringing in the surfers' long-awaited giant waves), beyond the town of Montauk, one approaches an outstanding example of the continuing tragedy of the land losing to the sea, in the perpetual wars that a sightseer can too easily think of as merely for fun, like a game, and not for desperate real. At the very eastern tip end of Long Island, on a gravel cliff at Montauk Point, President George Washington ordered a lighthouse constructed. A 168-foot tower was designed and built, in 1793, by the noted architect John McComb; it originally stood all of 293 feet back from the edge of the gravel cliff and the threat of the pounding Atlantic surf. Today the distance has been reduced to a mere 65 feet that is still continuing to diminish rapidly. Here the land generals—for a proper defense—should perhaps have employed a granite foundation rather than gravel? Surely this battle is a mismatch approaching an inevitable one-sided victory. All around the perimeter of Long Island Sound, old granite lighthouses are today being replaced by automated beacons set on plain steel towers, and very soon it will also be farewell to Washington's Montauk lighthouse.

Worrying about this light's demise, one also worries about the White Cliffs of Dover, alongside *La Manche,* which the insular British call the English Channel. One estimate has the famous chalk cliffs presently retreating at a rate between ten inches and a yard per year. Some North American seaside chalk cliffs are reported to be giving way at twice that rate. One trembles for the loss of the many-hued clays of Gay Head, on Martha's Vineyard. Notable evidence, all this, that ours is a constantly changing world; it is the rapidity of change that is so shocking. If François Villon had climbed as a young lad and returned later, he might have mourned, *"Ou sont les rochers escarpes d'anton?"* for the ocean-honed diminishment seems not much swifter than the sun-melting of snowdrifts.

Some of the land-ocean changes are due to the apparent "tipping"—rearing and rocking—of the continents. The American northeast coast is considered to be "drowned topography" (which may still have some rise left in it, from the long-departed tremendous downpush of the last Ice Age), as is the northwest coast around Puget Sound. And the mountainous California coast is supposed to be rising.

If continental drift is a reality, and the United States is being pushed very slowly westward, then the pressure of Atlantic waves beating on the cliffs of Monhegan Island, Maine, has been the maritime force giving a push, so to speak, to the tiny tail of the dog. Since mid-1968 the research ship *Glomar Challenger* has been drilling holes in the floor of the Atlantic and Pacific oceans. Examination of borings taken from the South Atlantic "basement" indicate that from 10,000,000 to 80,000,000 years ago, South America and Africa were being pushed apart at about two inches a year, whereas those from the North Atlantic floor show the United States and Europe to be diverging at about half that rate. At the other edge of North America, California's two major cities, perched precariously above the famous San Andreas Fault, where violent slippage caused the disastrous San Francisco earthquake of 1906, are said to be moving slowly on their way toward each other, so that by about 50,000,000 years from now, San Francisco and Los Angeles may be one, as unbelievable as would be any future conjoining of Dallas and Fort Worth or that of any other unlikely and incompatible siblings.

Dr. Richard P. Von Herzen, of the Woods Hole Oceanographic Institution, has suggested that about 10,000,000 years ago California may have been pushed across a Pacific counterpart of the mid-Atlantic ridge; the buried ridge would account for the new young mountains between the Rockies and the Pacific coast, with their hot springs, geysers, and recently alive volcanoes. For the immediate future, experts have begun warning Californians that the fault zone beneath them is being very sharply loaded with stress and that the situation is fast becoming critical. Dr. William T. Pecora, of the Geological Survey, has forecast a major San Francisco disaster repeat surely within thirty years, "but probably within the next decade"! Sightseers are disaster-prone in that while they would not "wish" such catastrophes on others, they *do* want to be somehow safely present to observe them if they happen to happen. It would be interesting to know how the Californian coast-slide warnings affect both residents and visitors. In October, 1969, a San Pedro oceanside cliff cracked open, leisurely sliding palatial homes about like checkers. When one thinks of the thousands of residents in many new housing subdivisions thrown up boldly and so foolishly within known San Andreas Fault areas, one is again reminded of the Matthew 7:26 parable of the unwise man who built his home on sand. Though all of us live dangerously, this dwelling in expectation of someday tumbling into the sea or into the earth seems as foolish, in our scientifically knowledgeable age, as the folly of unknowing Pompeiians and Herculaneans dwelling at the foot of drowsing Vesuvius.

The northern seashores are to be visited in winter, when a wholly different aspect of the earth-sea warfare is to be observed. There are wide ice sheets over the low-tide areas. The inevitable sea gulls stand happily about in the ice water, refusing as always to dive *under* for their food as a true water bird would do. This is the time of year for building great fires of driftwood, for simple picnics of hot dogs toasted on sticks over the flames, of opened cans of pork and beans heated in midfire, and of throwing leftovers into the sky to the sea gulls, who by midwinter will have become almost as adept as terns at flying by to catch food in midair. This is the time of year when the shore offers a great sea escape from citified, winterized, shut-in living. So few people go to the shore in midwinter that it is far easier to experience it personally at this time. Tropical seas are a happy alternative from the rigors of northern winters, but the cold edges of the northern oceans have a special kind of lonely difference from home that is like nothing else in the world.

Vasco Nuñez de Balboa viewed the Pacific Ocean from a peak in Darien in 1513. John Keats, carefully measuring out the beat of his lines, took poetic license to substitute the two-syllable name of Hernán Cortés as a better-metered discoverer:

> Or like stout Cortez when with eagle eyes
> He star'd at the Pacific—and all his men
> Look'd at each other with a wild surmise—
> Silent, upon a peak in Darien.

(Clifton Fadiman, oh, superb punster, once drew on this rich, vintage Keats to describe a rare, high cheese.) Poor Balboa's wild surmising may even have included premonitions of decapitation, which he was to suffer only four years later, on suspicion of plotting a revolt.

Balboa got to see only one ocean at a time. Today, by visiting the top of Mount Irazú, a few miles north of Balboa's lookout, in Costa Rica, one may view *two oceans at once*—both the Atlantic and the Pacific. The only other way you can accomplish this global cartographic adventure is by traveling all the way south to the tip of South America, at Cape Horn, and there trying to surmise, wildly, just where the Atlantic Ocean ends and the Pacific Ocean begins.

One may make the transcontinental journey across America— from sea to shining sea, all the way from one ocean to the other —for less than $2 train fare, which turns out to be the Isthmus railroad journey alongside the Panama Canal. From the top of a small mountain on the island of Tobago, it is possible also to see two oceans—the Atlantic and the Caribbean, one called an ocean and the other a sea. "I never was on the dull, tame shore, but I loved the great sea more and more." The poet longs to go to sea, while the sailor dreams of coming ashore. But to see the three great elemental *forces* of the Planet Water—the sea, the land, and the air—at their finest or worst, we must stand on the edge, the meeting place, in time of stress and storm, for here *is* the perpetual battle royal, the living planet's utmost expression of violent livingness. Here is nature's place called Armageddon, the standpoint of the first and last battle of the world, where the hurly-burly is never done and where the battle is forever both lost and also won.

IV Man Goes to Sea

W E are inevitably conditioned by our everyday surroundings, and I find myself especially made sea-minded daily because of a wall-wide 1965 *National Geographic* Van der Grinten projection map labeled, simply, "The World," in my bedroom that shows the United States as a tiny node in the narrow vertical terrestrial sliver of North America between two immense watery-blue oceanic vastnesses, the Atlantic and Pacific—with the lesser land masses of Europe and Asia out beyond. Of course, in this Mercator-like projection, Greenland is disproportionately enormous. But one is immediately made conscious, in looking at this map, of the fact that we live on the Planet Water; also, seeing the tiny United States at mid-map, no private American citizen in his right mind could begin to acquire imperialist ideas of world domination. Inevitably, he'd meantime become ocean-minded and eager to embark on voyages of investigation overseas.

The map's been put down, naturally; in *Mapping*, David Greenhood called it "pleasing, though its value is pictorial rather than technical." But at wake-up time, who could become "technical" about the world? Meantime, I have visited a U.S.S.R. tourist office in New York City where there is an immense Eurasian map that carries the Soviet Union practically wall-wide, so that the rest of the world—all Europe, China, the Atlantic and Pacific oceans, the Americas—are crowded together along the extreme peripheral map *edges*. How could anyone, using such a land-centered map daily, have any idea of

the vast extent of the planet's *watery* surfaces and of the wonder of faraway places out beyond the land-centered condensation that is Eurasian Mother Russia?

This present-day Soviet map is surprisingly typical also of
early Mediterranean man's kind of misconceptions, especially
his firm conviction that the planet's surface was flat, surrounded by the Ocean River, and mostly made of dry land.
Such is the oldest map to come down to us, a Babylonian clay
tablet of 2500 B.C., which is on view today in the Semitic Museum at Harvard University. By 580 B.C. a Greek scholar, Anax-
imander of Miletus, had put together "the whole circuit of the
earth, every sea and all rivers"; it was spherical, with longitude
and latitude, but still flat, mostly land, and, of course, circled
by the River Oceanus. One wonders if these early scientists ever
worried about a population explosion, or whether they thought
of their flat earth as Gertrude Stein did of North America: "In
the United States there is more space where nobody is than
where anybody is."

"Hail, earth, Mother of all!" the Greek poet Meleager sup-
plicated her, in 30 B.C., and so did all other poets for the next
1,500 years, until Henry the Navigator at last discovered that
the planet's surface was more watery than earthy.

The study of maps appears usually to be mostly a male addic-
tion. When a family plans an automobile voyage, and maps are
secured from the AAA or one of the gasoline companies, it is
the males—grandfathers, fathers, and sons—who examine them
most carefully. The advance pleasure of the maps is as joyous
for men as the actual traveling. Phyllis McGinley has soundly
expressed the female view of such male nonsense: "A woman
gets where she is going with a minimum of fuss and temper; she
is not too proud to inquire directions and when they are being
given to her, she listens; men would rather pore endlessly over
maps, however inadequate, or else make out by intuition."

In a breathtaking work published in 1966, *Maps of the Ancient Sea Kings*, Dr. Charles Hapgood suggested that as long
ago as 12,000 years there was a civilization of worldwide sea
travelers "that must have dominated much of the world; the evidence is rather plentiful—at least potentially." The first
exhibit was a sea chart drawn by a Turkish admiral, Piri Re'is,
dated A.D. 1513, which was discovered at the Topkapi Palace in

Istanbul in 1929. This map apparently showed the peninsulas of Antarctica as they had looked *before* they acquired their latest mile-thick covering of ice (seismic soundings in 1946 were said to have confirmed the map's accuracy) and even portrayed the topography of the headwaters of South American rivers and other dimensions unknown in the 1920's. Hapgood suggested that the Turkish admiral's map must have been based on an actual examination of original maps or copies dating back to this supposed age of supermariners. We cannot very well search for ancient seaports buried beneath a mile of Antarctic ice. Hapgood placed the possible world headquarters of this remarkable ancient civilization at Cuicuilco, Mexico, near Mexico City, where a pyramid was inundated by lava about A.D. 200. Carbon-14 dating of material from the sediments above the surrounding pavement indicates an age of more than 6,000 years. Here, Hapgood suggested, "We may have a relic of the people who navigated the whole earth, and possessed the advanced sciences necessary to make our ancient maps." The "world capital" buried beneath acres of lava at Cuicuilco isn't likely to be dug up for a long time to come, but in October, 1969, the announcement came out of Cambridge University that "the first large-scale attempt at radar-charting of the ice-buried continent surrounding the South Pole is about to be made." What an outcry will be raised if even one small possession of an ancient sea king should be discovered beneath Marie Byrd Land!

Scholars at the Smithsonian Institution announced in 1966 the discovery of Japanese-like pottery in Ecuador which would seem to indicate that prehistoric men *must* have crossed the Pacific at least as long ago as 5,000 years. In 1966 a Roman scholar announced that discoveries in Peru and Colombia of similarities between Italian and South American polygonal walls and design of jewelry, pottery, and burial urn lids seemed to indicate that either the ancient Etruscans had visited the New World 2,500 years ago or the still more ancient Pelasgians had made the journey more than 3,000 years ago. Vilhjalmur Stefansson has stated: "It is probable that at least those parts of the three continents which border on the Mediterranean were known to each other from the time of the earliest navigators, thus from 30,000 or perhaps 40,000 B.C." Cretans and Phoenicians probably knew of the oceanic worlds beyond the Red Sea and the Mediterranean. In *The Ancient Mariners,* Lionel Casson wondered: "How far did the primitive Mediterranean mariners sail? There are tantalizing archaeological clues which seem to imply trade links between the older civilizations of the eastern Mediterranean and western Europe of prehistoric times: beads of Egyptian faience have turned up in Britain, and there are carvings on Stonehenge that look for all the world like the symbol of the double-ax which the Cretans favored; in Brittany necklaces of a mineral, a rare green phosphate native to the Near East; Spanish pots and figurines bear an odd resemblance to types found in Asia Minor." Carried by ship in remote prehistory or conveyed by long overland journeys in caravans? Lacking any maritime evidence, Casson concluded that the exotic goods had most likely reached far places by land delivery, "passing from hand to hand in village after village." During the 1970's, we may find an entire new maritime history of these early days emerging, as underwater archaeologists begin to piece together a new picture based for the first time on objects found beneath man's sea routes, at the bottom of the oceans.

Man apparently first went to sea in quiet waters, notably in the Nile River, using punting poles to move himself about. On the upper Thames River, about St. John's Lock, you can to this day try the ancient mode of poling your way on a punt, a trying ordeal, indeed, with a 20-foot pole. By 3000 B.C. the Egyptians had to be building extremely large, sound cargo vessels, in order to be able to carry the great stones (1½ tons each, totaling 2,300,000 tons) that would go into the construction of the pyramids at Giza. The *Geographical Review* has presented a remarkable new theory by Edward J. Kunkel, who suggests that the great pyramid of Khufu was perhaps designed and built as a wholly hydraulic structure! This would mean that all the way, from the quarries far up Nile downriver, through dug canals to the base, then vertically upward into place! The vast walls were watertight, Kunkel suggested, raised by the operation of a huge water pump set up *inside* the pyramid, with canal locks zigzagging up the outer pyramid face as it was built. A sort of Panama Canal operation: "There are notches on the inside of the top of each stone to provide clearances for the supporting beams when the next layer of stones was laid. Hitherto these notches have been explained as fulcrums for levers used in placing the stones." Kunkel even made a model of the pump. It is also interesting that the pyramids, monuments erected both to the glory of megalomania and to a firm belief in the afterlife, are made of nummulitic limestone laid down—as slavishly, perhaps?—by the death of large protozoans some 50,000,000 years ago at the bottom of a prehistoric Afroeurasian sea. It is thus much more of a funerary monument to the innumerable nummulites buried here by the billions than to the one Hamitic human king who is no longer in residence.

As important for King Khufu's afterlife as his immense tombstone-pyramid was his solar ship, in which his soul could sail throughout all eternity in pursuit of the sun. In 1954, his 5,000-year-old ship was revealed in a pit opened in the sandy plain on the south side of the great pyramid, where it may be seen today.

In 1493 B.C., Queen Hatshepsut of Egypt, whom historian James H. Breasted called "the first great lady in world history," sent an expedition southward down the Red Sea to Punt, the Land of God, which brought back not only gold but much more expensive incense—used in vast quantities in burnt offerings on the altars of the temples of Amon. This trade to an unknown far-southern land on the other side of the equator had been going on since before 3000 B.C. In about 1481, this first lady was murdered by her young husband, but she had meanwhile portrayed the journey in rich detail in bas-relief and inscription on the walls of her famous temple of Dehr el Bahri, where we can still view the remarkable wall plaques; but we do not yet know where Punt was, though it may have been on the delta of the Zambezi River, and the gold fields may have been in the vicinity of Africa's mysterious giant fortress of Zimbabwe.

Queen Hatshepsut also had large vessels constructed, to carry two 100-foot-long obelisks totaling 700 tons down the Nile. Since Egypt had no forests, the very lumber for these vessels had to be imported. From Byblos, Phoenician ships brought the famous cedars of Lebanon. In 3000 B.C., King Snefru sent a fleet of forty Egyptian vessels to carry back home the precious timbers. Later, in a period of decline when the seaways were no longer open to Byblos, the wail went up from the city of the Egyptian dead, "What shall we do for cedar for our mummies, those trees with whose produce our priests were buried and with whose oil nobles were embalmed?" In 3000 B.C., Mesopotamian princes were importing diorite, a black stone useful for statuary, from the Arabian shore of the Persian Gulf, and evidently the traders of this era also went on eastward all the way across the Arabian Sea to visit the western coast of India.

How did man, a land-surface animal that had come down out of the trees, ever chance to go to sea? Among the ingenious answers offered is an "accidental" concept, by Charles E. Gibson. In *Story of the Ship*, he says that since man is "by nature a land animal, preferring to draw his daily bread from the soil, it is only when the latter fails to satisfy his demands that he turns to the water." Then a bit of maritime philosophizing: "There was a time when man, as a species, knew nothing whatsoever of water transport. He began to learn probably through a liking for fish—grubbing for roots, gathering berries, fruits and leaves, primitive hunting and fishing from the banks. . . . He was forced to improve his fishing catch. . . . The first 'crisis' produced the first 'ship,' a chance floating log, a bundle of reeds which, grasped with one hand, left the other free for fishing." One may make fun of this as oversimplification, but the old salt's theory still holds on shipboard today: "One hand for the ship, one hand for yourself."

What makes men go to sea? During the five years he spent traveling around the world on the *Beagle* (a journey that resulted in his publishing the revolutionary *On the Origin of Species* a quarter of a century later), Charles Darwin was seasick most of the time. So his assessment of the lure of the sea is surely prejudiced: "Even the greatest number of sailors, as it appears to me, have little real liking for the sea itself; if not compelled to it by necessity, visions of glory when very young and force of habit when old are the sole bonds of attraction." In 1970, a 1918 letter by John Masefield ("I must go down to the seas again") says he was seasick all the way.

Dr. Samuel Johnson, who in contrast had spent little or no time at sea, was nevertheless equally unfavorable: "A ship is worse than a jail. There is, in a jail, better air, better company, better conveniency of every kind; and a ship has the additional disadvantage of being in danger. When men come to like a sea-life, they are not fit to live on land."

What makes men go to sea? Charles E. Gibson has given the ultimate reason for the earliest voyages, and it is still apt: ships go "seeking tin and copper ores, gold, silver, precious stones, perfumes, spices, incense, peacocks, apes and other exotic luxuries to grace the persons and homes of the noble classes." Times change, and tastes, too. But the basic fact of international commerce continues—overland, oversea, carrying the exotic, strange merchandise which is not conveniently available on the home market. Gold has always been perhaps the most extreme of sought-after treasures. Columbus' first act, after landing, was to inquire where the gold was to be found. And Balboa, naming the newly discovered "South Sea" (he saw it in that direction), first called it the Golden Sea, since the precious metal was topmost in his mind. Virgil sorrowed, "O cursed lust for gold, to what dost thou not drive the hearts of men!" and an early metal-philosopher found the lovely, glowing stuff has "a power that radiates out into space, a power by which man himself would like to be carried away: That is why he wants to take possession of gold." The *Wall Street Journal*, surely a pro-gold publication ordinarily, fulminated recently on the fearful mineral's evils: "The metal has spurred feuds, vendettas and wars. It has helped create, and later destroy, communities large and small. It has appeared in all the world's mythologies and, in more cases than not, as a kind of curse that is passed continuously from man to man."

In the Mediterranean, the coastal trade and exchange of goods between Egypt and the islands to the north was presently taken over by the Minoans of Crete, who have become romanticized as the Sea Kings, the People of the Isles. For about 300 years after 1800 B.C., their ships ruled the seas so securely that their great seaside cities and palaces on Crete were not even protected by walls. Meanwhile, weapons, clothes, jewelry, and pottery of Cretan manufacture were bought avidly by the rulers of Egypt, Phoenicia, and the Greek islands. The ruins of the great palace-temple of Knossos, on Crete, were not revealed until Sir Arthur Evans bought the site from the Turks in 1898 and began to dig. He uncovered countless frescoes—vivid portrayals of the graceful bull-dancers seizing the horns and leaping over the backs of the beasts—a stately throne room, the queen's bathroom, and strange subterranean labyrinths that appeared to be the home of the legendary bull-man minotaur, and palace-wide plumbing facilities comparable to modern water-operated bathrooms.

We are still not positive as to just what brought Knossos down, whether it was nature (earthquake and fire) or man (conquest) or both; but it is recognized that the Minoans were conquered by Greek mainland Mycenaeans soon after 1500 B.C. Most recently wonderers have been trying to associate Minoan Crete with mythological Atlantis. The new sea kings were great traders, but they were also at the same time perpetual sea raiders, pirates. The formerly peaceful, policed trade of the East Mediterranean became engulfed in a confused era wherein gangsters and sea raiders from all sides—Lycians and other rovers from the shores of Asia Minor, Libyans from the west, and Mycenaeans from the north—attacked the civilized centers. At about the same time that the kings of Mycenae and Tiryns, Pylos and Thebes laid the great siege of Greek marauders against Troy, another formidable alliance of sea raiders was repelled not once but three times by Egypt (1221–1190 B.C.). We know of this Egyptian victory because of the records of Ramses III. We know of the contrary Greek victory at Troy because of the hero tales of Homer and his sons, the *Homeridae* guild of royal court entertainers who composed/created the *Iliad* and *Odyssey* (and many other splendid epics, all long since lost, alas) at least 300 years after the event, and long after Agamemnon and the other Mycenaean kings' city-states had been overwhelmed, pillaged, and destroyed by the invasion of Dorian Greeks from the north.

These Mycenaeans, as interpreted by Homer, and equally wonderfully by our present-day bard, Robert Graves, were true seagoing companions, whether traveling in the "round" type of ship used for carrying cargo or in the swifter "long" galleys intended for making war. The leader and his men were one, unlike the master and slaves of the later Roman and medieval galleys. Whenever winds were available, they sailed rather than rowed. There was an almost indefinable difference between trading and raiding, and on a bigger scale, between raiding and migrating.

In war at sea, the enemy is always the pirates. The American sea captain Stephen Decatur expressed the abiding rule for all time for loyal seamen: "Our country, right or wrong!" Wherever one has lived, the name of the game has always been patriotism, and one must support the cause of friends and neighbors if he is to survive: there is no place for dissidence. "War is a nation's way of eating," the Durants have expressed the cruel truth. "In the last 3,421 years of recorded history, only 268 have seen no war."

The oldest sea tale of the early Greek seamen is of Jason and his Argonauts, who journeyed through the Black Sea in search of the Golden Fleece. *Hercules, My Shipmate,* composed by Robert Graves in 1945, has portrayed this voyage of many of the best-known heroes of mythology on a typical sea journey: if they drank too much in a host city, raped some ladies, and killed a few of their hosts, the next day they were honorably repentant, sufficiently hung over, and determinedly went ashore to build an altar and solemnly sacrifice bulls to Venus or some other appropriate Olympian divinity as a confessional device to make up for their sins, thereafter going forward on their voyage as joyously "innocent" as any modern sinner who's been cleansed and shriven by confession to a priest: "All together, Argonauts and Dolionians heaped pyres and set the . . . corpses upon them, with rosemary and other sweet-smelling herbs to disguise the reek of roasting manflesh, and with all the gifts of food that had been put into the *Argo,* except the wine. Together they danced in armor about the pyre, three times about each, clashing their weapons together, while servants blew on conches and beat drums to frighten off the ghosts of the slain."

Greatest of all the early sea tales is that of Odysseus' journey home to his island of Ithaca from the sack of Troy—and the *sea* is the most important part of the story all the way. Hermes, the gods' messenger, "skimmed the waves like a sea-mew drenching the feathers of its wings with spray," and later, "Odysseus spread his sail to catch the wind and used his seamanship to keep his boat straight with the steering-oar. There he sat and never closed his eyes in sleep, but kept them on the Pleiads, or watched Boötes slowly set, or the Great Bear, nicknamed the Wain, which always wheels round in the same place and looks across at Orion the Hunter with a wary eye." Weather? "A mountainous wave, advancing with majestic sweep, crashed down upon him from above and whirled his vessel round. The steering-oar was torn from his hands, and he himself was tossed off the boat, while at the same moment the warring winds joined forces in one tremendous gust, which snapped the mast in two and flung the sail and yard-arm far out into the sea."

Odysseus on the long journey home (lasting ten years) was not a trader or a raider or a warrior. In fact, the nearest comparison one can discover is the modern yachtsman cruising along a new shore, discovering new harbors and coasts, raising the appropriate flag at cocktail hour, adventuring and making friends with other pleasure-seeking modern sea raiders all along the way. Bill Robinson asserted, in *The World of Yachting*: "Cruising is a ridiculous way to get somewhere. Under sail it is slow and inefficient, and in a high-speed powerboat it is quite expensive. Cruising's rewards are of the spirit, and they resist definition in any reasonable manner. A harbor that might be passed in the flick of an eye by a car zooming along the turnpike at 60 m.p.h. becomes a symbol of achievement when it is attained after a day of cruising. Its possibly pedestrian shores take on a special glow as they fold in upon a newly arrived cruising boat in late afternoon."

Homer was presumably a Mycenaean descendant who was telling the Ionians of his own time what the "good old days" had been like—mostly by a glorious, Shakespearian kind of imagination. He is rather like the Greek scholars who later converted the Romans, after those outlanders and unsea people had taken over the Mediterranean world, to a respectful knowledge and understanding of the ancient Greek sea wisdom. Bard Homer possibly never went seafaring, like so many other scholars of oceanic wisdom. He was only in part interpreting true memory of the dead past, with considerable room for imagination, surely one of the richest in all so-called history. The *Odyssey* journey would seem to have taken ten years. The siege of Troy also took a decade. But Agamemnon, faced with the task of commanding a group of uncontrollable pirate-kings, could scarcely have kept them on shore and besieging for so long; perhaps it lasted (if it ever did happen in reality) two or three years, scarcely more.

The war would seem to have been caused by Troy's attempting to close the Dardanelles to trade (thus cutting off the Greek city-states from the grain trade out of the Black Sea), rather than the abduction of Helen, wife of Menelaus. But for sightseers ever since, the site of Troy has been one of the great crossroads of history, to be visited and viewed and experienced in a personal and always very Homeric way.

Alexander the Great, who believed himself to be a direct descendant of Achilles, ran naked around his supposed ancestor's tomb (correct behavior, by protocol), on his way to dismantle the Persian Empire. Julius Caesar, who claimed descent from the Trojan side, built an altar of turf at the ruins and promised to restore Troy. (What anti-Greek feeling could have inspired this pledge?) Centuries later, visitors for a thousand years or so would mistake the ruins of Alexandria Troas, on the nearby seacoast of the Dardanelles, as the site of Homer's Troy, and there suffer just as genuine "Trojan raptures," with as much pleasure, presumably, as if this other sad ruin had been the real thing. The original Troy was by now silted up far inland, as many newer cities were, having been built by sensible choice safely far from shore so as to be at a distance from the ever-menacing sea raiders.

In the centuries immediately after Homer, the new variety of Greek colonists settled all along the northern edge of the Mediterranean and the Black Sea ("like frogs around a pond," Plato called it). And meantime the most ambitious sea people of ancient times, the Sidonians, whom the Greeks named Phoenicians (from *phoinos,* "dark red," after their famous dyes of Tyrian purple), became the greatest merchants of early history. Their colonies spanned the *southern* Mediterranean shores (Queen Dido, legendary founder of Carthage, around 800 B.C., who killed herself when Aeneas sailed away, is one of the few remembered ones). A group of early Phoenician seamen was sent by King Hiram to man a fleet sent by King Solomon from Ezion-geber to Ophir (India) about 970 B.C. In 700 B.C., Phoenician mariners in the service of Pharaoh Necho II of Egypt sailed all the way around Africa, returning home through the Strait of Gibraltar. In 500 B.C., Hanno of Carthage sailed down the west coast of Africa, establishing colonies that were to endure for centuries. It was at about this time that the Phoenicians (like the Trojans earlier at the Dardanelles) formally "closed" the Strait of Gibraltar to the ships of other sea nations. It is interesting that in 1968 the U.S.S.R. protested bitterly when two American destroyers of the Sixth Fleet passed through the supposedly international Bosporus on a "tour" of the Black Sea.

In 325 B.C., a Greek geographer, Pytheas, from Massilia (Marseilles) slipped through the blockade of Gibraltar to make a journey northward. He was the first mariner to recognize the peculiar mother-child connection between the moon and tides (the Mediterranean, one must remember, being practically tideless), and he was the first scholar to use the name "Britain." He visited the interior, maybe even circumnavigated it, and went on northward to visit Thule, which could have been either Iceland or Norway. Somewhere along the shores of the North Sea, he discovered a source of amber. His book, *The Ocean,* was long ago lost, and we know of it chiefly from detractors. But his northward sea journey was surely a match for Queen Hatshepsut's southward sea expedition to Punt more than a thousand years earlier.

An inscription was discovered on a stone at Paraíba, Brazil, in A.D. 1872, which scrivening specialists estimated to have been incised about 600 B.C. by Phoenicians (this would have been conveniently at the time when the Phoenician sailors employed by Pharaoh Necho II circumnavigated Africa). The inscription was translated in part to read: "We are Canaan's sons from the King's town of Sidon on a trading voyage, stranded on this far shore in a land of hills. We offered a youth to the high gods in the 19th Year of our great King Hiram and sailed from Ezion-Geber to the Red Sea with 10 ships. For two years we were on the sea rounding the Land of Ham until a storm from Baal drove us away from our companions. May the high gods bring us good fortune." There is also in Brazil a considerable collection of strange pottery, found around the mouth of the Amazon, and now in the Goeldi Museum at Belém. The inscribed stone has disappeared, as original monuments tend to do. Meanwhile, in 1968, Dr. Cyrus Gordon, of Brandeis University, studying an early transcription made in 1874, only two years after the glyptic rock was discovered, suggested that certain *uses* of Phoenician terminology not known to archaeologists at the time of the discovery of the stone ruled out the possibility of a forgery. Gordon further suggested that this recorded landing must have been only one of many visits to the New World— "There may have been many intentional landings in the centuries, even millennia, before Columbus"—and that the visitors brought with them architectural ideas, such as pyramid building and monumental stone structures "supported by forests of stone columns in the Egyptian manner, which served to train the Mayans and Toltecs in their raising of gigantic temples." How many of us when visiting foreign places (enlightening the local citizenry with our brilliant suggestions, architectural or decorational) are in a position to record our advice with momentous incisions on stone tablets?

Whether or not early Phoenicians ever reached the New World, there was a long interval afterward before anyone else attempted the transatlantic crossing. Then, around A.D. 650, peaceful Irish monks, who had already reached Iceland and Greenland earlier, were apparently driven westward by advancing Viking warriors, all the way to North America, settling peaceably along the Canadian waterfront and later merging into the culture of the Algonkian Indians. "The monks and their retinues crossed to Baffin Island," Dr. Carl Sauer, a geographer at the University of California, has suggested in *Northern Mists.* They "followed the shore, turning west into the Gulf of Saint Lawrence." At New Salem, New Hampshire, there are some curious rock structures, labeled, displayed, and promoted today as "Mystery Hill Caves," which their explorer, William Goodwin, purchased, just as Sir Arthur Evans had purchased the Knossos Palace site in Crete from the Turks. Goodwin had a splendid time rearranging things as he supposed they may once have been, at the same time managing to enrage later-day archaeologists who thought he should have left everything untouched.

The rearranging of ancient monuments began in ancient Egypt, usually because somebody needed the stone to build a new monument. Just as the pyramids at Giza have been quarried endlessly, the strange rock structures on a New Hampshire hillside were in time quarried to build the first sewers in nearby Lawrence, Massachusetts. "All day long," an old resident is quoted in Charles Michael Boland's *They All Discov-*

ered America, "wagon after wagon came out of the woods loaded with stone from the caves, possibly carting off the most valuable archaeological evidence in North America." Vandals also carried away bits and pieces. Goodwin announced discovery of "a human sacrificial stone" which would fit the idea of the Phoenician inscription on the Paraíba stone of a "youth" offered to the "high gods."

This 30-acre complex of remnants of walls and structures on an isolated New Hampshire hilltop, 25 miles west of the Atlantic Ocean, with the same strange air of the preserved past that one finds at solitary Stonehenge in the Salisbury Plain, just *might* be our most remarkable monument to seafaring discoverers from far across the North Atlantic and beyond—from the far eastern end of the Mediterranean. New methods of dating and other forms of tracing true origins may bring a resolution to the mystery of New Salem, New Hampshire, during the 1970's.

The Viking explorers came overseas in their long ships to North America by way of Iceland and Greenland during the three centuries after A.D. 900, when the area was in a "climatic optimum" much warmer than today, so warm that the famous grapes could have grown in Newfoundland, "Vinland," and farming would have been possible in Greenland. Leif Ericson is given the Viking credit for discovering America in A.D. 1002, though he was, of course, no more the discoverer than Columbus, who came along 490 years later in search of the Great Khan, carrying his elegant presentation robes throughout the West Indies and donning them whenever he thought there might be a chance of being presented at the court of Cathay. Columbus died believing that he'd discovered a direct route to China, which was still another 5,000 miles away to the west. Jean Nicolet, exploring the St. Lawrence River for France in the next century, also brought along a flowered Oriental robe. Lachine Rapids (China Falls), on the St. Lawrence, were named partly in mockery of Nicolet's delusion. So difficult it was for seamen during the age of exploration to grasp the sheer immensity of *surface* of the Planet Water!

The Vikings ranged more widely over the surface of the planet than any other European sea people. During the ninth century, they first entered the Mediterranean, penetrating ultimately as far as Baghdad. In A.D. 885, a great armada of 700 boats carrying an army of perhaps 40,000 men swarmed up the Seine River to besiege Paris. Later King Charles III of France bought them off with the gift of Normandy and his daughter's hand to Rolf, who promptly settled down to become "civilized," whatever that may be. His sea-roving descendants then went on to conquer Sicily, Naples, and England. The Norse King Roger of Sicily, at whose palace northern Viking and southern Arabic seafarers met and exchanged views in the twelfth century, must have been a high point in man's enjoyment of acquiring new sea knowledge. In Oslo, Norway, we can still view an original Viking longship, buried with its chieftain-owner about A.D. 1000 at Gokstad. In Thailand, when the royal barges go on parade every October down the Chao Phraya River, faint wonderment about ancient Viking vessels inevitably stirs in the viewer's memory.

The most fascinating fact about Viking voyagers to America is that they left so many runic inscriptions everywhere, to enrage unbelievers and delight trusting Vikingites. There's a rude runestone at Kingiktorsuak in Baffin Bay, maybe dated 1135. I've examined, with considerable awe, the scratchings on Dighton Rock, alongside the Taunton River on Assonet Neck, Rhode Island, and also some even fainter marks on the side of a rock on Manassas, a tiny islet beside the harbor of Monhegan Island, Maine. At Newport, Rhode Island, is the tower that Vikingites have proved to their own satisfaction is the ruin of a fortified church. At Heavener, Oklahoma, a runestone discovered in 1912 carries a purported date of November 11, 1012. The scholars who interpreted this date, which they called a "cryptopuzzle," then went to work on the most famous relic in America, the Kensington runestone found by farmer Olaf Ohman at Solem, Minnesota, in 1898. In a learned 1967 work, *Norse Medieval Cryptography in Runic Carvings,* guaranteed to confuse unbelievers and drive them to despair, authors Dr. O. G. Landsverk and Alf Monge showed that the Kensington date was May 7, 1244. This stone, and finder Ohman, have been alternately honored and abused for a half-century now. In 1948, when Vikingites were apparently in the ascendant, the stone was even carried off to Washington, D.C., to be put on honorable display alongside another runestone found near Upernivik, Greenland.

It is interesting that cryptographers Landsverk and Monge found that the Norse incisions were made by runemasters in an eleventh-century colloquial style that could not have been imitated by forgers or pranksters in 1898, just as Professor Gordon stated of the Brazilian Paraíba Phoenician carving that 1872 Brazilian wits could not have imitated correctly the Phoenician colloquial writing style of 600 B.C. In 1965, Landsverk headed a successful campaign to have Congress designate October 9 as Leif Ericson Day, and the Post Office Department even issued a gracious stamp portraying Leif, but cautiously evading any mention of exploration, discovery, or founding of colonies in the New World.

Finally, before leaving the Viking explorers of America, there remains the unique peculiarity that in order to anchor their ships they always drilled holes in huge anchor rocks, then thrust in an iron ringbolt. Mooring-rock holes have now been discovered along many northern American rivers, and if you keep your eyes open and at the same time successfully estimate what the water level of the particular stream may have been some 800 years ago, you may discover another one. The Viking-ites will love you for it and the unbelievers will hate you, but it is an interesting waterside game.

Another transatlantic candidate for Discoverer of America has long been Madoc ab Owain Gwynedd, an obscure Welsh prince who may have sailed to the New World in 1170. In *Madoc and the Discovery of America,* Richard Deacon suggested he may have landed at Mobile Bay, Alabama (the Daughters of the American Revolution put up a monument to him there, which should be enough accreditation for any First Family claimant). Deacon, a British historian, once sailed a flat-bottomed boat from Norfolk, Virginia, to North Africa; he discovered an ancient manuscript in Poitiers, France, ruins of forts in several Southern states, and Welsh words among certain fair-skinned American Indian tribes; obviously New World Welsh descendants, Deacon decided. As much fun, this, as moving and rearranging stones around the Knossos palace in Crete or the caves at New Salem, New Hampshire.

All of the Indian nations of Central and South America greeted the Spanish conquistadors as gods who must surely be descendants of earlier gods who had once visited them before by sea, led by Quetzalcoatl, or Tiki, who was a tall, bearded, white, kindly, very godlike person. The more stalwart supporters of each group of supposed early explorers suggest that they surely visited Yucatán and somehow went inland to teach the simple inhabitants of the New World the finer architectural skills of the Old, such as pyramid and temple building. The later native populations soon learned, the hard way, that the Spaniards were not the old gods or descendants of gods. If the earlier explorers *had* visited mid-America, it's doubtful they'd have left godlike memories, either, since sea raiders have never been kindly or godlike, but merely piratical practitioners of the free-enterprise school of pillage and plundering. There is one oddly possible "actuality," that Sir Thomas More, on one of his diplomatic journeys to the Netherlands for then kindly King Henry VIII (who later had him beheaded), heard a remarkable legend of a faraway country that had to be the Inca empire from some waterfront seafarers who'd obviously been to America and returned; he then rushed home to London to write his famous *Utopia,* which would thus be not at all a piece and place of fiction, like Plato's *Republic,* but an actual factual report of the land of the Incas before Pizarro's brutal conquest. (People meantime still debate where Plato's republic may have been, whether it was the "lost" Atlantis, wherever that might be.)

The greatest of sea travelers were surely the Polynesians, who made unbelievably long voyages across the vast Pacific empty wastes, wind-propelled journeys up to 2,500 miles (Samoa to Hawaii), somehow miraculously managing to manipulate perfect landings on faraway tiny islands as neatly as the present-day space vehicles' moon landings, arrivals most carefully advance-planned by elaborate computations. Harold Gatty, Wiley Post's navigator on the famous 1931 primordial flight around the world, later made a detailed study of Polynesian navigational methods, and Guy Murchie had carefully studied Gatty before writing, in *Song of the Sky,* that their primary navigational instrument was the ocean *wave*: "To the islanders the wave was like a tool, for it was studied and measured to a degree not to be exceeded anywhere until the later days of oceanography. As we use radio and radar today, so did the South Sea navigator a thousand years ago use the ocean wave. He did not merely steer by the angle of the wave, but he observed the whole pattern it made around an island. . . . In mid-ocean the sky was for him a compass, clock and map."

The Polynesians began to make their great exploratory voyages up to perhaps 2,000 years ago. If they came out of southern Asia, it is presumed that they were pressured from behind by the Malays, as the peaceable West Indian Arawaks were later pushed northward by the more warlike Caribs (who gave the word "cannibal" to our language). After careful advance preparation in Peru and in the South Sea islands, Thor Heyerdahl set out on his *Kon-Tiki* raft journey to prove that the Polynesians may actually have originally migrated *westward* from South America. In *Kon-Tiki*, he stated frankly that he'd also consulted numerous texts, that "an armchair student can, in his library bookshelves, travel wider beyond time and horizons than can any modern outdoor explorer. Scientific works, journals from the time of the earliest explorations, and endless collections in museums in Europe and America offered a wealth of material for use in the puzzle." He postulated two westward transpacific migrations, one in A.D. 500 from South America, and a second from northwest North America in A.D. 1000, at just about the same time that the Norse Vikings were making the same kind of daring long voyages to the eastward side of North America, over the North Atlantic.

The most exotic candidates for Polynesian ancestry are the members of Alexander the Great's fleet. In *Men out of Asia*, Harold Sterling Gladwin says the fleet started eastward from Susa in 323 B.C., immediately after Alexander's death, under the command of Alexander's admiral Nearchus. His story propels them along the coast of southern Asia, picking up new crew members, as vacancies occurred, from ports along the way, "men and women from the coasts of India, from the valley of the Ganges, from Burma, Sumatra, Java—polyglot, polygamous, polygenous. We are going to call the product Polynesian."

The age of modern scientific maritime exploration may be said to have begun when a young prince of Portugal, Henry, third son of King John I (who'd married an English princess), in A.D. 1420 set up the first great "modern" school for pilots and explorers at Sagres, in the southernmost Algarve province of his father's kingdom. "Upon the windswept promontory of

Cape St. Vincent, above the stony shores of Sagres Bay, with Portugal and all Europe behind, he faced infinity across a boundless sea." Elaine Sanceau described the scene in *Henry the Navigator*: "Lagos of the Infantes time was not only a busy port and starting-point of all long-distance voyages, but it was the center around which gathered students of the new science of navigation. In the observatory of Lagos astronomy was studied, not as the superterrestrial mystery influencing the destinies of man, expounded by medieval stargazers and fortunetellers, but as a sure guide to accurate navigation. In the same way mathematics and geometry, from abstruse speculations of the sage became a practical science bearing on daily life; and at Lagos expert cartographers drew out new maps—maps that no longer were compiled from guesswork and hearsay, but which showed islands where they really were, and coastlines as they had actually been seen."

This remarkable man was a true chief of staff: he never made a single *exploratory* voyage himself, though he had command of numerous military sea expeditions against the Moors in North Africa. He started sending out the "discovery" ships when he was only twenty-five years old, and long after his death in 1460, the power of his personal forcefulness kept the fervent maritime exploration under way until more than half of the globe's surface had become known, and European sailors had at last reached Asia by *both* of the two possible routes—around Africa and straight westward all the way around the Planet Water.

The roster of his captains—Ziroc, Teixeira, Velho (his finding of the Azores, an 800-mile journey straight westward into the unknown North Atlantic *void*, was comparable to and co-equal with the far-reaching journeys of the Polynesians), Tristao, Díaz, Cadamosto, Gomes—may readily be added to the names of the great discoverers who sailed after he had died. Had he still been alive, many of them would surely have sailed from Lagos—Diogo Cam, Bartholomew Díaz (who first rounded Africa's Cape of Good Hope), Vasco da Gama (who first reached India), Christopher Columbus (in the service of Spain), John Cabot (for England), Giovanni da Verrazano (for France), and Ferdinand Magellan (for Spain). Prince Henry's biographer, Elaine Sanceau, has expressed the mystery of the man: "He awoke to scientific curiosity early in life. This serious and reserved young man, who cared for study more than for the pleasures of his age, who harbored no political ambitions, and put all thought of love and marriage from his life, pondered unceasingly upon the mystery of the earth. The world was wide, and stretching far to lands unknown. . . .

"The world owes the Infante Henrique more than it often remembers, for he inaugurated a new age. The end of the medieval period is commonly supposed to coincide with the fall of Constantinople. With far more truth it could be put back thirty years, to the date when Henrique first sent forth his caravels. . . . In all the millenniums of human history, only during the last four hundred years has there been intercourse amongst all races of mankind around the globe. Henrique was the first to find the key that opened wide the gate of man's inheritance."

As enigmatic as Henry the Navigator is Christopher Columbus, admiral of the Ocean Sea and viceroy and governor of the Indies. Was there ever a more determined man in all the history of exploration? He tried to get backing from his birthplace, the city-state of Genoa, in 1480, then from Henry VII of England, from Charles VIII of France, from John II of Portugal, before he finally approached Ferdinand and Isabella. Every reasonable monarch had turned him down. The man was obviously mad, and far too demanding.

Isabella, queen of Castile, was a deeply religious woman, dedicated to the defeat of the infidel Moors. On January 2, 1492, Mohammed Abu Abdullah surrendered the kingdom of Granada, bringing to an end the 780 years of Islamic reign in Spain. Columbus, pleading for backing for the transatlantic crossing, had promised, "I declare to your Highnesses that the gains of my enterprise must facilitate the conquest of Jerusalem." And so, when she and Ferdinand signed the agreement, on April 17, 1492, she was already dreaming of a great new crusade—*eastward*—to the Holy Land. Since Constantinople had fallen in 1453, and the Arab curtain had closed, the silks, scents, and spices of the Orient were in shorter supply than ever: a successful crusade would make both good Catholic and sound commercial sense.

Holiness and religion were similarly combined in Columbus' thinking with the determination to discover a shortcut to Oriental riches. He knew that time was running out in the race with Portugal to reach India first, for Columbus had been in Portugal when Admiral Díaz arrived home after having rounded the Cape of Good Hope in 1487. The next step could only be a Portuguese voyage all the way across the Arabian Sea to India, which the Portuguese proceeded to achieve under Vasco da Gama in 1497 (Díaz went along, captaining a ship, and was lost at sea).

Columbus was a strange sort of withdrawn person, almost a Joan of Arc in his firm belief in his God-given mission. The Maid of Orléans had gone to the stake only sixty-one years earlier, still positive of her ordained fate to save France. Cristóbal Colón left Palos, Spain, on August 3, 1492—exactly the wrong season for such a voyage. After putting in at the Canary Islands for repairs, the true voyage of the three relatively unseaworthy little caravels began on September 6. Though this was in mid-hurricane season, they had excellent weather all the way. When the men threatened to mutiny, and the commander of the *Pinta*, Martin Alonso Pinzon, suggested, "Sir, let your honor hang half a dozen of them, or throw them overboard," Columbus mildly replied, "Martin, let us keep on good terms with them and sail on for a few days more," and once more buried himself in his own thoughts. This bespeaks a holy man, positive of his mission. One must remember that most of the Spanish conquistadors were peasants from simple, brutal backgrounds. Columbus was born in Genoa, never gave up his citizenship, and married the daughter of a Portuguese sea captain; though he went to sea at the age of fourteen, he was widely self-educated in the medieval lore of the times.

Not enough is remembered of the vivid colorfulness and powerful perfumery of Columbus' discovery of the New World. Today on a West Indies cruise, we encounter a modified but nevertheless exotic reflection of it. On October 7, Columbus' sailors saw brilliant parrots, flying far out to sea, and on Discovery Day, naked Indian girls came swimming out to greet the caravels of gods with gifts of gorgeous flowers and parrots. When Columbus went home to Spain in triumph, he carried not gold, but great numbers of the wonderfully colorful birds. To this day, the Caribbean isles continue to be one of the richest tropical paradises that a sea-cruising visitor may discover.

When the islands threw off colonial European rule a few years ago, many hoped that things might revert, that once more exotic-colored parrots and beautiful maidens with gorgeous flowers in their hair would come swimming out to greet all visitors. Alas, this has not yet happened.

After October 12, the great Discovery Day, Columbus' story was really over. Returning to Spain, along the way he first visited Portugal and had a triumphal reception from Admiral Díaz and all the other great explorers to whom at long last he had the chance to exclaim, "I told you so!" Hadn't he reached China? He knew so (and remained sure until his death many years later). Then, in Spain, there was the great homecoming triumph, but no cargo of golden treasure to finance a holy crusade to free Jerusalem from the infidel. Instead, Isabella proceeded to finance three costly additional Columbian ships, all far more extravagant than the original. Columbus' reports to Isabella remained private until after her death. Since she was a deeply religious person, his letters were always most discreet, like a Sunday school scholar's reports to his teacher. Samuel Eliot Morison, Columbus' most thorough American scholar, suggested (with his own kind of New England reticence), that "there must have been considerable sporting between the seamen and the Indian girls, for the habits of the Tainos were completely promiscuous; but Columbus said nothing of that, since his *Journal* was intended for the eyes of a modest queen."

The New World was "sold" to the men of the Old World by one of the most flamboyant seafaring men of this in-between time, Amerigo Vespucci. Born in Florence in the great days of Lorenzo the Magnificent, he was the brother-in-law of the loveliest woman who ever lived: Simonetta, the wife of Marco Vespucci, whose portrait, by Sandro Botticelli, is familiar to us in the great sea-goddess painting of all time, the *Birth of Venus,* also called *The Renaissance.*

From Spain, where Amerigo worked in a branch of the Medici family international bank, he wrote magical tales to Piero de' Medici, now living in exile in France, and to another friend, Piero Soderini, in Florence. The letters were passed about and widely read around Europe, and were a chief reason why every man in any European country soon began to think of going to the New World to renew his fortunes, but, more importantly, to begin to live life more fully. In *Caribbean, Sea of the New World*, German Arciniegas, Vespucci's Colombian biographer, described how "Vespucci speaks of Dante and Petrarch, but he also brings to mind Boccaccio. He draws an unforgettable picture of the Caribbean. He is the Botticelli of the new sea opening before his eyes. A wild sea, peopled by savages. The women appealed most to Vespucci, the Venuses of the Caribbean, somewhat more naked than those of Botticelli, with their reddish skin, their handsome, graceful well-formed bodies. Next to the women, the hammock. How pleasant he found those nets, swaying in the breeze, where one can sleep far better than in the stuffy beds of Europe. Vespucci was the first person to describe the New World in terms that fired the enthusiasm of the men of the Renaissance. His letters were passed from hand to hand. They were translated into every tongue, published everywhere. In this period, in which an entertaining writer was held in greater esteem than a navigator who had devoted his whole soul to his vast undertaking, it may be said that the first prize for the *novel* was awarded to Amerigo Vespucci, the Florentine. And the New World received its baptismal name, though Vespucci did not live to know it."

Did Vespucci make four voyages to "America"? Did he make even one? One tends to doubt it. One of the chief doubters, Alan Villiers, examined the case like a modern detective, finding that Vespucci "recorded nothing in Spanish of these great voyages of his, only wrote of them in Italian, which a man might do if his accounts were meant for the consumption of those who were in no position to check his statements. These were often contradictory, frequently wild, and sometimes downright falsehoods. . . . He had 'sailed' by his own account, to somewhere in what is now British Columbia, but *overland*— not in a prairie schooner, but in a *ship*. Amerigo told a good yarn!"

It is too bad that we cannot simply take it thus. William Shakespeare, the finest tale-teller of all time, lived in this era of explosive exploration. In his great moments of reality, so frequent in the plays, we often see the most *exact* bits and pieces of truth from the great age of exploration in which he lived. He must often have talked with (interviewed, in fact) such great sea wanderers as Francis Drake and John Hawkins, and probably made extensive notes that would later turn up as fantastically *correct* "realistic" scenes in the plays. If we respect Shakespeare for his creative fantasy, surely we can recognize the richness of that other Renaissance "reporter," Amerigo.

"I did find a new continent south of the Equator," Amerigo wrote, "which has a milder and pleasanter climate than other continents known to us." And, "if paradise exists anywhere, it cannot be very far from here." Of the compliant and lovely Indian maidens, he wrote: "The greatest sign of friendship which they show you is that they give you their wives and their daughters and are highly honored, when they bring you a daughter, even though she be a young virgin, if you sleep with her. . . . A woman here has as much liberty as the man; they are not jealous and are immoderately libidinous, and the women much more so than the men, so that for decency I omit to tell you the artifice they practice to gratify their inordinate lust."

We celebrate Columbus Day, but not Amerigo Day, and also not Magellan Day. Fernando de Magalhães was perhaps the bravest and most daring explorer of seas in all history. Unlike Columbus, he knew where he was going. Though he sailed for Spain, he followed in the original scientific spirit of Henry the Navigator. But let us face truth: Columbus, a typical fanatic, "knew" where he was going, too, and died in the positive conviction of his misinformation about having discovered a new route to China. Like Columbus, Magellan could get no support from the Portuguese king, and so he renounced his citizenship and "went over" to Spain. The Portuguese, to this day, have never really forgiven him.

Magellan's circumnavigatory dream came real when he was only thirty-five years old and had already gone halfway around the globe—in the other direction to the Far East, around Africa. Only four years later, he was on his way, with five dilapidated old vessels, on the grand voyage of all the ages. We are fortunate to have the Italian passenger Antonio Pigafetta's diary of the voyage, the sight-seeing adventurer who went along "to experience and see with my own eyes a part of the very great and awful things of the Ocean." Which is, of course, the reason why each one of us wishes to set out upon the greatest of planetary journeys—our own personal circumnavigation of the Planet Water. And while we hope to experience and enjoy the great moments, nobody relishes the dread prospect of undergoing the awful as well: for ninety-six days, Magellan sailed the immensity of the empty Pacific with the trade winds behind him, and no sight of land. "We ate old biscuit reduced to powder and full of grubs," Pigafetta reported, "and drank water that was yellow and stinking. We ate the oxhides from under the yardarms, and also the sawdust of wood, and rats."

Many of the men died, consumed by scurvy—the disease caused by deficiency of vitamin C—while the sides of their wooden ships were consumed by the deadly teredo worm. By 1798, lime juice was being issued regularly to prevent scurvy, and the metal hulls of today's ships are painted regularly with new types of "saltwater protection"—antifouling paints that resist both corrosion and various marine growths. Magellan died on the tiny Philippine island of Mactan. In mid-1969, someone stated on American network television that he "was eaten," which the Philippine Embassy was prompt to deny vigorously. Juan Sebastian del Cano captained the vessel home, lied about Magellan, and thereby almost ruined the dramatic story and glory of man's first great sea voyage around the planet, along with the reputation of the great navigator who brought it off with such single-minded purposefulness.

Admirers of the great maritime explorers tend to put down the space-age astronauts. Alan Villiers, surely the world's greatest authority on sail, said Magellan's achievement was "a great one and his voyage the greatest, perhaps, ever made by man. Compared with the pioneers of the space age, briefly flung in cocooned capsules upon passages carefully calculated by computer and brought into existence by the joint efforts of a horde of scientists backed by long-massed knowhow and enormous wealth, the Portuguese worked virtually alone. His vision, his leadership, his organization, and his achievement were personal triumphs of his own spirit, endurance and limitless courage, handicapped by numerous persons who in the course of his wonderful voyages had time for mutiny, treachery and endless intrigue. He did know where he was going, yes, but neither he nor anyone else had any real conception of the difficulties, or even of the tremendous distances involved. His ships were unwieldy, unsafe and primitive, and full of headstrong, ill-assorted, difficult and largely reluctant men, for most of whom the only certain outcome of the voyage was death." No matter what the glory of the commander, this was the inevitable role of the ordinary seaman—to go swiftly to death at sea by way of fevers, traumatic fears, and scurvy. And yet, from time to time, men did go to sea in the great age of exploration who had as much adventure and even fun as their officers. This was true of the second great global circumnavigation.

Sir Francis Drake was England's greatest hero when he set out in 1577 on the—unannounced—possibly greatest and most joyous voyage of all time around the world. To the Spanish enemy whom he would be robbing all along the way, he was the monstrous pirate Francisco Draque, or, to the more foul-mouthed, *Cacafuego* (Shitfire). The Spaniards had claimed that no other nation could sell Negro slaves from Africa to Spanish mine owners in the West Indies, since the Pope had drawn a line giving all lands on one side to Portugal and all on the other side to Spain. Drake believed in his "free-trading" right to sell slaves. The Spaniards were enriching themselves by what may be called the "legal" land piracy of institutional robbing of the original peoples of America of their gold, silver, and whatever other riches could be pilfered from them to be shipped home to Spain. Naturally, Drake knew it was his own God-given right in turn to rob the Spanish ships of their precious cargos. Finally he went ashore and even robbed the mule trains in Panama before the metal could be loaded aboard the galleons. He once climbed a tree there, and in 1573, looking southward, he saw the Pacific Ocean. Balboa had claimed it for Spain as, first, the Golden, and then as the *Mer del Sur,* Sea of the South. Magellan gave the final incorrect name on the peaceful day when he emerged from the channel that he named Strait of All Saints and that others later renamed for him. Drake now claimed, "That shall be *my* sea." All of us are still enchanted with Balboa's second thought, for "South Seas" once meant a paradise on earth.

Drake traveled in great style. On his flagship was an orchestra of musicians, and he ate off the finest plate of gold and silver. In 1578, just before he passed through the Strait of Magellan into the Pacific, he preached a sermon that put the men of the *Pelican* (he renamed it the *Golden Hind* upon entering the

Pacific, thus honoring the principal financial backer of his piracy) into the co-equal fellowship of the ancient Argonauts: "I must have the gentlemen to haul and draw with the mariner and the mariner with the gentlemen. Let us show ourselves to be all of a company, and let us not give occasion to the enemy to rejoice at our decay and overthrow. I would know him that would refuse to set his hand to a rope, but I know there is not any such here." Here are Jason and Hercules, Ancaeus and Autolycus, all together again on a jolly piratical golden-fleece quest, 2,500 years later! Of this dramatic declaration, Frank Knight said in *The Sea Story*, "This was revolutionary. It cut across all the established motions of class-distinctions; it destroyed the old separation of the soldier from, and superiority over, the mariner."

All the way up the Pacific coasts of the Americas, Drake proceeded to capture and loot, courageously, joyously, flamboyantly, a vast number of Spanish vessels and towns, a journey made very much as Jason had once made his way along the Black Sea littoral. The Spaniards were astounded and flabbergasted to see the dreaded pirate *Cacafuego* in person, and on the "wrong" side of the continent. How *could* he have reached there? When he landed in California, Drake was feted, crowned king, and given a gala Golden State sight-see tour by a large tribe of Indians. He promptly named the area New Albion and set up a high post with a metal plate inscribed with the name of Queen Elizabeth I before departing for the great transpacific voyage. In 1936, a California automobilist stopped near Laguna Ranch to change a tire and picked up alongside the highway a metal plate that Drakites claim is the very one tacked up by the great admiral 354 years before. This is an "explorer's calling card" that is truly worth viewing.

The Drake journey was adventure, fun, and derring-do with the accompanying threat of destruction all the way. But it was surely the *shared* kind of voyage that the ancient Mycenaeans, Vikings, and Polynesians had once experienced in their long-ago long journeys and that today's vast new private navies of yachtsmen take part in—long, happy days and nights of calm punctured with terrifying storms. "Don't give in, God is with us!" Drake pleaded during the typhoons, cyclones, and hurricanes (he did not have Columbus' divine good luck of the first "discovery" voyage); and, afterward (he was a preacher's son, and often gave the tiresome sermon Sundays on board), "What did I tell you? God *is* with us!" Modern yacht travelers, let's face it, have none of the genuine joys of piracy that enriched these earlier voyages, from Jason to Drake. They're far more likely to be mulcted by a larcenous marina operator. Modern yachtsmen are either rich or poor, but they never rob and murder and rape when calling on romantic new ports: some of the excitement of the legendary past has surely departed.

The voyages of both Magellan and Drake produced for the first time the great *calendric* surprise of the westward journeying of men around the planet: somewhere along the way they had both "lost" a day! Magellan's crew members were so upset that, back in Spain, they very religiously did special penance in Seville Cathedral to make it up to God for all the saints' days they'd been celebrating one day ahead of the correct date. Most sinful! What could have happened? And Drake was stunned when he found that he'd arrived back at Plymouth, England, on what proved to be a Monday, not a Sunday. After all, he had carefully ticked off the days, as we all should do when journeying afar.

And so man had to come to artifice, to recognize that he must create a make-believe, a simulacrum, an artificial, twirling globe and then try to figure out on its surface where the "lost" day came in, perhaps how it arrived or disappeared. Magic, this! The Alexandrian Greek mathematical whiz Eratosthenes had figured this wonder out, way back in 200 B.C. He had even estimated the earth's diameter—and come within 12 percent of the exact truth! Naturally, his prime meridian of longitude ran through Alexandria. When maritime nations began making globes, some 1,700 years later, each one proudly mapped the prime meridian through the capital of his own nation; this still goes on. However, in 1884, twenty-five nations got together in Washington, D.C., and agreed that the prime meridian for all of them would run through Royal Observatory at Greenwich, England. Most globes show this today. But if you own a "foreign" map, best check your meridians before you begin to figure where you are.

On a globe, the meridian of longitude through Greenwich is, simply, zero degrees—a dramatic line that stretches vertically the length of the Planet Water from North Pole to South. Travel down this line with your eye, on a globe, and at the point where the prime meridian crosses the equator, you will reach the *no-latitude no-longitude "zero point."* There should be a Zero on Earth Club for the very few mortals who have visited this unmarked watery spot in the Gulf of Guinea. Ghana, to the north, is sometimes called "the nearest land to nowhere."

And, of course, over in the Pacific Ocean, there's a sort of *anti-zero* point "where two days, two oceans and two continents meet," a spot on the international date line between Alaska and Siberia where the Arctic and Pacific oceans "merge." Alaska Airlines, which will fly you there, claims that "you look from today into tomorrow, from Alaska into Russia, and you are beyond the farthest west point of land on the North American continent."

In order to give each day a place to "begin," an international date line was set along the 180th meridian of longitude (the farthest or antipodal parallel east or west of Greenwich), and there is, right on this line, an archipelago of farthest-out islands called, appropriately, the Antipodes. They were discovered in 1800, and not long thereafter American fur dealers had managed to wipe out their sole animal population. Maybe someday the World Wildlife Fund or some other such international lifesaving foundation will set out a new colony of fur seals there. I have never met any global traveler who has visited the Antipodes, or "point zero," for that matter. Perhaps Bert Hemphill or Lars-Eric Lindblad are contemplating tours to both places.

The most startling fact that Henry the Navigator's expeditions soon revealed was that most of the planet's surface is covered with water. Before the fifteenth century, scholars had *always* assumed most of the earth's surface must be dry land. As the Portuguese caravels crept down the west coast of Africa, they soon crossed the Tropic of Cancer, the imaginary line that marks the sun's farthest declination northward, and entered the dreaded torrid zone. The heat in the tropics turned out to be no greater than during a hot summer back home in Portugal! In 1483, when Diogo Cam actually crossed the equator, the waters around his ship did *not* boil, as legend had always predicted, nor did his ships catch fire from the intense heat of the sun. When they turned around, south of the equator, to go home, like the 600 B.C. Egyptian voyagers around Africa reported by Herodotus, they, too, *"beheld the sun on their right hand"*—i.e., to the *north,* which only happens when we go south of the equator and come about northward again. Herodotus reported but didn't believe this; oddly, this seems to offer genuine proof that Pharaoh Necho II's sailors really *did* circumnavigate Africa.

Sailors began ducking each other on the homeward journey long before the age of exploration began. There were ceremonies for passing through the dangerous Straits of Gibralter, and probably Jason's Argonauts celebrated their first passage through the Dardanelles with ritual ablutions. Nowadays, many cruise-ship passengers are turned from "pollywogs" into "trusty shellbacks," and inducted into the domain of Neptunus Rex, when they cross the equator for the first time. When they cross the international date line, others are given a certificate honoring their initiation into the Realm of the Golden Dragon. When one crosses the Arctic Circle (and on a globe, this appears as a voyage through the Bering Straits or, in the Norwegian Sea, away up to Narvik or Hammerfest), he joins the Polar Bear Club.

In 1594, one of the earliest *passengers* (i.e., *not* a working crewman), a twenty-one-year-old Florentine named Francesco Carletti, set out on a part-pleasure, part-business trip around the world, and we have his chronicle of the journey, full of the same astonished notes you or I might make, describing such wonders as pineapples and coconuts, and the more unusual sexual customs observed or joined in along the way. Exactly 430 years later, the *President Harrison* of the Dollar Line inaugurated the first regular around-the-world steamship passenger service.

Circling the Planet Water can even be a funny stunt. In 1958 the "shortest cruise around the world" took place, a 50-minute journey in the U.S. nuclear submarine *Skate,* which simply made a circular journey of less than two miles, around the North Pole, beneath the Arctic polar ice pack. The strangest long-distance sea journey ever (36,000 miles) was that of the U.S. nuclear submarine *Triton,* which crossed the equator four times, always underwater, and then went all the way around the planet underwater! Captain Edward Beach has told of the strange journey in *Around the World Submerged.*

Sky travelers during the 1970's will journey without privacy, packed up to 500 persons per plane, in long rows, with absolutely none of the sight-seeing joys of travel left. It is reminiscent of the miserable transatlantic mass migrations of most Americans' ancestors: either as immigrants packed belowdecks —more than 16,000,000 of them that way—or carried as between-deck slaves—more than 15,000,000 in the transatlantic trade (another 9,000,000 died in transit).

"Flight-seeing" will apparently be reserved for shorter journeys, in smaller planes, when the pleasure-passenger should go provided with a copy of Elizabeth A. Wood's interpretive *Science for the Airplane Passenger,* which explains why *every* airline passenger should be provided with *a big picture window* at his elbow. An example of the many goodies best observed way up there is that watery phenomenon, the rainbow, which, "seen from the ground as we stand with our backs to the sun (or to the moon) is a splendid sight, but it is incomplete. Only when we look *down* on it can we see the whole rainbow."

Replogle Globes published a charming work in 1951 by Mercedes Guyette, *See the World on a Globe.* It is full of the puzzling wonders of distance: If Columbus and Magellan and all the other great explorers, with their ancient maps composed of half-fantasy and quarter-truth, could have each had a few minutes to play the game, how less romantic would their voyages be to us now! Miss Guyette listed many of the Great Circle surprises: Maine is nearer to Ireland than to Los Angeles. The distance from Chicago to Wake Island is about the same as to Vladivostock, Siberia. Alaska, not Hawaii, lies between the U.S.A. and Japan. Casablanca, Madrid, Paris, London, Stockholm, Oslo, and Nome are all about equidistant from New York City.

Direct American concern with sea travel began necessarily with the first British vessels carrying colonists to the New World. In 1957, Captain Alan Villiers reenacted the voyage of the first Pilgrims, sailing the *Mayflower II* to Plymouth, Massachusetts. When you go aboard the careful replica, at Plymouth, it is possible (1) to realize how tiny the Pilgrim generation were and (2) to see that there was no *democracy* aboard: the elect occupied the cabins while ordinary folk were stashed belowstairs, or belowdeck. New Englanders were soon going to sea in their own right, and by the time the sailing ship was reaching its great climax before the takeover by steam, the American-built clippers, first in the China trade, then rushing gold-mad dreamers to California and later to Australia (a latter-day search for instant riches that is sort of equivalent to Vespucci's New World instant-happy-life dream 350 years earlier), turned out to be the greatest (and final) *sailing* vessels of all time.

The American search for whale oil also caused a major invasion by New England sailors into South Sea islands not unlike that of the Europeans into the West Indies after Columbus' first voyage and Vespucci's letters. In part, this was due to the initial "combined" voyage of exploration and oceanography by what might be called the first of all "modern" sea captains, James Cook. Writing of Yankees seeking after paradise (divided remarkably between Columbus' medieval and Vespucci's Renaissance approach) in *New England and the South Seas,* Ernest S. Dodge, head of the Peabody Museum of Salem, Massachusetts, suggested that "not until spacemen bring back records from the moon shall we see such excitement and public interest as Cook's voyages produced . . . the stories of the beauties of the islands, the salubrious climate, the fruit and other food so bountifully and easily produced, and the engaging, handsome, happy Polynesians. Here was the paradise on earth already philosophically produced in the mid-eighteenth-century European mind."

In 1809, the *Phoenix* "sailed," the first steamship run successfully from Hoboken, New Jersey, to Philadelphia, Pennsylvania, only two years after Robert Fulton's *Clermont* had made her introductory successful try-out. One hundred and fifty years after the *Phoenix*'s steam-off, Peter Freuchen summed up: "The steamship had swept sail from the Seven Seas, except for sport, pleasure, training and a little odd trade in out-of-the-way places."

By the early 1940's, when Frank Braynard had begun work on his *Lives of the Liners,* the maritime world of travel had shifted totally to steamers. An odd sidelight is that sea-minded people were soon able to express the same kind of sentiment and dedication to the new "floating teakettles" that had once been so religiously reserved for wind-driven vessels. "Ships possess an individuality more evident and real than any other vehicles of transportation, more, perhaps, than any other man-made object," Braynard wrote, perhaps expressing man's graduation from dependence on the elements to the expectation of accomplishment by vehicles of his own invention. "More than bridges, hotels, railroads, automobiles, airplanes, or buses, ships take on almost *human* qualities." Braynard is, of course, hung up on ships, but he knows the new means we shall soon have of transversing the seas. He was primarily instrumental in naming the first nuclear vessel *Savannah II*, for the original *Savannah*, the first steamship to cross the Atlantic Ocean, and looks forward to future unbelievable ships that shall soon find their way (perhaps without human aid) across the seas, using "handfuls" of atomic fuel instead of the old space-taking tons of coal or gallons of oil. These superlong vessels will carry immense containers: "25 ships with the capacity of handling 2,000 containers will handle the entire U.S.-European general cargo-trade," McKinsey & Co., of London, predicted in a 1968 survey of future shipping.

Somewhere along the way of intercontinental travel, the discovery was made that oceanic voyages could be periods of in-between relaxed fun. This became true for a large number of businessmen crossing the Atlantic Ocean—the only way to go until the airplane put the men back on a worrisome, tight flying schedule. In-between living had become one of the greatest relaxations that intercontinental businessmen "on duty" and others could indulge in, because they could explain (both to home offices and to wives) that this was a *necessary* interval at sea.

In November, 1969, the S.S. *United States*, driven out of her former business by low-fare fast plane service, transferred from transatlantic ferrying into cruising, symbolizing the major shift-over of most passenger surface vessels to fun-voyaging. Noah's ark was the first cruise ship. It was filled with honeymoon couples: "These went in two and two unto Noah into the ark, the male and the female, as God had commanded." (In 1970, once more an international expedition will climb Mount Ararat, seeking timbers from the supposed ark.) Noah's, or Gilgamesh's, cruise took place sometime between 4500 B.C. and 2500 B.C. In "modern" cruising, the first luxury American one took place in 1867, chronicled by Mark Twain in *The Innocents Abroad,* the work that made his fame. It was a cruel journal and not worthy of the great humorist's later, better efforts. All people, when they go off on a cruise, are living a dream life away from home, the kind of thing that usually only the members of a victorious army get to practice in a foreign land. In his later years and around-the-world travels, Samuel Clemens behaved just as outrageously as the "patriarchs" and "venerable fossils" had carried on aboard the *Quaker City* in 1867. There just wasn't a younger Twain along with the courage or cruelty to make fun of him.

Today there's plenty of room for making fun of our older cruise travelers, and for the same old reasons. The cruel movie *Mondo Cane* made tragic fun of elderly Americans trying to dance the hula in Hawaii. Most dreamers of visits to faraway places just haven't been able to make the great, long ocean voyage (or pay for it) until they were older and had earned it. But now we have come into a fantastic new age when vast numbers of people are at last going to sea at a much younger and more vigorous age—"for fun," into a make-believe world.

The West Indies cruise business has come to life, offering a make-believe world into which people float who have dreams remarkably similar to those of Amerigo and Cristóbal half a millennium ago. Statistics change so rapidly that they often have little long-range significance. Nevertheless, in the winter-spring cruise season of 1968-69, a half-million Americans took off for the Caribbean, the Mediterranean, the South Seas, and even around-the-world cruising—four times as many as had let themselves go to sea in this leisurely fashion a decade earlier.

Cruise planners today show a remarkable wisdom for carrying their passengers to the romantic sea-lanes where anyone who has read Homer or Columbus or Vespucci or Melville can almost sense reenactment of his favorite dreams of paradise, as he goes among the Greek, Caribbean, or South Sea islands—and islanders. The *Wall Street Journal* reported in 1969 that wise island merchants welcome the arrival of cruise ships in harbor; often, in season, up to four or five such giant floating palaces are present at a time, "bringing up to $20,000 worth of business in three hours for each big cruise vessel!" And if you go ashore, and if you do not turn the article over and see a Japan or Brooklyn label you can pretend for real that you are a Phoenician sea trader landing on a strip of sand, scrawling a message with a stick, leaving your traveler's checks, and then waiting for the smoke signal from the Minoan islanders that indicates that the barter deal is agreed to. Island-hopping and island-visiting is much easier in our times, and perhaps our present-day cruise passengers are truly the sea kings, queens, and princesses of all time. The only objection to pleasure cruising, which is constantly expressed by the lady cruisers, is that there are never enough young princes aboard to consort with them romantically on the romantic island visits. Perhaps all cruise passengers shall one day get to recognize the original tenet of Amerigo in visiting strange islands, that the best romance comes from mingling ashore with the native population, getting introduced to the sons and daughters, and maybe getting to share sleep in the local double hammocks.

Cruise passengers expect to visit faraway places. Temperate zoners demand a sailaway into the tropics. Europeans have always wanted to visit the New World, and Americans as eagerly wish to cruise the Mediterranean or the South Seas. If one cannot afford the ticket or the time, it remains possible to cruise briefly near home. There are ferryboat rides that are brief dreams of what sea voyaging may be. For New Yorkers, for example, there is the Staten Island Ferry, a five-cent journey that, enjoyed regularly, keeps a man from becoming a landbound creature. Walt Whitman called ferry voyaging "inimitable, streaming, never-failing, living poems." Richard Bissell, who's been known to make ferryboat crossings numerous times (always an uneven number, so as to end up on the other side), once expressed his antibridge venom: "Crossing a river on a bridge is as rewarding as seeing the sights of Manhattan in a subway train."

Ferryboat cruising can even, in time of fog or storm, be as terrifying as a run-in with a northeaster aboard an ocean liner. In February, 1969, three Staten Island ferries spent several hours cruising around upper New York Bay because tides were running 6 feet higher than usual.

Man's first duty, in going to sea, has always been to find food, also the reason why he first descended out of the trees to the land, and why he first came ashore (in so extremely different a form from his present disguise), and finally why he has gone back to sea. Fishing fundamentals have changed little since the first prehistoric man picked up a sharpened stick and stuck it into a fish, perhaps crying out, "Thar she blows!" if he happened to throw it. Today's snorkler has a powered harpoon, which is quicker and slicker but is still a simple hunting device. In *The Frail Ocean,* Wesley Marx described recent methods of hooking giant South Pacific tuna, methods that preceded the new gigantic purse seines and power blocks that today make fish harvesting a matter of massive mechanics: "At a tuna 'boil,' a crew member would 'chum' (toss out live anchovetas or other bait fish scooped inshore and kept in bait wells). Other crew members unhinged ramps on the side of the clipper. They stepped down onto these ramps, their legs awash in the Pacific, their hands gripping bamboo poles that dangled a barbless hook shrouded in chicken feathers. The feather lures were flicked into the boil. The frenzied tuna failed to discriminate between the lures and the anchovetas. Once he felt a wrench, the fisherman, like a human crane, would arc a forty-pound tuna overhead. At the top of the arc, the fisherman would release the barbless hook by simply letting up on the tension. . . . In schools of large-size tuna, as many as five fishermen would link their poles to a common lure, hook a tropical tuna, pull together, and arc an iridescent, hundred-pound torso over their backs to the clipper deck."

Perhaps we Americans do not eat enough fish. John von Glahn, of the Fishery Council, has devoted much of his life to preaching two fundamental sermons—first, eat more fish; second, don't overcook fish. We could learn much from the Japanese, whose diet includes a large proportion of sea creatures, much of it eaten raw. Since many of us already enjoy raw oysters and clams, the way is open to octopus, fish, eels, and crustaceans, marinated and seasoned to taste.

At Fish Expo '68, a gathering of sea people in Boston, Congressman William Bates bemoaned the fact that fish make up only 2.5 percent of all U.S. food consumption. Representing several fishing ports, he was, of course, promoting home industry. Oddly, our diet is never made up of what we believe represents a best nutritional balance, but of what we like, and this is influenced—in selecting meat, fish, fowl, breakfast cereal, and desserts—not only by personal taste and experience but also by advertising and even the TV commercials which influence our children.

Fish are coming to market nowadays from farther and farther away. "Fishermen generally have stayed close to home," John Bardach reported in *Harvest of the Sea,* "with such notable exceptions as the British, the Portuguese and the French, who have long participated in the Newfoundland cod fisheries, and the Yankee whalers, who once combed all the seas for their quarry. Following World War II, however, the technologically advanced nations spread so rapidly over hitherto unexploited reaches of the sea that the southern oceans now supply about 35 percent of the total world catch. Between 1952 and 1962 the catch was approximately doubled, and in so doing it has kept ahead of the increase in world human population."

"Freedom of the seas" has different dimensions for each nation. President Harry Truman extended U.S. federal control out over the continental shelf, and in 1966 the nominal 3-mile limit was extended to 12 for fishing. Since that time, fleets of Soviet trawlers in the North Atlantic are occasionally encountered crossing this inexact "barrier." The CEP countries of South America's West Coast in 1954 extended their control of fishing *200 miles* out into the Pacific, and since that time armed vessels from Chile, Ecuador, and Peru have been seizing and fining American yellowfin tuna trawlers. In 1970 there are 140 clippers in the American tuna fleet, manned by 2,000 fishermen. Korea claims fishing rights 250 miles out, which impedes Japanese trawling of the nearby waters. Great Britain and Iceland have been quarreling since 1958, when Iceland extended her territorial waters from 4 to 12 nautical miles out and the British sent in warships. In 1961, a new treaty allowed for part-time British fishing. The Russian fishing fleet has meantime increased until it is the world's largest and most modern—operating off North America, South Africa, Japan, and even in the Indian Ocean. Oceanography's task, for the fishing industries, is to find out where there are more *new* fishing grounds, and also to learn more about fish—for example, whether perhaps there are immense unknown populations in the lower depths that may be harvested.

In all man's history of going to sea, the toughest life was that of the old Grand Banks dorymen off the coast of Newfoundland. In his *Wild Ocean,* Alan Villiers (who himself spent time on the Grand Banks) told how "the poor doryman had to set out in his little box of a boat at dawn *every* morning (unless a gale was blowing and his ship was jumping too much to work fish). Each and every day, sometimes for six months at a stretch, he had to take his chance alone against squalls, ice, fog, collision with steamers, and the usual hazards of being over-turned, swamped, or otherwise drowned." Today he's disap-peared into history. But today a fantastic armada sets forth out of Plymouth, England, every four years, on the *Observer* Sin-glehanded Transatlantic Race. In the latest contest, 34 men, 1 woman, and 1 dog set forth from Plymouth in June, 1968. The *Observer* reported the progress of the craft, breathlessly: "They set sail at 11 A.M. today (June 2), bound for the new land of North America. Ahead of them lie 3,000 miles of turbulent ocean, at least a couple of gales and the loneliness of a single-handed passage which may last 20 days for some; others may take 60 days or even more. They do it for no material reward, but merely for their own satisfaction in attempting one of the boldest undertakings in this modern world, the toughest, lone-liest and longest race in world sport."

Geoffrey Williams, the winner, arrived at Newport, Rhode Island, in 26 days, 20 hours, 32 minutes, beating the 1964 rec-ord by almost a day, and the first record, of 1960, by 14 days. All alone, Williams nevertheless carried a considerable variety of equipment—compasses and sextant, barometer, depth-sounder, and chronometers, even an electric computer which "as a result of the information fed into it was able to simulate my progress and advise on hundreds of possible courses, though the choice remained inevitably mine."

There is a deep vicarious thrill in following one of these re-cent journeys that is far more immediately personal even than reading the journals of the great explorers of long ago. Vicari-ous transatlantic loners are now waiting breathlessly for the June, 1972, Singlehanded Transatlantic Race to begin, so that they can rush out and daily purchase the London *Observer* to see how the lonely contestants are making progress in that "toughest and longest race in world sport" across the wildest and roughest ocean on the planet. It makes one extremely con-scious of the fact that man—and woman—is still going to sea in the only way that is correct: alone—with courage, curiosity, and a special kind of human-oceanic affection for the great im-mensity of saline waters.

V Lakes, Rivers, and Streams

TODAY'S planet-wide urbanization of man's customs and expectations is the fulfillment and expansion of his first settlement into riverside communities, when he had learned to plant crops and domesticate animals. River valleys were and are the best of environments for an agricultural civilization. The American Mississippi Valley, the San Joaquin Valley, even the half-billion Chinese who today live precariously in river valleys—our world is still very much in an age of river-valley living, for the best of reasons: convenient drinking water, water for crops and herds, silt for gardens and herbage, endless "soft" water for washing, and sewage transportation. The worst derivation of river-valley culture is the fact that in the United States already we've poisoned too many of our rivers and are now engaged in a belated program to create secondary water systems for supply, sewage, and transportation—much as the human body's lymphatic, blood, intestinal, uremic, and other channels handle separate river "systems."

The three greatest early river-valley civilizations, which all began at relatively the same time, were along 1,000 miles of the Indus River in what is now West Pakistan; in the combined valley of the Euphrates and Tigris rivers in what are now Iraq and Iran; and in the Nile Valley, in what is now the United Arab Republic. The Indus' name in ancient Sanskrit was *Sindbu*, which the Greeks called India and the Persians called Hindu. The river gave its name to the entire great subcontinent, as well as to the Indian Ocean and, by way-out extension, also to the red men of the Western Hemisphere whom the lost admiral, Columbus, taught us to call Indians. The intensely rich Tigris-Euphrates ancient civilization is continually being revealed to us in greater detail as explorer-archaeologists continue to dig up more and more of the buried libraries of "books"—the inscribed clay tablets that look so much like tiny Shredded Wheat biscuits, and that form the microfilm archives of this highly civilized river-valley way of life. The Nile Valley is the only one of the three early river settlements which continues to be operated today as a tremendously fertile region with an agricultural continuity stretching from before 5000 B.C. (although human habitation of the valley goes back 10,000 years or even much longer) to a recent projected vast expansion of agriculture by more than 2,000,000 acres, made possible by the new Aswan High Dam.

When Willard Price, adventuring down the Nile on a small boat a few years ago, asked some Nile River islanders "who" they were, they proudly answered, "We are the people of Ramses!"—surely the greatest human family record for staying on and working papa's farm, and meantime living a happy life.

Very little is known about the ancient Indus River Valley cities, whose chief sites examined thus far have been at Harappa and Mohenjo Daro. The writing of their inhabitants remains to be deciphered. We know nothing of their history or why their civilization came to an end sometime after 2000 B.C. One possibility is that volcanic activity formed an immense dam a hundred miles or so downriver from Mohenjo Daro, and that the great city was destroyed not once but many times by vast mud floods. The courageous citizens apparently rebuilt their drowned town several times, but at last gave up, and the entire area is today suffering from increasing salinity of the soil. A museum was opened nearby by President Ayub Khan of Pakistan in 1967; it displays some of the remarkable pottery once manufactured there, and before long scholars will undoubtedly begin to unravel the history, as archaeologists continue to winnow the soil.

The most exciting fertile region of the early farmers is Mesopotamia, the once rich valley between the Tigris and the Euphrates. Men may have begun planting and harvesting crops there as long ago as 5,000 to 10,000 years. Of the congenial folk of this valley, Will Durant has suggested that twentieth-century men would probably have felt more at home in ancient Babylon than in the Dark Ages environment of medieval Europe. The study of the entire area was first called Assyriology, after those heartless warriors whose ruthless barbarity, described by Lord Byron, still makes schoolboys' blood run cold:

> The Assyrian came down like the wolf on the fold
> And his cohorts were gleaming in purple and gold.

Only much later did scholars gradually discover that Assyrian and Babylonian were merely dialects of a great Mesopotamia-wide language now called Akkadian.

Professor Edward Chiera went further than Dr. Durant. After soberly wondering if our own present-day leftovers would give future archaeologists the idea that we were even more materialistic than we are, he assessed that after the Akkadian tablets have been fully translated, future scholars "will probably decide that the 'golden age of mankind' was in the second and third millenniums b.c., after which barbarians took command and messed things up thoroughly."

Many of our current attributions of invention and creativeness in philosophy and the sciences to Greece may someday be projected back beyond the Greeks to this great river-valley home of many civilizations. Ferdinand C. Lane summed up the astonishing variety of knowledge here where "magicians, soothsayers and other wise men developed the basis of modern astronomy, divided the great circle into 360 degrees, gave the day its twenty-four hours, the week its seven days, and inaugurated other innovations that mathematicians wish might have been retained. Our numerical system, based upon tens, is inferior to the Babylonian twelves; such was the homage man has paid to his fingers in making quick calculations." Dr. Chiera flatly found the Greeks to be mere imitators, not originators: "Would the Greek colonists in Asia Minor start 'inventing' scientific theories about the origin of the world, when all this previous development was at their disposal and carried with it the prestige of hoary antiquity? A priori, we must think that the great contribution Greece gave to the world was not in the main original: the Greeks took what they found, adapted it to their own needs, and carried it on to still greater perfection. It is idle at present to meditate about Sumerian influence on Greek myths and legends and on the speculations of ancient Greek philosophers. Resemblances can already be traced, but the safest thing to do before attempting comparisons is to wait and first piece together and translate the Sumerian (Akkadian) texts. There is no doubt whatsoever in my mind that, when such a study is possible, we shall be astonished by the results."

Life afloat along the Euphrates or the Tigris hasn't changed greatly in the past 6,000 years. Herodotus described the boats coming downriver to Babylon nearly 2,500 years ago as "circular and made of skins, managed by two men who stand upright in them, each plying an oar, one pulling, one pushing." Today, down past "modern" Baghdad (now on the opposite side of the river), one can still see the same type of round, black, tar-caulked saucer-vessels, called gufas, twirling downriver or ferrying between shores. That is, if there is peace. For as I write this, there is restrained hostility along the Shatt al Arab, the Tigris-Euphrates estuary between Iraq and Iran.

Modern Cairo dominates a waterway far easier to navigate than the Euphrates or the Dardanelles. "To this day, uneducated Egyptians refer to their river as *al-bahr*, or 'the sea,' " Desmond Stewart, writing about 2,500 years after Herodotus, said of the city and the river, "and this was the first sea on which men learned to sail. Apart from being sheltered, the Nile, as a sea, had two remarkable advantages: its constant tide was from the south to the north; its dominant wind was in the opposite direction. The man who wished to travel downriver north from the first cataract had merely to launch a raft upon the Nile and the impetus of the river would carry him and his goods as far as he wished to go. And the man who wished to journey upriver to the south did not need to fight the current with oars. A strong and persistent wind blew steadily south. It made the up-river journey, against the stream, easy for any craft with sails."

In the Egyptian Antiquities Museum at Cairo are models of the ancient boats, but out on the river sail real ones that today are little changed from the ancient feluccas. The earliest vessels were made of papyrus, the magical *byplus* that was also the first writing paper. None grows along the river anymore—it was wiped out by a termite that also attacks old papyrus documents in libraries. To see papyrus boats, one has only to go up-Nile to the Ethiopian lakes where today's *tankwas* closely resemble the ancient Egyptian vessels, and since the early Egyptians were Hamites from Ethiopia, perhaps their papyrus vessels originated there. Farther afield, one can also see a sort of papyrus reed vessel on Lake Titicaca, in the Western Hemisphere's South American Andes Mountains, 12,506 feet above sea level (Planet Water's highest "navigable" lake; there are higher—Yandok Tso, in Tibet, 13,800 feet; Walau, Hawaii, at 13,020 feet).

The Nile River Valley is mankind's most ancient family-ancestral museum of stone monuments, of which surely the hypostyle hall before the temple of Amen-Ra at Karnak is the most massively impressive of all—the largest pre-space-age great-hall known to be built by man, with a forest of massive inscribed columns. Jean François Champollion, the man who discovered how to translate hieroglyphics, said, "They conceived this temple like men a hundred feet tall!"

For two and a half millennia, sightseers have been voyaging up the Nile to see what's left at Thebes (the Egyptians called it No-Amen). But most of the ruins of Assyria still lie beneath immense mounds of sheer dust—congealed, compounded silt. Brick is the most long-lasting of all the building materials used by man, outlasting even granite, limestone, or iron—but only if it has been properly burned first at a very high temperature. Alas for those great Mesopotamian mounds of rubble, the rubble of simmered, *sun-dried* brick palaces. Just as the great brick-builders Sennacherib, Nebuchadnezzer, Sargon, Tiglath-pileser, and all the rest of the Mesopotamian great ones had no stone with which to construct their palaces, they also had no wood to burn to fire their bricks into truly permanent form.

We still know very little of the early river cultures. One scholar, Alan Gardiner, once exclaimed: "What is advertised as Egyptian 'history' is merely a collection of rags and tatters," but in the past century or so, ancient Egypt and Mesopotamia *began* to come to light, and who knows, one day the Etruscans, the Hittites, the Phoenicians, the Harappans, and all the other mysterious great nations of the past may yet become better known.

From what we have learned thus far about the Nile and the

Euphrates-Tigris valley civilizations, there were two almost un-
related kinds of life in both. One was that of everyday people,
living and working in relatively simple happiness. The other
was that of what makes for history—the hatred, competition,
and rivalry of vanity-ridden kings, a grim picture of generations
raised like Spartans to the arts of waging war, conquering, acquiring slaves, and raising monuments to each king's personal
pride and arrogance. The word "rivalry" derives from "river."

All of today's human "civilized" arts apparently began in
these great river valleys, including the art of "civilized" warfare
as the game of the great powers way of life that still exists
among nations. There existed then, as there exists now, the perpetual drive among rural people to "move to the big city."

A German scholar of where, why, and when cities developed,
all offspring of the original mother-city, Babylon, German
scholar Wolf Schneider, summed up the *drang nach burg* that
is in most of us, in *Babylon Is Everywhere: The City as Man's
Fate:* "In Babylon was assembled for the first time everything
that constitutes the attractiveness and the danger of giant cities:
culture and depravity, arrogance and money, temples of faith
and those of hectic amusement, splendor and misery. . . . Like
octopuses, the cities extend their arms far out into the country
today. They reach out over the countryside, over countries,
over continents. . . . The division between city and country
becomes increasingly vague. The city, of course, will not become rural; rather, the country will become urban: the earth
will become a city."

Willy-nilly, we're moving rapidly toward worldwide
cityhood. Lord Ritchie-Calder told a gathering of London ur-
banite conservationists in 1969 that world population, about 38
percent urban now, will be up to 100 percent urban within the
half-century, and he gallantly predicted a "hell on earth" in the
future world-city of 1.3 billion neighbors: "Civilizations were
once linked to a particular river basin or region, and so buried
themselves in their own mistakes. But today we have a global
civilization, a community so interdependent that every mistake
is on a world scale. The really dangerous stuff around today is
radioactive waste in nuclear 'burial grounds,' like that in the
state of Washington, a twentieth century Giza that cost more,

in the burial of live atoms, than it cost to entomb all the mummies of the pyramid kings of Egypt!"

All of us are beginning to realize that we really may be—or even are—the next-to-last generation of human beings that will get to live in this world. Back in the earliest Near Eastern days, the Prophet Isaiah dreamed of a hopefully near-future time when "nations shall beat their swords into ploughshares, and their spears into pruning-hooks: nation shall not lift up sword against nation, neither shall they learn war any more." This simple wisdom of live and let live, this great agricultural platitude, was never tried out, nor was the Jehovic commandment "Thou shalt not kill," or the modest "Pity it is to slay," or the extreme sense of universal Satyagraha, Gandhi's direct way of nonviolence.

In the Western Hemisphere began a race whose contestants apparently had instincts similar to those of the builders of river cities along the Euphrates and the Nile. Settlers began to gather in urban communities within the Mississippi and Ohio river valleys in about 300 B.C. Mound builders, they were called, for the immense number of man-made earth hills that are still to be found in the American Midwest. Scholars now call them the Hopewellian and Adena people. Farmers and also traders, preliterate, they left only some pottery, elaborate copper jewelry, and the immense pyramid-shaped burial and temple mounds, one of them actually covering an area wider than the great pyramid of Khufu in Egypt. Robert Silverberg, a scholar of these ancient Americans, has reported that we still do not know how or why their civilization ended, but that probably the culture was "shattered by the arrival of the white man with his contagious diseases and his fondness for collecting slaves who could be worked to death . . . a combination of syphilis, measles and despair snuffing out the villagers."

The first dramatic European exploration and penetration of the interior of North America came by river, and it began with the voyage of the Frenchman Jacques Cartier up the St. Lawrence River in 1534. By this time, a dozen years after Magellan's circumnavigation, European explorers knew they had to go farther to reach China. Some, like Jean Nicolet, still thought China might be just a few miles inland. One wonders why the early explorers didn't recognize that Canadian red men could scarcely be Oriental yellows. Then, as intrepid French explorers penetrated farther westward, each one who found a new Great Lake tasted it quickly, hoping for the brine of the great western ocean beyond which lay Cathay. But these advance rivermen were moving into the flowing *freshwater* heart of the Watery Continent—a rich, soppy, seepy, soggy land mass representing the final stages of defrosting of the last great Northern Hemisphere deep-freeze Ice Age: we North Americans live in the swiftly diminishing midst of a vast plenitude of water, and ours is what hydrologists and geologists have called the Lacustrine Era, the age of lakes.

All of the freshwater-wet land portions of the planet are in the process of drying out, aided and abetted today by the industrial and urbanic demands and activities of mankind. As much as a third of the planet's land surface was depressed beneath ice during the last Ice Age, which came to an end when the wide ice blanket melted some 10,000 years ago. When ice melts, puddles are the natural result, and puddles begin drying up the minute they're born (the way that we, as living creatures, begin our journey toward ultimate desiccation, desuetude, and death, from the moment we're born). Some 40 percent of the planet's land surface is outright dry deserts, stony mountaintops, or polar permafrost areas; this leaves only 60 percent of the land surfaces of the globe that are freshwatered by standing lakes and flowing rivers.

The greatest natural wonder within the United States is *not* the Grand Canyon, great opened-up-wide history book of rocks of all ages though it be. Our finest national natural wonder is that massive chain of watery phenomena, the Great Lakes, which today, even though much diminished and dried out, still contain well over a third of *all* the fresh waters on the surface of the Planet Water. "The immemorial surprise of Middle America," Noel Mostert called them, "the one dramatic and colorful frontier in this continent's history that has never been popularized, an oversight that is scarcely credible. The impeccable freshness and purity of their beauty, the quite astonishing scenery that unfolds along their shores, seems as uncelebrated as the fact that certainly no other natural resource has had a greater impact and influence on the development of the continent, and scant place in literature." Not even Hemingway, who sailed the lake boats as a boy, ever wrote of them. For a poet's picture of Lake Superior we must go back to Henry Wadsworth Longfellow, who drew so much of his *Song of Hiawatha* about the fine young Ojibwa brave from the writings of Henry Schoolcraft, the scholarly first Indian agent (because his wife was Indian, derisively called a "squaw man") in the Sault Ste. Marie area. Again, like Melville and Shakespeare in dealing with the factual tales of Moby Dick and the Bahamas shipwreck, the poetic writer who never was there brings the tale of Hiawatha to life for us:

> By the shore of Gitche Gumee,
> By the shining Big-Sea-Water,
> At the doorway of his wigwam,
> In the pleasant Summer morning,
> Hiawatha stood and waited.
> All the air was full of freshness,
> All the earth was bright and joyous. . . .

Living alongside Lake Superior-Gitche Gumee, Prince Hiawatha was obviously one of the truly happy people, the children of nature that Jean Jacques Rousseau had begun writing about a hundred years before Longfellow. Maybe both of them were right: in 1637, a century before Rousseau discovered children of nature at long distance, Thomas Morton, a resident of the Puritan colony in Massachusetts, who was much despised by his bigoted fellow colonists, had written of his Indian neighbors: "According to human reason, guided only by the light of nature, these people leade the more happy and freer life, being voyde of care, which torments the mindes of so many Christians." Another scholar of the innocence of Indianhood, Arthur Tourtellot, described these inhabitants of paradise: "They respected age for its wisdom and they could look upon the forest without seeing it as so many cords of timber. They could snatch salmon from the river, but they found companionship in the river too. Their lives were probably a closer parallel to the life of the river than those of any other men who have lived near it, if the poets and philosophers be excepted; for, inarticulate as they may have been to the rest of the world, nearly every Indian was himself a poet and philosopher."

Today's Great Lakes are but a diminutive watery relic of the far-waterier recent geological past. Then the Missouri River probably flowed northward, as the Red River of the North still does. "What are now Lakes Michigan and Superior emptied into the Mississippi," Ferdinand C. Lane describes the immediate post-glacial landscape, "but even they were dwarfed by that glacial monstrosity, Lake Agassiz (or Algonquin), which sprawled over Minnesota, North Dakota and the Canadian provinces of Manitoba and Saskatchewan. Some remnants of its original 110,000 square miles survive in Lakes Winnipeg, Manitoba, Winnipegosis, the Lake of the Woods, and countless lesser lakes that dot the landscape."

Though he was disappointed that Lake Huron's waters turned out to be fresh, Samuel Champlain nevertheless named it the Fresh Sea. Étienne Brulé, the first European to view Huron, was devoured by the Huron Indians two decades later. North American Indians did not eat brave enemies in the hope of thereby encompassing their spiritual virtues along with the vitamins. Winters could be very lean, especially if game had moved away to another part of the forest. Any gourmet inevitably is curious about the taste of this king of viands, long pig, as the Maoris or Polynesians call human flesh from the stewpot.

One of the greatest New World water journeys was that of Robert Cavelier, sieur de la Salle, down the Mississippi in 1682. He set out in midwinter, dragging his loaded canoes on sledges over the frozen rivers, and finally arrived at the Gulf of Mexico in the glorious greenery of a Louisiana springtime. "There was in him an imaginative splendor which shows that the Renaissance was not dead," Bernard De Voto has described this direct heir to Vespucci. "He was Seventeenth-century France, France as expanding capitalism with its primordial business ethics, and so kin to Colbert. But he was a man of the next century too, he is the first of a line that includes Pitt and Thomas Jefferson." Near the mouth of the river, there was one of those taking-possession ceremonies—with cross-raising and the naming of the vast, still only slightly known territory after Louis XIV, who now *owned* "all the nations, peoples, provinces, cities, towns, villages, mines, minerals, fisheries, streams, and rivers" in the vast watershed.

Cartier, Champlain, La Salle, Vérendrye, Lewis and Clark— all traveled without maps; the rivers, mountains, and valleys that they viewed were nameless, or else bore as many names as there were local Indian tribes around them. Champlain complained in his diary of the troublesome mosquitoes: "It was wonderful how cruelly they persecuted us." Another explorer called them "the vexatious, glory-minded, musical-winged, bold denizens of the shady forest," and still another complained in his diary: "Muschgetters tormented us all night long." Many river-valley Indians slept slung up in hammocks over smoke fires, half-suffocated by preference. Only one early explorer, Father Sagard, was known to have sensibly carried along a mosquito net. Fortunately, malarial parasites had not reached North America. One visitor to the Indians commented, "Tame cattle have they none, excepting Lice."

All the travelers expressed the beauty of what they saw. Ohio means "beautiful river" in Iroquois. It was idyllic—buffalo grazed on the river islands, great canebrakes often formed a green jungle along the banks, and flocks of birds were everywhere—ducks and geese on the river; partridges, turkeys, and quail in the riverbank forests.

After several false starts, the English made their first permanent settlement alongside the James River, in Tidewater Virginia, soon beginning their penetration westward by following the network of rivers and streams inland into the primeval forest. The Pilgrims at Plymouth, Massachusetts, were soon followed by Puritans who began moving westward. But the French were the truly successful invaders in mining the prime riches of northern North America—fish and furs. The tiny islands of St. Pierre and Miquelon, off the southern coast of Newfoundland at the doorsill of the Grand Banks, are the last remnants of the once vast dominion of New World France. During the height of the fur trade, when the *coureurs de bois* and voyageurs were traveling far inland on the Canadian lakes and rivers to exchange European goods for the animal pelts, Frenchmen discovered in this spacious primitive wilderness something of the savage, simple happy life that Rousseau had dreamed of. The canoes they traveled in, some as long as 45 feet, with a crew of as many as fourteen, "often managed up to eighty miles, between earliest dawn and summer's dark," Henry Beston has estimated, "at about forty strokes of the paddle to the minute. Mile after mile they sang the old ballads and songs of France, singing together with the thrust of their swift strokes, the gay, choral sound echoing back upon them from the enclosing walls of the forest or floating off across the stillness of lakes into the north and the unknown." Longfellow expressed the feeling of this vast wilderness in the opening lines of *Evangeline*:

> This is the forest primeval. The murmuring pines and the
>   hemlocks,
> Bearded with moss, and in garments green, indistinct in the
>   twilight,
> Stand like Druids of eld, with voices sad and prophetic,
> Stand like harpers hoar, with beards that rest on their bosoms.

The Europeans gutted this virgin wilderness in rapacious style, and Americans and Canadians have continued the predacious haul—"Let him take who take can," Rabelais expressed it —with never a thought of the morrow. First the beaver and other furbearers were cleaned (or skinned) out. Next came the mighty woodsmen, and the vast virgin forests were stripped (or skinned). Finally, and we are in that age now, the Great Lakes themselves are in the midst of being ruined from having pollutants dumped in them, both from human waste products of the great new cities and from the leftover wastes of the riches taken from underground. In 1969, an iron-mining company at the western end of Lake Superior was "discovered" to be dumping some 60,000 tons a day of ore waste, and it was only one of many such companies. And so we turn the miraculous wilderness into that other kind of awful, *empty* wilderness—wasteland.

After the entrepreneurs, the fur trappers, lumber barons, and mining specialists, were done, the forests and lakes began coming back into public domain. New trees are now growing in the Great Lakes area; in national forests, wildlife is making a comeback; maybe the lakes will be given a chance. "The Green Woods Wilderness of eastern America is the biggest, richest, most hospitable wilderness on the face of the earth," Rutherford Platt says, inviting us into today's remaining but also regaining forest, which is still a great wonder for a city person to behold.

Rivers may be tractable and mild, or cruel and heartless, and they can murder entire communities of men with droughts or floods. More than half a billion people live in river valleys and deltas in the Far East, where there is the lifelong threat of death by drowning. Americans in the Mississippi River basin have had to battle the Father of Waters endlessly. One of De Soto's companions on his discovery-voyage, Garcilasso de la Vega, described the 1543 Mississippi flood: "Forty days in reaching its greatest height which was the twentieth of April, and it was a beautiful thing to look upon the sea where there had been fields on each side." Four centuries later, William Faulkner described the intensely personal warfare waged in time of flood between Old Man River and man; the cruel Mississippi was "piling up the water while white man and Negro worked side by side in shifts in the mud and the rain . . . lapping, tentative, almost innocently, merely inexorable (no hurry, his) among and beneath and between and finally over the frantic sandbags, as if his whole purpose had been merely to give man another chance to prove not to him but to man, just how much the human body could bear, stand, endure."

The spring, 1969, 50-mile-long flood crest of the Mississippi was the third highest in history, but the $100,000,000 damage was only a third of what could have happened. In Operation Foresight, more than 200 miles of emergency dikes were built, and 10,000,000 sandbags placed. Plastic foam was sprayed 4 inches thick over levees to prevent seepage and erosion.

One of the worst flood years was 1937, when waters rose nearly 60 feet at Cairo, Illinois, and a lake formed in the lower valley that was almost as large as Lake Superior. Great rivers have always *demanded* a wide "meander belt" of potential flood plains in which to operate—eroding and depositing silt—much as the oceans *demand* an intertidal zone along all their continental shores. When man comes along and builds riverside homes and factories, he usually ignores any such natural "riparian rights" of the river, blandly considering such things as floods and droughts as "unnatural" phenomena in what ought to be an adjusted, regulated, man-controlled world.

More and more river channels are being canalized, and new canals dug, so that within the eastern and central United States there are today more than 25,000 miles of navigable inland waterway channels, exclusive of the Great Lakes. In December, 1969, the once-turbulent Arkansas River was opened to Fort Smith and the Oklahoma line, at a cost of $1.2 billion, the costliest single public works project in the history of the country. When the project to tame the wild river was first proposed, Will Rogers, the humorist, said: "It would be easier and cheaper to pave the Arkansas than to develop it."

The rivers and lakes are busier than ever today, carrying more than 15 percent of all the nation's cargo. In place of the early canoes, bateaux, rafts, flatboats, and broadhorns, today's immense barges are push-towed by powerful tugboats of up to 9,000 horsepower. Except for the New York State Barge Canal, the first artificial waterway, all are now under federal control.

The first Erie Canal, from the Hudson River to Lake Erie, was opened in 1825, making a water highway to the western plains that was crowded for the next several decades with eager European immigrants bound for a new chance and a new life in the New World. The canal was rebuilt larger twice, the present one in 1905–18 as part of the enlarged New York State Barge Canal system. Well over 1,000,000 tons of cargo today pass through it toll-free annually, and thousands of pleasure boaters also ply it for passage between New York Harbor and Lake Erie, using one branch, the Oswego Canal, to reach Lake Ontario, and the Champlain Canal to voyage northward by way of Lake Champlain to Montreal and other St. Lawrence River riverports. The Ohio River has been gradually "canalized" until today it's practically a man-made stream. When the completed canalized river was officially opened, in October, 1929, President Herbert Hoover said that the cost had been half that of the Panama Canal, and that this was only the beginning of the never-ending need to give perpetual care to the Ohio as a great artery of commercial river traffic. One is reminded, in the twentieth century, of the perpetual care that once made the Mesopotamian Valley a well-watered garden of paradise.

The first steamboat down the Mississippi was the *New Orleans*, built in Pittsburgh for Nicholas and Lydia Roosevelt. Two years earlier, the couple had floated down the Ohio and

Mississippi on an immense raft-houseboat, on one of the great wonder honeymoons of all time. On the steamboat journey in 1811, Lydia gave birth to a baby, and there was a mighty earthquake, an onboard fire, a Mississippi flood, and even dangerous boarders (Indians who demanded, and were given, a bottle of firewater). The vessel made the one-way trip somehow. In 1816 the first round-trip voyage was made by the *Washington*.

Of the joy of rafting down the Big River, which the Spaniards called *Espíritu Santo,* River of the Holy Ghost, and the English tried to name Malabanchia—*Misi* (big) *Sipi* (river) is so much more exact—Huckleberry Finn is the great unwashed poet: "Soon as it was night out we shoved; when we got her out to about the middle we let her alone, and let her float wherever the current wanted her to; then we lit the pipes, and dangled our legs in the water, and talked about all kinds of things—we was always naked, day and night, whenever the mosquitoes would let us. . . . Sometimes we'd have that whole river all to ourselves for the longest time. . . . It's lovely to live on a raft. We had the sky up there, all speckled with stars, and we used to lay on our backs and look up at them, and discuss about whether they was made or only just happened."

Mark Twain's first love was always the Mississippi River steamboat, "finer than anything on shore. Compared with superior dwelling houses and first class hotels in the Valley, they were indubitably magnificent, they were palaces." However, he did add honestly that "they provided everything—everything but safety." For the loss annually to sandbars, to fire, and especially to boiler explosions was devastating. After the total lull of the Civil War, there came two final splendid decades of supersteamboats—palatial vessels with sumptuous imported carpets, massive furniture, and elegant service. And then suddenly it was all over—river passengers switched to travel by locomotive railway. The last of the great riverboats, *Delta Queen,* is scheduled to end operations after 1970, and it's doubtful if she can be replaced with a costly new sternwheeler.

Since the opening of the St. Lawrence Seaway in 1959, great oceangoing vessels now come to port within the Great Lakes in the very heartland of North America. The digging of the Erie Canal, linking the far-inland Great Lakes with the seacoast port of New York, gave that city precedence over her rival, Philadelphia. Today one wonders whether perhaps the Great Lakes may be on their way to at last supersede the port of New York City.

Mark Twain, a great student of every facet of change in the river's obstreperous objection to casual passage, would have taken delight in the human capability expressed in today's truly massive inland waterway freightage. Master pilot Howard Tait, of the *Delta Queen,* on a mid-'69 voyage, pointed out to his guests: "That big brute of a tow coming up is the *John H. MacMillan*—9,000 horsepower, pushing *forty-eight* barges, six abreast and a third of a mile long, carrying about 2,000 tons of aluminum ore per barge—more than what 500 freight cars could manage!"

The pleasure voyagers, more than 40,000,000 of them annually, travel over the lakes, rivers, and canals by sailboat, outboard motor, canoe, motorboat, yacht, but always in the summertime: when primitive weather, old-time wilderness, returns for four months out of every year, the Great Lakes and Midwestern rivers return to the frozen old-time primitive ways. During the rest of the year—two-thirds, that is—this is the most crowded and busiest set of waterways on the planet. But, during that one-third hiatus, Richard Bissell, a Mississippi River pilot worthy of S. Clemens in stature, has complained, in *High Water,* that the temperature and all that "gets so mighty chilly out here in the Middle West in the springtime after dark! First it is winter and they are breaking ice with a couple of chartered boats up the Illinois River trying to keep the coal moving into Chicago to Commonwealth Edison and the others, and the deckhands they put on two sweatshirts under their sheep-lined coats and they still freeze to death waiting for the lock tender to get the big cakes of ice unstuck so they can open the gates—and then it is spring and the ice goes out and in the evening the boys and girls stroll downtown for a hot fudge sundae, but after midnight take it from me out on the river it is cold after midnight until well into May or sometimes even June."

Farther afield, one can adventure safely today down the Green and Colorado rivers on inflatable rubber rafts guided by experts. Father Garcés named the Colorado for its muddy red color, nearly 200 years ago, when he climbed down the side of the great canyon to visit the Havasupai Indians, who are still there to be visited on their *insular* Colorado River hideout.

The most way-out North American river journey is a repeat of Sir Alexander Mackenzie's 1789 voyage down the river later named after him to the Arctic (which he called the Frozen Sea). During the summers of 1966 and 1967, Constance Helmericks and her two young daughters made the lonely passage *down the wild river north*. From within the protection of her mosquito netting, she wrote: "You can hear all kinds of voices in the whiny insects' wings. You hear voices in the river and in the forest. But most of all, the voices are inside yourself. Subterranean layers you never knew you had. Snatches of old tunes you haven't thought of since childhood go around in your head for days . . . gradually you succumb to nature's enticing lullaby. The lullaby goes that nothing in civilization is really important anyway. And after a while, if you stay in the wilderness, you will believe it."

There are waterway journeys all over Planet Water, on civilized and on wild rivers: the inland waterway north to Alaska; cruises up the Rhine, the Nile, along the riverine waterways of France, England, Finland (which has 31,000 miles), down the Volga and Dnieper, along the Tapirapé River in Brazil (André Rakowitsch's boatel customers even carry along beads to barter with the friendly natives!).

Since the earliest historical times, men have especially sought the headwaters of famous rivers. Homer calmly accepted that "the Nile flows down from heaven." Herodotus went up-Nile south as far as the first cataract, but reported: "No man of all the Egyptians, Libyans or Grecians with whom I have conversed ever pretended to know anything" about where the life-giving river came from. Nero sent an expedition that went much farther upstream but bogged down in swamps. Leonardo da Vinci wrote that the Nile "issues from the Mountains of the Moon by several unexplained sources." Alexander the Great, finding crocodiles in the rivers of India, half-believed that the Nile, which also had crocodiles, might curl about in a great, mysterious loop from a source there. Not until A.D. 1858 did John Speke see Victoria Nyanza, source of the White Nile. Or is the Kagera River that empties into Lake Victoria the true source? Similarly, Pedro Paez reached, in 1618, the source of the Blue Nile, "two round fountains, each about four palms in diameter, what neither Cyrus, king of the Persians, nor Cambyses, nor Alexander the Great, nor the famous Julius Caesar, could ever discover." In 1625, Father Jerome Lobo peered into the "two holes each about two feet in diameter" and then followed upstream to Lake Tana, to view Ethiopia's Tisisat Falls (from an Amharic word meaning "smoke of fire"), pouring from the lake, and somewhere along about here is the Blue Nile's source, but where, oh, where can one pretend that there is a beginning for the planet's hydrologic recircling cycle?

The Congo (world's second-largest river), the Zambezi, and the White Nile all rise in the central African mountain range, the Ruwenzori, Mountains of the Moon, just as Leonardo had so brilliantly foretold. The River Niger, originating in Africa's far northwest, loops down through the Sahara to form a fourth, equatorial rain-belt river. The earliest river explorers went up all of them—in search of Zambezi gold, ivory, and the greatest black-gold treasure of all, human slaves, "free" manpower, the machinery of the pre-industrial-mechanical age.

The greatest mountains in the world—the Karakoram, the Kunlun, the Great Khingan, the Tien Shan, and the Himalayas —are thrust upward out of Eastern Asia as though they had been half-torn out or were about to be ejected from the Planet Water to form another circling moon. Some of our planet's greatest rivers pour down from these gigantic mountain ranges. Northward the Yenisey, Ob, and Lena flow into the Arctic Ocean. The Amur, Hwang Ho, and Yangtze Kiang course eastward through China to the Pacific. Southward flow the Mekong, Salween, and Irrawaddy. To the west, the Ganges, the Brahmaputra, and the Indus run down the Indian subcontinent—all three of these rivers rise out of the Kubi glaciers, which ice-flow out of Planet Water's loftiest mountain peaks. To visit any of these great rivers' sources would be to inspect the origin point where the unending freshwater wars begin between earth and rivers. If earth did not continue the eternal internal upward-thrusting (the Himalayas, planetary highest, are still rising), then the rivers and the watery storms of the atmosphere would long ago have reduced all the planet's land surfaces to uniform sea level.

The handsomest available monument (others lie beneath sea level) to the eternal water cycles of uplift and erosion is the mile-deep cleft of the Grand Canyon of the Colorado River. The sculptor-river has now been working endlessly in the great studio for 9,000,000 years. As the studio's walls once rose, the artist-river worked on them. Today it's not only a great library of geology but also fun to clamber down the sides of the canyon, on foot or on mule.

Americans seldom get to visit the headwaters of China's great rivers. Joseph Rock, who went to the source of the Hwang Ho (or Yellow River, "China's Sorrow") in 1930 for *National Geographic,* expressed his altitude fascination in frantic style: "I shouted for joy to view the highest mountains in our world: Tibetans worship these snowy peaks as emblems of purity," and he then proceeded to study the deep chasms and roaring waterfalls where the great river is steadily engaged in carving deep gorges in the Himalayan cliffs. This is the stark, soaring land of lonely monasteries set high on cliffs—the Potala of the Dalai Lama is propped on a height over the Kyi Chu, a tributary of the Brahmaputra—and where Buddhist anchorites spend their lives within mountain caves fasting and meditating upon the sins and sorrows of the rest of us. When one rides a mule to the top of Half Dome, in Yosemite Park, where the waterfalls come pouring purely out of cliffs, one might almost expect to encounter holy men dwelling in caves. But our mountain meditators are usually much more joyous and pagan: one cannot picture John Muir *immured* within a mountain cavern, fasting and praying. But one would like to visit that holy cave, 10,000 feet up, where the Ganges River begins in the melting waters of a glacier, turning miraculously into the waters of the world's holiest river.

When a traveler visits *Ganga Ma,* Mother Ganges, he is seeing the holy waters that received the ashes of Mahatma Gandhi, the father of nonviolence and devoted votary of civil resistance. Jawaharlal Nehru, India's prime minister, choking with emotion, told the nation a few hours after the murder in 1948: "The light has gone out of our lives and there is darkness everywhere. Our beloved leader, Bapu as we call him, the father of our nation, is no more. The light that has illumined this country for these many years will illumine this country for many more years, and a thousand years later that light will still be seen in this country, and the world will see it and it will give solace to innumerable hearts. A madman has put an end to his life."

In 1963–64, British author Eric Newby took the 1,200-mile journey which he described in *Slowly down the Ganges*. He wrote of the sacred river: "To bathe in it is to wash away guilt. To drink the water . . . is meritorious. To be cremated on its banks, having died there, and to have one's ashes cast on its waters, is the wish of every Hindu." To ejaculate, "Ganga, Ganga," may atone for the sins committed during three previous lifetimes! Hindu pilgrims slowly travel the route, taking six years. They start at the source in an ice cave near Gangotri, far up in the Himalayas at the very roof of the Planet Water, and its tributaries' sources depend on the melting snows of the planet's highest mountains—Everest, Kinchinjunga, Gosainthan, where Indian gods reside in an upper atmosphere far more rarefied than that of Greece's modest Mount Olympus. The pilgrimage is two-way, down to the estuary in the Bay of Bengal, where Sagar Island is as sacred a visiting place as the ice cavern high in the mountains, and then back to which the pilgrim must walk to complete the holy *pradak-shina*. If the votary is unusually inspired, he'll also "measure his length" along certain portions of the journey. Returning pilgrims carry home bottles of holy Ganges water as faithfully as Christians have long carried back home holy Jordan water to Europe and the Americas.

Benares is the most holy city alongside the Ganges. Where the visitor hears the faithful forever praising the gods, "Hare Rama, Hare Krishna, Hare, Hare" (Lord Rama, Lord Krishna, Lord, Lord). Marshal Tito, president of Yugoslavia, visiting, commented, "I have seen cities for learning and cities for earning, but this is the first time I have seen a city for dying." In 1968, Joseph Lelyveld reported in the New York *Times* that "the 'tourist *sadhus*,' young hippies from the West, are now an authentic part of the Benares scene—high on ganja and charas, intoxicating weeds from the surrounding countryside, but so are many of the Indian *sadhus* they meet."

"Oh! to die in Benares: to die on the banks of Ganges. To have one's body bathed for the last time, and then to have one's ashes strewn into the river!" said Pierre Loti. In the early

1950's, Gordon Cooper, an inveterate British traveler, gave what to me is the finest description of the massive *river worship* that takes place at Benares, where "on the waterfront are magnificent palaces and the most fantastic skyline in the world, a frieze of granite temples, rosy pyramids, golden shafts; altogether there are said to be 1,500 temples and large mosques, and also many sacred bathing places, approached by the famous ghats or flights of stone steps.

"These massive tiers of steps, which stretch along the bank and reach to the water's edge even in times of drought, where fallen temples emerge from their slimy beds, were made in honor of Ganges, and on each landing there are little granite altars, shaped like niches, in which diminutive gods are placed. These images are like those of the temples, but they are of more massive constructions, so as to withstand the swirl of waters which cover them during the annual floods. Here and there funeral pyres (burning ghats) burst into flames, while the smoke of burning flesh rises as an almost continuous incense."

Visitors to New York City can journey northward to Lake Tear in the Clouds, on Mount Marcy, there to discover the source of the Hudson River. The source of the mighty Mississippi is Lake Itasca, in northern Minnesota (almost in Canada!). Willard Price, journeying to the headwaters of London's Thames River, found an almost dry spring: "There was a thin film of water on the tip of my finger. 'That,' I said solemnly to my wife, 'is the Thames.' I wiped the Thames off on my slacks." Patrick Leigh Fermor once followed the great Danube River from one of its three recognized sources, a tiny spring at Donaueschingen, in the Schlosspark of the Fürstenberg princes, to its marshy outlets in the Black Sea. The Danube is one of the great rivers of history because of the massive armies that have swept up and down its corridor course. You can still see an inscription, high on the side of the famed Iron Gates, that marks the Roman Emperor Trajan's construction of a cliffside road for his troops. Herodotus called the Danube "mightiest of rivers." Attila the Hun led his Mongolian hordes up the Danube Valley, was defeated, and settled down in the plains of Hungary. In A.D. 1096 armies moved the other way, downriver, thousands of ships carrying 40,000 crusaders toward the First Crusade in the Holy Land. In 1241 came the Mongols under Batu the Splendid, to defeat Bela IV of Hungary and sweep onward to the Adriatic. Fortunately for whoever happened to have been left alive, they presently swept back down the valley on their return to Asia. In 1453 came the Turks, up the Danube to besiege Vienna, unsuccessfully. Today the visitor can sail peaceably down the "brown" waters of the "blue" Danube, to the sound of the familiar waltz on an Austrian riverboat, down through the historically alarming Cazane Defile, and presently try a Yugoslav hydrofoil overwater journey onward into the Black Sea.

Names—names—names! The riverine past that is also mankind's history. The greatest promise and least fulfillment of men's riparian dreams are wrapped up in the most watery mystery of all, the Planet Water's greatest river, the Amazon. Nearly *half* of the South American continent belongs to the Amazon and its tributaries—draining nearly 3,000,000 square miles, pouring out to sea a fifth (*20 percent!*) of all the moving freshwaters of the globe, 1,100 tributaries (15 of them great rivers in their own right), 30,000 miles of navigable inland waterways. In human values, the great Amazon Valley has always been one of the most poverty-stricken regions of the world, in the sheer splendor of animal and vegetable "explosion," one of the richest; its frondiferous green-leafiness forms the planet's largest jungle. A century ago, after a dozen years of dedicated solitary research in the Amazon Basin, the British botanist Henry Walter Bates explained his own personal Amazonian involvement: "There's something in a tropical forest akin to the ocean in its effect on the mind. Man feels so completely his insignificance there and the vastness of nature: here each plant and tree seems to be striving to outlive its fellow, struggling upward towards light and air; live and let live is clearly not the maxim taught in the wilderness."

The tribes in the Amazon Valley have always made war on one another. The supposition has been raised, ever since discoverer Francisco de Orellana first reported in 1542 that a race of lady warriors, the Amazons, ruled the lower valley from stone-walled cities, that maybe the Amazons really *did* exist, and in 1969 David St. Clair, in *The Mighty, Mighty Amazon*, once more suggested that "somewhere in there, on the Jamundá

River, there are hundreds of weed-encrusted walls, dozens of overgrown roads, and possibly millions of dollars in gold and ornaments." For total belief, can some explorer please produce just *one* statuette of an Amazon queen?

Another recent visitor, Leonard Clark, in *The Rivers Ran East,* has portrayed the fearful part taken by human blood as a real and ritualistic part of the hydrologic cycle of waters in the Amazon Basin: "Headhunting and scalp-taking in the Amazon is very often a part of the ceremonies for the harvest (or again, of the planting) season. The idea is that *flowing* blood represents the sap of new life, that death itself is necessary for the continuous flow in all its manifestations of life in matter. Thus, a human is a human today, but tomorrow might be a yuca stalk or a beast—no matter!—for the undying spirit is God Itself, and cannot be wetted, cannot be hurt, cannot have beginning or end." V. S. Pritchett called the Amazon's vast flow "a continent bleeding into the sea."

If Cartier or La Salle had gone exploring along the tropical Amazon instead of the temperate St. Lawrence and Mississippi, they should *surely* have brought along mosquito nets—for use against the vampire bats. These thirsty creatures never even bothered to grow legs or feet, since they never have occasion to stand up; also, they do not *suck* blood: they drill neat, cone-shaped holes in any available, exposed flesh (horse, human, or otherwise), with a pleasant accompanying anesthetic fluid, then sit around like dainty pussycats, delicately *lapping* the blood as it flows neatly into the tiny demitasse saucers. The other most outrageous denizen of the Amazon is the piranha fish; until recently piranhas were imported by American fish fanciers as "pets." The tiny, voracious monsters attack in merciless packs and can easily trim any waterlogged beast quickly to a bare skeleton. Since piranhas are endowed with tasty, sweet, white flesh, Amazonian Indians hoist them by their own greedy petard, so to speak: the slashed body of a long-legged flamingo is thrust down into the river just long enough for the toothsome piranha to fasten jaws onto it, then whipped back out and shaken over the boat. This is repeated until there is a boatful of piranha for lunch. The barefoot fishermen meanwhile must keep their feet off the floorboards to avoid a double feast.

The Amazon is the greatest river of them all, surely to be visited and enjoyed by any explorer who ever expects to call himself a knowing riverman.

Deepest of freshwater lakes is Baikal, *Dalai-nor*, in east Siberia. Its level is 1,486 feet above sea level, and its 5,712-foot depth goes down 1,226 feet below sea level—only 60 feet less than the lowest pocket on a continent, the Dead Sea area of Israel-Jordan. Baikal's 11,780 square miles is almost as big as Maryland, but still less than half the size of the planet's largest freshwater lake, Superior, 31,800 square miles, nearly as big as Maine. Soviet conservationists have warned that new pulp plants are rapidly killing Lake Baikal.

The lakes that most of us cherish in memory are small, quiet, serene. They also used to be quiet and motorless. Arthur Schopenhauer complained, a century ago, that "the most inexcusable and disgraceful of all noises is the cracking of whips—a truly infernal thing when it is done in the narrow resounding streets of a town. I denounce it as making a peaceful life impossible; it puts an end to all quiet thoughts." This is the way most of us feel about outboard motors on quiet rural ponds, about motor-scooters on country lanes, about snowmobiles roaring through snow country, about all the other hellish new motor noises. In contrast, Schopenhauer's whip-cracking seems in retrospect an innocent, inconsequential, gentle clatter. All sounds are, of course, relative, so that when the great sonic booms begin crashing all about, as they inevitably will during the 1970's, maybe today's outboard motors, motorbikes, scooters and even snowmobiles will seem, in violent "silent" contrast, extremely innocent, inconsequential clatter, entirely endurable.

North America is the Planet Water's continent of freshwater lakes; it contains at least half of all the world's fresh lakes. Shall one try to name every one of Minnesota's claimed 10,000? Maps of most states reveal thousands of lakes and ponds, small and large, all over, everywhere. Far better, public lakes and ponds, than private backyard swimming pools, though these, like apartment balconies, are sequestered family blessings. But lakesides are for sharing, though rather privately.

Henry David Thoreau wrote endlessly about Walden Pond. "A lake is the landscape's most beautiful and expressive feature. It is earth's eye; looking into which the beholder measures the depth of his own nature. The fluviatile trees next the shore are the slender eyelashes which fringe it, and the wooded hills and cliffs around are its overhanging brows." One can imagine his rage when he learned that the villagers of Concord, "who scarcely know where it lies, instead of going to the pond to bathe or drink, are now thinking to bring its waters, which should be as sacred as the Ganges at least, to the village in a *pipe*, to wash their dishes with!—to earn their Walden by the turning of a cock or drawing of a plug!"

What places Thoreau among the great natural philosophers is his constant sympathy and recognition for the *livingness* of the nonhuman things in his world: "Of all the characters I have known, perhaps Walden Pond wears best, and best preserves its purity . . . it is itself unchanged, the same water which my youthful eyes fell on; all the change is in me. It has not acquired one permanent wrinkle after all its ripples. It is perennially young." In fact, he was usually more at home with his lakes and rivers than with most people. His diary *A Week on the Concord and Merrimac Rivers* remains a classic. It was influenced by his discovery of the sacred writings of India, notably the Bhagavad Gita, which perhaps caused him to write so strikingly that "the ears were made not for such trivial uses as men are wont to suppose, but to hear celestial sounds. The eyes were not made for such groveling uses as they are now put to and worn out by, but to behold beauty now invisible. May we not *see* God?"

I grew up near the confluence of the Concord and Merrimac a mere century afterward, yet my generation never would have thought of canoeing on either of these once lovely streams, for they have become among the nation's worst-polluted rivers. It's almost unbelievable that so short a while ago the poet Lucy Larcom, changing bobbins as a doffer in a cotton mill, could look out upon the "Laughing River" as it was sometimes called, and sing,

> I do not own an inch of land,
> But all I see is mine.

Congress has begun to declare certain American rivers "wild" and others "scenic" (those with less-swift current and set in more-pastoral country); this action may protect or regain a few streams which man has not yet ruined. But what of Lucy Larcom's Laughing Merrimac, the ruined Connecticut, and all the other *lost*, once beautiful streams that today have the aroma and appearance of open sewers?When shall such a massive ecological turnaround begin to take place that can return them to their pristine, sweet-flowing condition?

When my son and I first followed the simple footpath around Thoreau's sacred Walden Pond, a small dog appeared and conducted us with great dignity, leaving to join the next group of pilgrims on the following hike as though he were some sort of hostly Concord canine cicerone. Thoreau found Concord's environs "over-civilized" in his day, but the area has since become truly inundated by burgeoning Boston, which will soon cover all of eastern Massachusetts with its suburbs, explosive symbol of the future worldcity. When we asked the guide in the Concord Museum if one might pronounce the great name Thor-*eau*, accenting the last syllable, she tartly told us that it was perfectly all right to use the "foreign" pronunciation, but that native Concordians prefer *Thor*-eau. So be it.

A lakeside walk can be an intensely soothing experience for anyone whose life is spent usually moving along paved sidewalks. For many years I lived alongside New York City's Central Park, and at that time I considered Central Park Reservoir and the circling cinder walkway to be my own personal Walled-in Pond. When I first began to tour it, there were many heel-and-toe walkers nervously ambulating along in their special costume that looked like old-fashioned long winter underwear. Nowadays, the cinder track has a new population of earnest joggers. Among all these trackmen in training, there is always a small, steady, mobile population of simple strollers like myself. This is, of course, no sylvan, pondy country retreat, but a walk alongside a tiny, metal-fence-enclosed lake in the midst of an immense city. Beyond the fringe of the park's towering trees and lawns, there is a stately silhouette of rigid, perpendicular skyscrapers that marches along each rectangular park edge in the distance, often, because of the smog, seen only mistily.

Many years ago, I discovered that as one comes hiking around the northern rim of the reservoir, it is possible for a walker to perform a remarkable act of legerdemain or *trompe d'oeil,* made possible by the visual phenomenon known as *parallax:* by walking along the cinder track, one causes the great skyscrapers of Manhattan's midtown skyline to *move* into different positions in relationship to one another. The best structures for this miracle-working are the RCA Building and the Empire State: near Central Park Lamppost #9534 (all park lampposts are numbered), it is possible to "walk" these two distant monoliths right up next to each other, and thus join them into what may be called, reverently, the Cathedral in the Sky, one of the Planet Water's stateliest and most stupendous manmade structures—with the RCA forming the huge basilica (containing, in imagination, the highest nave of any church), and the Empire State Building forming the cathedral's dramatically soaring spire. "Man was never so happily inspired," Robert Louis Stevenson has urged us imaginative parallax architects onward, "as when he made a cathedral."

Abroad there are many and many poetic small lakes—Como, Maggiore, Killarney, Kashmir (Dal Lake)—but surprisingly beloved beyond most others is little Windermere, in the British Lake Country, in whose vicinity Scott, Tennyson, Coleridge, Southey, and the best-known lakeman of all poesy, William Wordsworth, penned their love of nature. Wordsworth was a lonely and aloof man who never made friends with his simple country neighbors and also rarely bothered with the written works of others:

> Books! 'Tis a dull and endless strife:
> Come, hear the woodland linnet,
> How sweet his music! On my life,
> There's more of wisdom in it!

Wordsworth's and Thoreau's placid, lacustral lives are remarkably similar in many ways. Wordsworth showed utter indifference to the usual country occupations and amusement of his country neighbors. He also cared little for reading. "Nature was his book." A. G. Bradley suggested, a half-century ago: "He was out-of-doors the whole of every fine day. One would suppose that he would have shared in some form or other the pursuits of his neighbors in the course of so long a life spent wholly in their midst. Wordsworth dreamed past them mostly, or looked upon them through colored spectacles."

Because of Wordsworth's Demosthenic habit of vociferously spouting his poetry as he walked, his neighbors would sometimes exclaim, "Auld Wudswuth's brocken lowce ageean," and a contemporary interpreted their country wisdom: "These mutterings and mouthings of the poet were taken by the people of the neighborhood as an indication of mental aberration." Few artists, of words or of visual representation, could continue to create without patronage. Wordsworth's poems never supported him. There was a small family income and also a government job as "stamp distributor" that was actually a sinecure (somewhere an unfortunate clerk did the work called for), to pay for upkeep of modest Dove Cottage, while its owner "wandered lonely as a cloud." One is reminded that Thoreau was also supported at least in part by the family *pencil* business—which depended presumably on somebody else's cruelly chopping down the trees necessary for their manufacture. We are greatly enriched by both lakemen's writings, but one must also feel an equal sympathy for their patient neighbors who lived more mundane lives of quiet desperation, farmed crops, raised kids, and so had no time for dramatic poetizing.

My generation, as kids, read the carefree books of Thornton Burgess and *Wind in the Willows*. How little science or learning—and how much sentiment—there used to be in such books about lakes and ponds and their inhabitants! Franklin Russell has described with brutal vigor the variety and volume of life that explodes forth every springtime in the smallest pond, which reminds one that this goblet of freshwater is merely a tiny replica of the salt waters of the great Ocean Sea, and the rugged miniature life-war of survival waged here is just as fierce and unmerciful: "This was the awakening in the pond, a prodigious expansion of life, diversified and interrelated . . . a common animation of spirit and objective that plants and animals would soon merge insensibly into the secret of the pond and the swarming days that now lay just ahead. At every level of existence, constant competition for space and a share of sunlight, oxygen and moisture made haphazard the lives of all creatures. There was little outward sign of any struggle. Yet the diversity of life in this miniature universe seemed infinite. All this life—

visible and invisible—appeared against countless blunt shoots springing from the bottom, from mud, from old roots, from dormant seeds. Many plants want to live with almost the same intensity and direction as animals and insects." Twice a year, in spring and fall, the wind-stirred waters of the ponds are turned over, *explode*, take "a deep breath of air," the warmed heavier water sinking, the lighter rising from the bottom. But the prodigious annual expansion-explosion of water life is nowadays dwindling because of the increasing pollution of all freshwater sources. In 1969 the Federal Water Pollution Control Administration announced that the Potomac River, after an extensive ten-year cleanup program, was just as badly polluted as it had been a decade before when the program was started. At least a third of the nation's 100,000 lakes are now endangered by cultural eutrophication, the indiscriminate dumping of wastes—with sewage the principal eutrophier. Biologist A. M. Beeton warned, "We've got to decide soon how we want to use the lakes: if we want a sewer, then we'd better forget about swimming and fishing; you can't have it both ways." A new peril came into public notice in 1968, the increasing danger of thermal pollution, as many new atomic plants began to release billions of gallons of hot water into streams as part of their cooling-system operations.

Certain of mankind's most successful cities have been so watery that the people who live in them have always taken a totally different view on life, living, happiness, and pleasure, a truly *watery* view. Venice, with its innumerable canals, piazzas, lagoons, pigeons, Tintorettos, traghetti (ferries), and gondolas, is such a city; it is now slowly settling ever deeper down into the Adriatic Sea and into its own canal streets. Every other city in the world that traffics at all in canals is called a Venice. Amsterdam is the North Sea Venice in the Netherlands (which in turn gets its name from the fact that so much of Holland lies below sea level). The heart of old Amsterdam is a carefully preserved seventeenth-century water city looped with rings of canals, more than fifty of them, on which the visitor can go sight-seeing in glass-sided canalboats that even take him out into Amsterdam's great harbor. From this Renaissance city of Rembrandts, Hals, Vermeers, Hans Brinker ("the finger"), Mondrians, and diamonds, one may go sailing along Holland's 2,000 miles of canals and among her 1,000 lakes. In contrast to slowly sinking Venice, Holland continues to *rise* out of the North Sea, as more land-reclamation dikes continue to be built. The Delta Works, still under construction, is one of man's most daring colossal fabrications in defiance of the sea's destructive power.

In the Far East, Bangkok (Krung Thep), the eighteenth-century royal city of the kings of Siam, has been a city of klongs (canals), the Oriental Venice. In its immense floating market, in the early morning, farmers sell such exotics as jujubes, guavas, mangoes, jackfruits, rose apples, and pomelos. When the royal barges are on parade past the old royal palaces and pagodas, one is reminded of the remarkable friendship of Anna Leonowens and King Chulalongkorn, when she joined his royal household as instructress to his many wives and children. But Bangkok, Thailand, is swiftly going modern twentieth century: the klongs are rapidly being filled in and *paved* to make more space for vehicular traffic. Meanwhile, in Florida, U.S.A., Fort Lauderdale is called the Venice of America, for its innumerable canals, inlets, and artificial islands. Fort Lauderdale is fast growing into a considerable seaport, a veritable Venice, as the original was in the Middle Ages.

London in the time of Elizabeth I was a great water city, its life swirling about the Thames, its royal barge as impressive then as is the royal carriage today that bore Elizabeth II to her coronation in 1952. Anyone reading Shakespeare's description of Cleopatra's barge knows whose river chariot he meant:

> The barge she sat in, like a burnish'd throne,
> Burn'd on the water: the poop was beaten gold;
> Purple the sails, and so perfumèd that
> The winds were love-sick with them. . . .

Agrippa, the Roman listening to this lush description, gasps, "O, rare for Antony!" and one may be sure that Shakespeare was making an admiring reference to the royal virgin whom he may long ago have seen, he being a teen-ager, she a glamorous, imperious vamp in her mid-forties, perhaps the greatest woman of all time. By the time he wrote his play, lovesick perhaps with tender-age memories, she was long dead, just as when Alessandro Botticelli got around to painting Miss Vespucci (especially the scene with her lover, Giuliano de Medici), both were long dead. How pallid are photographs alongside records made of creative words or drawings!

Antony and Cleopatra has always struck me as a glorious paean to the womanhood of Elizabeth Tudor, in her royal Thames barge; if she'd been alive to witness it, she would probably have been as surprised and delighted as any mirror-peering lady could be, to find herself compared with the historic serpent-beauty of the Nile:

> For her own person,
> It beggar'd all description: she did lie
> In her pavilion—cloth-of-gold of tissue—
> O'er-picturing that Venus where we see
> The fancy outwork nature. . . .

Even the fancy footwork of royal horses prancing before a great coach cannot equal the splendor of the river vessel powered by handsome oarsmen working all in unison: no galley slaves these, but honored members of the queen's own royal household.

Oh, to have an American capital water city! John Adams used to stroll beside the Potomac in the early morning, hang his clothes on a hickory limb, and take a swim in the Presidential buff. George Washington, as we all know, *must* have thrown coins across the river, in 1750. There have always been Presidential yachts, and a highwater mark in their use may have been the day when President Taft got stuck in the yacht's too-narrow bathtub. In July, 1961, a water event took place on the Potomac that equaled in glamor any episode on Elizabeth I's Thames or Cleopatra's Nile. Jacqueline Kennedy, wife of the thirty-fifth President of the United States, carried 136 guests downriver to Mount Vernon aboard four pleasure boats. The occasion honored President Ayub Khan of Pakistan and his daughter the Begum Nasir Akhtar Aurangzeb; the other guests were prominent Americans and members of the foreign diplomatic corps. There was a lawn party such as Elizabeth I might have given up-Thames at Hampton Court—with music by an Air Force orchestra and the National Symphony. And there was in the oligarchic/geriatric pronouncements of U.S. Senators and Representatives the next day (uninvited ones, doubtless), all hell to pay about undemocratic high jinks and the spending of too much public money on showiness. But what a lovely water show this must have been!

This American water journey down the Potomac River to Mount Vernon was of the high order of the annual "wedding to the Adriatic" ceremony that used to take place annually in Venice. In the first one, during the summer of 1177, Pope Alexander III handed to Doge Sebastiano Ziani a consecrated ring with the words "Receive this as a pledge of the sovereignty which you and your successors shall have in perpetuity over the sea." This splendid sea-marrying ceremony was reenacted annually for the next six centuries: embarked on a large gilded barge, the *Bucintoro,* the doge sailed through the Porto di Lido into the open Adriatic, was handed the ring blessed by the patriarch of Venice, and threw it into the sea with the words: "Sea, we wed thee in token of our true and perpetual dominion over thee."

If our government ever quits forming ineffective committees that don't clean up the Potomac River, and instead gives drastic punitive powers to ecologists for a change, the Recovery Age for Rivers could well begin with a handsome ring ceremony at riverside: "River, we wed thee in token of our true and perpetual dedication to never again pollute thee."

VI Waterfalls and Fountains

WATERFALLS are a kind of upstream-down-leaping wild water that civilized man has had to become used to. All the great early river-valley civilizations came to life in the wide lower river reaches where the Nile, the Euphrates-Tigris, and the Indus had become relatively calm and placid. When Europeans began exploring and settling the eastern shores of North America, they penetrated the great rivers inland only until they came to the sharp upward stretch down over which each of the rivers came tumbling in cataracts and falls of wild water. No one has yet learned how to sail a ship up over a Nilotic cataract or a St. Lawrence River waterfall.

Unfortunately, that first view of the falls by a ship captain left no room for extraneous, inutile aesthetic appreciation of either the thundering roar or the eye-filling reach of tumbling waters; he saw only an impediment to his vessel's progress upstream. Alas, this transportation specialist was in time succeeded by a manufacturing genius who in turn saw in the waterfalls merely a means of creating free waterpower to turn the looms inside his factories.

North America was and is a new world, utterly different from Europe. If the early explorers had cared to listen, they would have found that American Indians had a lore of water nymphs and spirits that was as beautiful as the Old World mythology of Greece. But the Puritan settlers were too deeply concerned with conversion of the Indian "salvages" to their own rigid ideas of Sabbath-keeping, present gloom, and afterlife joy to recognize that possibly the wilderness pagans and the wilderness itself might contain a wonderful new world of beauty and happiness to be enjoyed *now*. Today we are still acting as crude exploiters and destroyers of the waters; we *still* need to learn, but *soon*, to use them as morally and sensibly as would aborigines: *"The moral necessity of the American people must be to become the aborigines of the American land!"* (Wendell Berry, of *Farmers of 40 Centuries*, F. H. King, in *Whole Earth Catalog*.)

The Appalachian Mountains are among the oldest on the Planet Water, reaching back over 500,000,000 years. Once they were higher than today's Rocky Mountains. At their easterly edge is the fall line, or what a riverman might better call the waterfalls line, where rivers pass from the stark resistance of the Piedmont granitic rocks to the softer coastal plain, in tumbling waterfalls. "All along the rivers of the Atlantic coastal plain," Peter Farb has traced the waterfalls line, "there are waterfalls: the Great Falls of the Potomac, the Schuylkill Falls at Philadelphia, the falls of the James River at Richmond, and many others. . . . The fall line marks the most easterly boundary of the Appalachians."

In Greece modern visitors find that local citizens still often believe as keenly in the presence and power of water spirits as did their ancestors. Patrick Leigh Fermor was told that "they are of a different and rarer essence from ordinary mortals and in some ways half divine. Their beauty never fades, nor do the charm and seduction of their voices." At Byblos, in Lebanon, the Adonis River still runs red because the god died there, and his lifeblood incessantly incarnadines the river: you can *see* it. In 1791, practical Alexander Hamilton visited the Great Falls of the Passaic, at what is now Paterson, New Jersey, and decided at once that here was the place for the Society for Establishment of Useful Manufactures to throw a waterfalls-murdering dam across the river. If you will visit the dam at Paterson today, the presence of water spirits, North American nereids, can be detected: they *are* there, even though they are now terribly overburdened with the pollution of industrialization.

We have very little poetry of falling waters in this country, though sightseers go increasingly to view them. One must still go back to read again Sidney Lanier's poem written a century ago of the Chattahoochee:

> Run the rapid and leap the fall,
> Split at the rock, and together again
> . . . With a lover's pain to attain the plain.

Its swift journey down the edge of the Appalachians, from a Blue Ridge source, and later separating Georgia from Alabama, has now been typically, constrictively bound up by numerous hydroelectric dams. Today the poet would perhaps be expected to express admiration for the rush of waters over the Bartlett's Ferry Dam. But something (almost everything) spiritual has been *lost* meantime. There is something about freely falling water that T. H. White once put into Lancelot's admiration for Guenevere's hair: "Not like silk; it is more like pouring water, only there is something cloudy about it too. The clouds are made of water, aren't they? Is it a pale mist, or a winter sea, or a waterfall . . . it is the sea in which I was born."

There was so much more to the original waterfalls than a barrier to progress upstream or a creation of waterpower! Beyond the aural and visual pounding beauty was the richness of contained life. When the Europeans first arrived in America, the eastern rivers teemed with Atlantic salmon. The Merrimac River was said to have been so filled with them during their spring migrations that those nearest the riverbanks were sometimes even *crowded onshore.*

The Merrimac, when the Indians lived beside and with it, was an especially blessed river—abounding in fish, fragrant, and refreshing. Especially convenient for catching migrating salmon was a 32-foot downtumble, Pawtucket Falls. Here was one of those great gathering places of Indians described by Thomas Morton in 1622: "At the spring, when fish comes in plentifully, they have meetinges from severall places, where they exercise themselves in givinge and playing of juglinge trickes and all manner of Revelees; which they are delighted in. Their naturall drinke is of the Cristall fountains, and this they take up in their hands, by joyning them close together. They take up a great quantity at a time, and drinke at the wrists. It was the sight of such a feat that made Diogenes to hurl away his dish."

To Pawtucket Falls came, in 1821, a group of Boston mill moguls seeking a waterpower base. Francis Lowell, for whom the town about to be founded would be named, had died four years previously. In 1811 he had committed what Hannah Josephson, in *The Golden Threads: New England's Mill Girls and Magnates,* labeled "piracy so monumental that it takes on the character of a patriotic act"—visiting British cotton textile centers and coming away with perfect blueprints of their operations, recorded by his remarkable photographic memory. This was the sort of James Bond deed that gave Europe the secret of China's silkworms, and the Soviet Union the American secret of the atom bomb. Pawtucket Falls became a dam, and its waters were cleverly channeled so as to turn the wheels of Spindle City, the first great industrial enterprise, "setting the pattern of industrialization," Miss Josephson suggested, "that the whole country was to follow in every field."

Somehow the processes of industrialization always turn a blessed river into a cursed river. Hydroelectric power—still making use of river power but requiring greater drops than the Pawtucket Falls' modest 32 feet—presently made the original Spindle City operation—which Charles Dickens had visited and admired so much in 1842—obsolete. Now there is just a smelly, polluted stream flowing through a town that gets its power from elsewhere.

If ever this sad river, once known as Laughing Waters, regains its purity and beauty, one would hope that some sort of reconstructed "scene" of Indian joyous festival might be set up, as has been done with the grim Pilgrim colony at Plymouth, to show how splendid life beside the river used to be when people —the American Indians—lived there who knew how to use and to live in mutual respect with and alongside a river.

Morton, who tended to be disliked by his fellow colonists because he respected New England's original inhabitants (all the rest regarded them as very low creatures indeed), was a rare universal man in the wilderness. His geography of rivers, alas, was all askew, for he pictured, for example, the Patomack River's source as the Lake of Erocoife (Lake Champlain). Nevertheless, his personal observation was sound enough: "I have seen such multitudes of codd passe out of a pond that it seemed to me one might go over their backs drishod!" A 1781 report stated: "Shad, bass and salmon more than half support the province of Connecticut. When the young ones return down-river to the sea, there are such multitudes as to fill the river." Today one would of course not dare or care to fish the Merrimac or the Connecticut, either of which could be called "the world's most beautiful sewer."

Soon after the French explorer Cartier made his first voyage up the St. Lawrence River in 1534, there were rumors of a great waterfall somewhere to the west. In 1648, Father Raqueneau, a Jesuit priest, repeated Indian reports of "a cataract of fearful height." At last, in December, 1678, Father Louis Hennepin, a Franciscan missionary, was led to the foot of Niagara Falls by Indians; there, among the frozen ice cakes, he promptly set up his traveling altar and said a Mass. A few years later, setting the tone for all future visitors to the most famous falls of all time, he trebled their actual height but called them rightly "more deafening than the loudest Thunder; when one looks down into this most dreadful Gulph, one is seized with Horror."

Niagara is a "receding" falls; it has retreated about seven miles in the past 10,000 or so years. Until 1969, the Canadian or Horseshoe Falls had been moving back toward Lake Erie at about 5 feet a year, while the American Falls retreated at a rate of from 2 to 7 inches a year. The Horseshoe Falls handle some 94 percent of the flow. In 1965, the Niagara Falls *Gazette* started a Save-the-Falls campaign to call a retreat to the falls' seemingly natural and inevitable recession. By June, 1969, work was under way to "dewater" the American Falls temporarily with a cofferdam stretched across to midstream Goat Island; during the summer of 1969, the lip of the falls, the talus of accumulated rock debris below, and the makeup of the riverbed above and below the falls was studied most intensively by means of rock borings and other engineering tests and devices. The cofferdam was then removed to allow a free flow of Lake Erie's ice downriver. The decision? Perhaps for the first time in all history *to create a truly man-made falls out of a natural one.*

Though world almanacs continue to list only the "natural" waterfalls of the world, many of the greatest, in terms of drop, are in fact man-made. But all of these are just so much more of the same "water over the dam" and surely greater drop is no basis for adjudging aesthetic beauty. There are more than 3,000 major dams throughout the United States, many of which, like the one turned on at Morrow Point Dam, Gunnison, Colorado, during 1970, are *twice* the height of "natural" Niagara. "No natural waterfall on the continent can rival the cascade that pours over the spillway of Grand Coulee Dam on the Columbia River," Peter Farb extolled the man-made water wonder. "It is about as long as Niagara, and four times as high." One must question any overcasual "no *natural* waterfall can rival," because these damned dams are as each like the other as are our similarly unimaginative rectilinear glass skyscrapers—all planned solely for economic use of each inch of space, never toward an enlargement of visual and aesthetic pleasure and enjoyment.

The French explorers gave the name of an Indian town, Ongniaahra, "point of land cut in two," to the local river and, later, to the falls. Ongniaahra became Ongiara and, presently, Niagara. There is surely some Freudian significance in the fact that for generations grooms have taken their newly married brides to behold the great falls on their honeymoon. Until 1961, the New York Central Railroad even ran a special Honeymoon Express.

Most daring of all Niagara Falls' daredevils was Blondin, the great French aerialist (Jean François Gravelet) who slung a rope across the falls in 1859 and then proceeded to prance, run, turn somersaults, walk backward blindfolded, and even carry his manager piggyback over the high rope, while brave men trembled and female viewers frequently fainted. In 1901 a crazy lady went over the falls sealed in a barrel, and madmen and madwomen have been going over it in weird contraptions ever since, seeking the worldwide notoriety and sometimes fortune that this sort of whacky daredeviltry so seldom wins.

The fascination of Niagara continues to haunt the world. When Europeans visit America today, one of their chief sight-seeing wishes is *still* to glimpse this first among world water wonders. Power plants on both sides of the falls create electricity amicably enough for the two owner nations, meantime allowing for high-falls sight-seeing within daylight hours during tourist season from April through October—a remarkable compromise among national, hydroelectric, conservation, and world-visitor interests.

Viewing the falls, one need hardly be conscious that more than forty powerful generators are hard at work, deep down below, invisible; or else one may turn welcomed visitor on a tour of the power plants to see how the waters, diverted around the falls, drop so heavily and powerfully through the hugh tubes to spin turbines and generate electric power. And here lies the truth, alas, of why Niagara Falls will *never* "recede" any farther. Because there *must* be a water drop here to operate the under-falls hydroelectric plants: for all the stories in the press about maintaining the "beauty" of the falls, the ultimate aim of the preservation—which has never chanced to be mentioned in the newspapers—must be to keep the differing levels of the Niagara River at this exact power-plant point. And so, nature's masterpiece must, of course, be in some way compromised to become one more masterpiece-by-permission-of-man, some sort of concealed high dam, with meantime enough of a "natural" look to pleasure the eye of the wonder-struck beholder. Perhaps they will build a concrete structure and then baste the top with granite boulders cemented irregularly along the brim? One often wonders why engineers have never attempted this sort of dam gingerbread variation against the inevitable insane, rigid, interminable *sameness* of the forever straight-as-a-rule hydroelectric dams throughout the nation and the entire world. Our too rectilinear age cries out for more gingerbread and pop art as sheer visual relief against the universal plainness, dullness, squareness and infinity of samenesses.

Nature always tries to achieve an ultimate symmetry, and the great wonder of a waterfall is that the work is forever but part finished, and so is *never* symmetrical. Martin Gardner, discussing symmetry and asymmetry in *The Ambidextrous Universe,* noted "the enormous preference that nature shows for vertical axes of symmetry due, of course, to the simple fact that gravity is a force that operates straight up and down. As a consequence, things tend to spread out equally in all horizontal dimensions. Water spreads out to form lakes with horizontal surfaces. A lake is indifferent as to whether it spreads north or south, east or west, but is incapable of spreading up in the air."

This is unquestionably the great wonder of every surprising waterfall, tiny or large: it is forever an unfinished, living work of art, especially delightful because of its uncertain, unbalanced shape, which also varies from season to season as the volume and power of water change.

I am enough of a realist to recognize that "natural" Niagara is finished, ended, and that one can only hope the *objet d'eau* to be created there in the next dozen years won't be too much of a monstrosity or too silly-artificial. I recently viewed a somewhat similar sibling falls in Iceland, Gullfoss, known as Golden Waterfall for its colors in bright sunlight (though I saw it during the midnight-sun season of perpetual daylight, the sun didn't chance to shine through), and for the rainbows reflected back from sunbeams. At one time, an attempt was made to purchase Gullfoss Falls for development of hydroelectric power, but it has instead remained a scenic natural wonder.

Iceland is called a part of Europe, and so these are considered to be the "highest falls in Europe." A glance at the map will show that both Iceland and the Faroe Islands are about as much a part of the continent of Europe as they are of, say, the imaginary continent of Atlantis. Vilhjalmur Stefansson once interpolated that "Iceland does not extend so far east as Greenland. . . . In my opinion, we are thoroughly justified in holding that Greenland and Iceland both belong to the North American continent rather than to the European." More recently, Sigurdur Thorarinsson called Iceland "a supramarine part of the Mid-Atlantic rift zone that is more accessible for geological and geophysical studies than its submarine parts." One of these days, geographers and geologists will calmly—and bravely—state the obvious fact that Iceland is a part of neither the Western nor the Eastern hemisphere, but indeed is the highest part of that mid-Atlantic mountain range that is so steadily *separating* North America and Europe from each other. In fact, nobody has ever managed to firmly define just what the "Western Hemisphere" or the "Eastern Hemisphere" limits may really be. Even President James Monroe, in pronouncing his famous Doctrine, never knew just what the exact defensive dimensions against belligerency were of the hemisphere that he was about to protect from invasion out of the other hemisphere.

In Iceland's primitive countryside, one approaches Gullfoss along the sheer edge of a deep canyon, on a black-gravel road that is especially scary in rainy weather. As the rains came down belligerently, our bus teetered along the edge of this— what I should like to call the Grand Canyon of the Hvítá— until suddenly we came to the torrential activity of the falls themselves. There are several succeeding banks of tumbling water enjoying itself—exactly such as Niagara might get to have and relish if she were left to her own device of receding.

The greatest water tumble in the world, into a long, slender chasm, is Africa's stupendous Musi-o-Tunya—"the smoke that thunders." The falls is usually called after the little old Englishwoman who once resided a half-planet away in Buck House, London, who never had the pleasure of viewing them: I cannot remember a single anecdote of Queen Victoria ever viewing anything that had not been brought, like General Tom Thumb, into the palace to be beheld. What a catastrophic misnomer!

Musi-o-Tunya plunges into a 360-foot-wide/narrow chasm in a half-mile-deep/long sheet of water. Musi then in reverse creates an immense ascending cloud of spray and mist that has created on the opposite side of the narrow chasm a famous rain forest. Gullfoss, alas, does well to give life to a few mosses and lichens—and yet the curling, thundering wonder of the water itself is all the more evident because of the lack of any alongside floral diversionary diversity. Gullfoss is incising at a rate of about 3 feet a year—creating ever more unexpected irregularities of tumbling jets. It is fortunate that freshwater, tumbling over falls, is whitened by the aeration taking place, just as breaking waves at the edge of the sea acquire spume, spray, foam, and froth—else we would have little visual pleasure out of either breaking-water *edge*.

There is another waterfall, in northern Iceland, that is most impressive, the *Godafoss*, or Fall of the Gods. In A.D. 1000, barely a half-century before the forming of the Icelandic Althing (the world's oldest parliament), Thorgeir the Law-Speaker courageously threw all of his sacred household gods over this falls when he abandoned his pagan gods to become a Christian. A more appropriate name, then, would be not Waterfall of the Gods but Downfall of the Gods. This is on the Wagnerian grand scale of local-god defiance shown by Mohammed when he so courageously (like Thorgeir) destroyed Hobal and the entire *shirk* of several hundred local nature gods of Mecca, after he'd captured the holy town in A.D. 630. But Mohammed then cautiously retained the sacred Black Stone, which most followers of Islam still honor at the Ka'ba, and so the nature gods of Arabia are somehow forever upheld, whereas the water and earth gods of Iceland have been wholly abandoned. When you gaze into the Godafoss waterfall, it is wholly possible that Wotan and his fellow nature Olympians may be staring angrily—and even vengefully—back. When nomadic peoples, whether Viking wanderers of the seas or Bedouin of the deserts, turn to monotheism and an intolerance of their ancestors' deities, it is only natural that these now neglected planetary divinities may experience a reactive divine wrath against mankind. Voltaire once expounded: "If there were no God, it would be necessary to invent him." But the nature gods continue, calmly, to proclaim, "We are *already* here!"

What did Father Hennepin experience when he first viewed the vast tumbling of waters over Niagara in 1678? With considerable pretending, as you today scurry across the base of the falls or ride the *Maid of the Mist* listening to the recorded history, it is perhaps conceivable to imagine that you are back in the primeval wilderness. But in the Hiawatha country of northern Michigan it is still possible to take a *true* wilderness cruise into the midst of a virgin forest and there view Tahquamenon Falls, a remarkable primitive experience in the 1970's.

Niagara is, like all other tall falls, a barrier, in that no salmon ever could bestride it upward. The fish in the Great Lakes got there thousands of years ago when the entire river was higher and the falls represented less of a climb-leap. In recent decades, men have been learning to ride the ocean waves shoreward, body-surfing and board-surfing, but they go only *with* the water currents and tides. Salmon fight upward *against* the stream, leaping powerfully high against and through the downflowing waters in what must be the greatest athletic sport on earth, something the human body is incapable even of attempting to do on a comparative scale. It is as though you or I were to take off, in the midst of our morning shower, and rise right up through the waters of the shower—and continue to soar upward *some thirty or forty feet*. Even a movie of the salmon joyfully leaping up and over a water cataract can give us a vicarious, robustious thrill that explains what life against/ into/with water might be like if one were a fish endowed with powerful fins. Why do salmon pursue the arduous upriver journey? Each is following his nose, scientists now know, seeking out the sweet smell of the tiny home stream.

The lost Atlantic salmon which once crowded New England rivers returned upriver not in one sole, terminal suicidal-parental journey but year after year—not unlike human joy-takers who have gone upriver in their sailboats and yachts for a joyous "annual" love festival at a marina, returning sadly down-river for another year of everyday living before going again back up for another orgy next springtime. Certain unrandy Pacific salmon are said never to return back up their birth rivers, but instead prefer to live out their cautious careers in unsexual but less demanding bachelorhood or spinsterhood. The usual experience, of course, is the once-in-a-lifetime journey of the Pacific salmon, up the Columbia and other great Western rivers, their anadromous bodies somehow adjusting to the switchover from salt to brackish to fresh waters. The seminal salmon, rich and fat, move upriver, the ladies matronly, the gentlemen fasting and experiencing a terminal transfer of substance from muscles to genital glands. At last, at the right place —apparently salmon cousins marry cousins, breaking every sacred law against consanguinity, which human near-relatives hold so sacred (are there therefore insane salmonoid Jukes and Kallikaks?)—each lady digs the cradle trench and deposits her eggs, and the male swims over, voiding his milt; bride and bride-groom bitterly contend for territory against near-cousin parents nesting nearby; no cousinly whist or bridge games here; there-after all the brides and bridegrooms, mamas and papas, sadly deteriorate and die. Honeymoon and parenthood were too much.

Before construction of the Dalles Dam on the Columbia River, known widely as "the dam that should never have been built," there was once a famous fishing grounds where Indians annually built wooden structures out over Celilo Falls. These have now disappeared behind the dam, and only a roadside sign marks their former site: ANCIENT INDIAN FISHING GROUNDS FULTON CANYON NEXT RIGHT.

Counting up the present 150 dams in the Columbia Basin, Oral Bullard penned a frantic plea, *Crisis on the Columbia,* in 1968, warning: "There is crisis on the Columbia River today; crisis born of man's compulsion to put the river to his immediate use without sufficient thought to the needs of future generations. The Corps of Engineers, the Bureau of Reclamation and/or local power interests are busy constructing dams at every possible site . . . projects that embrace virtually every Northwest stream of consequence from the Skagit in northwest Washington to the McKenzie in southern Oregon and on east to Idaho and Montana. Where will it end? A Corps of Engineers spokesman has said, 'the goal of optimum development is far from reached.' "

In the high Rockies are many of the most spectacular waterfalls in the entire nation, most notably within Yellowstone and Yosemite national parks. John Colter was the first white man to enter the Yellowstone region. He and a trapping companion, paddling around a bend in a river, encountered a swarm of dozens, or perhaps hundreds, of Indians. Hastily they dropped their beaver traps overside. His companion was shot, and Colter was stripped and offered the chance to run the gauntlet across a cactus field with the entire pack of braves in pursuit. He escaped, killing one warrior who ran ahead of the others. Then he crawled up inside a beaver house in the Madison River and there hid in the "penthouse" while harking to the death-rattle threat of naked Indian feet tramping about overhead.

Hours later, after dark, Colter set out, naked and hungry, on an impossible eleven-day journey back to the trappers' fort. Somehow he made it. And next spring, this remarkable man returned again, in search of his beaver traps. Rutherford Platt called Colter's runaway river journey "perhaps the most exciting one-man sight-seeing trip in human history."

Big country apparently always makes for tall tales. Jim Bridger (Old Gabe) followed Colter as an early Yellowstone visitor, and his descriptions, Munchausened-up, got to be known as "Jim Bridger's lies." But the wonders *were* all there, and an 1870 expedition brought the commonsense decision to create a national park—the first, and still our largest (until and unless the New York State Adirondack Mountains area, some

8,500 square miles, much of it now within state parks, ever becomes federal). Most of us will agree with Hiram Chittenden's 1895 assessment: "There are three distinct features which unite their peculiar glories to enhance the beauty of this Grand Canyon of the Yellowstone: the canyon itself, the waterfall at its head and the river below." Of the falls, he wrote: "A deep-toned thunder rises in ceaseless cadence and jars the air for miles around." It is interesting that audial observers usually find that waterfalls *thunder:* the primeval meteorological description is oddly appropriate, since the water is discharged in an almost electric holocaust that doesn't detonate and stop, and is therefore even more thunderous than an electric storm.

Inspiration Point is a good place at which to reread Freeman Tilden's 1954 plea: "If a great waterfall is in question, it is much easier to explain that you are going to use it for water-power than to explain why you are forgoing that industrial use in favor of preserving it as a thing of beauty and inspiration."

And so Colter's Hell became, in 1872, "a reservation withdrawn from settlement"—or, as elsewhere described, "a public park or pleasuring-ground."

"We are looking at the handiwork of Nature the Demolisher." Nathaniel Pitt Langford described the sculpturing of water in 1871: "Beauty is the by-product." A lot of beauty was created in the spring-summer of 1969, following the fantastically heavy snowfall of the 1968–69 winter. The 30-year annual average depth of snow in the High Sierras is 72 inches, as contrasted with the 1968–69 doublefall of 146 inches, containing a water content increased by 25 percent.

Most of us visit the Yellowstone in midsummer, when much of the heavy snow water has completed its thunderous journey, and the midsummer visitor simply does not know what a falls *anywhere* may be like, at its greatest strength and violence. On the other hand, a wholly overburdened falls is also not at its best—even its sound can be overdone and less musical. The midsummer sound and sight of 109-foot Upper Falls and 308-foot Lower Falls may even be the original reason why Americans have national parks today.

Not until 1961 was the Tioga Road completed, in Yosemite National Park, up to a place called Olmsted View. From this site a visitor can see the panorama of three terrific ribbons of water: upper Yosemite, 1,430 feet (9 Niagaras); middle, 675 feet; lower, 320 feet—a total of 2,425 feet, about a half-mile, creating altogether one of the highest waterfalls on the Planet Water. "On windy days," Philip King Brown has described this tied-down tornado, "Yosemite Falls sometimes swings back and forth like a giant silver pendulum, and the tremor of the water crashing into the boulders below can be felt for a half-mile around." Also, the thundering roar—felt and heard.

Freeman Tilden has superbly described water the destroyer/ creator in its Yosemite studio, in a 1954 work, *The National Parks*, which maintains a hydrohuman or hydropomorphic point of view throughout. He says that "standing on the valley floor of Yosemite, staring up at granite walls that tower three to four thousand feet above us, sometimes almost sheer, we can only gasp and wonder; it was all done by *water*, after the up-lift and tilting of the Sierra Nevada block gave the existing streams the impetus. By a flow of glacial ice later, yes; but ice is only the mineral form of water. . . . Like a granite-cutter in Barre, Vermont, with an edged tool and a mallet, the moun-tain glaciers found their edged tools in the form of loose rock masses, breaking away on natural joints and loosened out of place by frosts and sun. Once gripped by the ice, these were tools enough, and the mallet was gravity, and the push of the ice masses that lay behind. The water torrents used the same de-vice: abrasive material, from quartz sand and pebbles to boulders, with an irresistible corroding force behind them." Thus, water the destroyer/creator.

Men have begun to make use of this vast power of water. In 1969, a new "water cannon" was created that is said to be a faster, more efficient, and more economical rock breaker than explosives or mechanical drills. The water cannon is a com-pressed-air jackhammer whose moving piston strikes a chamber full of water, forcing continuous bursts of water out through a nozzle and against the rock at pressures of up to 100,000 pounds per square inch. The lesson for construction of this man-made waterpower jackhammer could have been learned from studying the rocky walls of Yosemite and the jackhammer of Yosemite Falls working on them today!

Tilden made a suggestion regarding the Grand Canyon of the Colorado that is surely apt for the entire Rocky Mountains area: "For all we know, the mountain-building forces may still be in progress here. The canyon is not a passive thing: every inch of this area is pulsating with life."

Conservationist Tilden expressed the power of "hard" water, laden with sharp tools, in carving out beautiful canyons on the surface of the Planet Water. Inevitably one must place alongside this the plea of a leading American water-conditioning specialist, Emmett J. Culligan, for the human consumption of pure, that is, "soft" water, in *Water* (1965): "Water molecules are forever coming and going in the human body. About two quarts of this water is eliminated daily and is replenished by drinking. If the new water is absolutely pure, it will eliminate sickness almost entirely. Most sicknesses are caused by feeding the body mineral-laden water. Mineral-laden water, fed to the body by drinking, will cause precipitates or sludges to form as a new compound in the intestines, much the same as hard water forms a sludge in the bathtub, kitchen sink and laundry. When the water fed the body is hard, laden with minerals, some of the body's three hundred million cells may be adversely stimulated by this foreign matter, and may grow malignantly as cancer." Since 70 percent of the human body consists of water, and the entire chassis is renewed every twelve months, one can well imagine the glorious internal canyons that may be carved in a much shorter time than the glacier rivers of ice and waterfalls of water require to create a beautiful High Sierra valley. All one must do is to drink the appropriate hard waters, which are armed with the right tools for the interior sculptoring job of "Nature the Demolisher, where Beauty is the by-product" (once more quoting Pitt Langford). Each kind and little drop of water in its correct place, and likewise tiny grains of sand, makes the beautiful canyon and the healthy man?

Just as classical façades of stark stone pillars require festoons of vast numbers—clouds—of doves flying before them to bring out their stark beauty by a contrasting softness, waterfalls take on a living quality when they have the added refinement of winged life. Most waterfalls in the American Sierras and Rockies give the careful viewer and bird-watcher a remarkable sight-see lagniappe: the dipper, or water ouzel, a chunky blue-gray bird with a tinge of dark brown on its head and shoulders.

Its habitat is the waterfalls and swift-flowing streams from the Sierra Nevada northward into Alaska, as well as some places in the Rockies. Peter Farb says: "There is scarcely a waterfall, whether in the foothills or in the High Sierras, that does not have a pair of these little birds flitting about in the spray or plunging headlong into the cascades themselves. The dipper . . . is one of the most indefatigable singers of the west, one of the few birds that sing the year round, in a tone as sweet as a flute and as liquid as a stream, with numerous trills and tremolos. The torrents of its song match the yearly flow of the waters; scarcely more than a trickle in the dry fall, it builds up during the winter and unleashes a flood of melody in the spring. Whereas other birds sing in response to the songs of their own kind, the dipper is tuned to the streams that furnish an accompaniment for its solo performance. . . . Its nest, a little hut of moss, is usually situated on a ledge alongside a waterfall; but sometimes it is built inside the fall, between the cascade and the cliff, so that to reach it the little bird must fly through the torrent."

Nobody has yet seen a dainty water ouzel flying in and out of the torrent of water tumbling so mathematically over a modern power dam, just as nobody has ever seen a salmon bravely swimming up through the dam falls—or, for that matter, as one does not see flocks of doves (which are, of course, merely pigeons on the wing, the way winged men become angels), flying in cloudy formations before high-rise glass skyscrapers. Both too-tall mathematical monstrosities (from a nature viewpoint, anyway) are well beyond the flight grasp of either fish or bird, so unnatural, unexpected, and artificial are they, just as they represent a different kind of visual pleasure for the intelligent sightseer as an art or man-made object. *Electrical World* pridefully called "the dam itself one of the few intrinsically beautiful products of machine civilization." No water ouzel or Chinook could ever agree. Higher power dams simply do not make automatically for higher hedonics. And fish "ladders" are a piscine reminder of human hogs routined through suffocating subways.

In 1954, Elmer Peterson, in *Big Dam Foolishness,* which describes the turning of living rivers into lengthy, vapid lakes ("The history of a lake is the history of its death"), quoted geologists who maintain that the average artificial reservoir's life in the typical American plowlands belt, because of silting up, is only about fifty years. Thus 1950's dams would be through by A.D. 2000. The U.S. Army Engineers, dam builders, are usually prejudged guilty in all cases; in 1954, they gave proof that silting does *not* take place up against the dam, but all along the new lake's edges

Beaver pelting and gold mining, along with the vast deforestation of the wilderness, transformed the natural balance of the waterways into an empty wasteland. Gone were the beavers' dams that had once ponded back the swift, scarifying streams; the sludge from gold smelting was an extreme form of pollution, a hydrocide comparable to the dendrocide of tree murder. "Wildness is a necessity," John Muir proclaimed in 1898, and conservationists continue to cry out the rest of his utterance: "Mountain parks and reservations are useful not only as fountains of timber and irrigating rivers, but as fountains of life."

The greatest falls on the Planet Water, Salto Angel, Angel Falls, was named not for inhabitants of heaven, but for a very real, earnest young American, Jimmy Angel, who flew over and found them as a side result of his pursuit of a mountaintop treasure of gold that was presumed to be hid nearby (and that you can still pursue, since it has not yet been revealed). Angel Falls is sufficiently remote to still be an angelic site, best seen by plane, and has not yet been turned into a gold mine as a tourist mecca. Nor have its waters been overpolluted by sludge from gold smelting in the mounts above, since the missing gold lode has not yet been put to work.

On one of Jimmy Angel's return journeys in his never-ending search for the pot of gold, he crashed right next to his falls. The plane is still up there, miraculously to be viewed along with and almost alongside the tumbling waters, almost as if by plan. Somehow he managed to walk, climb, crawl, and tumble downward away from the wreck. He died in 1956, and his widow later managed to have his ashes scattered over the falls named after him. Though Angel never stopped looking for the dollars-in-the-bank treasure-trove richness that powers our civilization, he seems also to have enjoyed the natural visual wealth healthily as well. Angel Falls remains a wonder of wild nature in great part because of its sheer inaccessibility. "For centuries, men have explored the Gran Sábana area for diamonds and gold," the Venezuelan tourist literature describes this watery wonder. "Today, it is still shrouded in mystery and superstition. The wild landscape of the Falls is so formidable, with sheer drops of 1,500 feet, that no one has actually ever reached the top on foot from any approach, much less climbed the face of Devil's Mountain, on the Fall's sheer side: This ascent remains one of the great challenges to the world's mountain-climbing fraternity."

In 1968, for the first time, men *did* climb to the top of Cerro Auyantepui, Devil's Mountain, and looked down in awe upon the greatest water fall-drop of all—3,200 feet. Dr. Roger Latham, a member of the first scientific expedition to scale the Auyantepui heights, has described his experience of "discovering" Angel Falls—and his words, a half-millennium or so after Father Hennepin's discovery of Niagara, could set a perceptive standard for waterfall viewing for all time: "It's almost impossible to describe my sensation when I first walked out on the shelf overhanging Angel Falls, the world's highest waterfall. Suddenly there was the jungle more than 3,000 feet straight down. In fact, more than straight down, because the great precipice curved back in under our ledge.

"The awful height gave the ethereal sensation of standing suspended in space. It was like having the whole world suddenly opened for inspection. But even more soul-stirring was Angel Falls itself. I lay down on the edge and inched my way out until my head and shoulders were over the edge. *And there it was.*

"The torrent of water bursts out of twin flumes and cascades down into that eternity of space—so far that even all those tons of water rarely make a whisper as they splash upon the rocks 3,200 feet below. The curtains of water enlarge as they fall, blending and widening, whipped by relentless updrafts, until they finally strike in slivers of fine particles, almost like a heavy rain, over acres and acres of algae-covered boulders and gravel. Rainbows come and go as the wind lifts the mists and the sun intermittently plays hide and seek with the ever-present white clouds. *One lies there spellbound and awestruck at the overwhelming immensity of this panorama and perhaps for the first time realizes how truly big this world is.*"

Inevitably we see the wonders in human terms. Dr. Latham's final comment takes one back to the queen's bedroom at Camelot, where Lancelot is forever brushing Guenevere's chevelure of tumbling hairfall, White's "It is more like pouring water, only there is something cloudy about it too." Lancelot brushes a lady's hair and thinks of falling water, and Latham views a waterfall and exclaims: "Eighteen men are never going to forget Auyantepui—the Devil's Mountain—and especially 'the Angel' —all 3,000 feet of *her!*"

The world abounds in rapids, cascades, and cataracts, the swift action of rivers intent upon wearing down the rocky earth surfaces—like human feet beating upon stone stair treads which ultimately wear down into scoops and hollows—and returning the land surfaces inevitably once more to ocean. The expected falls are such as Niagara, which simply pour down over the top of a cliff edge. The unexpected and almost unbelievable pour out from great openings in the cliff wall, and most surprising of all these is the Angel Falls, in the strange, wild area of Gran Sábana, Venezuela. Sir Arthur Conan Doyle wrote about a prehistoric mountaintop in this area in *The Lost World,* and W. H. Hudson wrote of a bird-genie in *Green Mansions.* The wonder and greatness of the Angel is in its unexpected, overwhelming *difference,* not its immense dimensions.

The *World Almanac,* annually listing Planet Water's superfalls, gives their importance in terms of height, volume of flow, steadiness of flow, crest width, drop over sheer or sloping surface, and one leap versus successions. Their dimensions should not count: it is the inexplicable beauty of each mantle of falling water that creates each falls' "importance." Thus, Iguazú, which "belongs" to Brazil, Argentina, and Paraguay, is barely higher than Niagara but nearly 2 miles in width. Tugela Falls, five of them, on the Umgeni River, Natal, almost require survey from aloft. Kukenaam (Cuquenán), on the Guyana-Venezuela border; Sutherland, in New Zealand—there are tens of thousands of waterfalls, many hundreds of great height or massive flow. These are the great *evidence* of the constancy of continuity of the hydrologic cycle: raindrops on their swift journey back down to the oceans, but with a vengeance. They recede presently from cataracts, as rockfalls take place, to become flumes and rapids, and finally smooth, tired old rivers moving languorously in a flat bed. Ovid, in *Ars Amatoria,* encouraged human lovers with the evidence of waterfalls: "What is harder than rock, or softer than water? Yet soft water hollows out hard rock. Only persevere!"

Iridescence is perhaps the most spectacular aspect of waterfalls: the rainbowlike play and display of interference colors from reflected sunlight glinting and glancing back out from the surface of the down-tumbling waters. Zambia and Rhodesia's Musi-o-Tunya (Victoria) has another name, Chongwe, "the place of the rainbow." A "reverse falls" of upgoing rain rises 350 feet, and mist goes on up another 5,000 feet. "The sun at our back, shining full on it, reflects two, sometimes three lovely rainbows," Gordon Cooper has described this opalescent wonder. "Rainbows so bright, so vivid, are never seen in the skies; the colors are reversed, the upper being blue, yellow, red, and the lower red, yellow, blue." Chongwe has another rare phenomenon, moonbows, or lunar rainbows, created in the spray in the light of the full moon. One of the few falls in the United States where this phenomenon is also regularly observed is the Cumberlands, in Kentucky.

Waterfalls are, of course, the greatest, as watery scenic wonders. A typical oddity of the Planet Water is that one of the greatest falls cannot be viewed properly by our eyes, adjusted as they are to seeing sights in the medium of the atmosphere. These are the great falls of the Hudson River, a vast waterfall that tumbles over the lip of the Hudson submarine canyon, at the edge of the continental shelf, a waterfall within water that's at least eight times the height of Niagara.

We may be entering upon a new age of "artificial" waterfalls. An excellent one, created in the 1780's, is at Kassel-Wilhelmshöhe, Germany. In 1967, a New York City television executive spent an estimated $1,000,000 to create a miniwaterfall in a minipark in mid-Manhattan with a 20-foot-drop waterfall that ringles and rundles as ingratiatingly down an artificial "cliff" as any exotic waterfall to be seen in a faraway wildwood: Paley's Percolation is an entrancing sight and escape for the urban soul in need of faraway water pleasure.

Much more of this creation of "artificial" waterfalls can be expected in the future. During the 1950's, the Horseshoe or

Canadian Falls of Niagara were altered, the flanks deepened to prevent the center from receding too swiftly. One may hope that future falls over dams may be manipulated so as to allow these artificial drops of water to furnish forth more natural sounds, appearances, and ungeometric satisfactions to the human eye, ear, and general receptive appreciative faculties.

A fountain is, basically, an artificial upward-shooting jet of water, playing streams of water that are all the more intriguing the more they are contrived, ingenious, and unexpected. Their first purpose was holy, and the holiest of Greek fountains was the Castalian Spring at Delphi, where visitors to the oracle first washed their hair or took a ritual bath before asking the important questions about their future. One may still drink of this spring's clear, cool waters and ponder holy answers. But the greatest purpose of fountains is the simplest—to provide ready, convenient drinking water to an urban populace. The most amazing fountain builder of all time was Marcus Agrippa, who constructed 500 of them in a single year, as imperial aedile under his close friend Octavian Augustus. Just as Octavian found Rome a city of ancient brick and left it a world capital of newly carved marble, Agrippa set up the Statio Aquarum department which thereafter cleaned sewers, repaired aqueducts, and constructed outlets. Agrippa built the new Aqua Julia aqueduct, and set water moving through half a thousand new fountains and several hundred new basins and pools. For the next 300 years (approximately 30 B.C. to A.D. 287), Rome was the most fountainous city on Planet Water, with all manner of *jets d'eau*, which I like to think of as *jeux d'eau*, or games of water, taking place.

After the barbarians had destroyed the aqueducts and carried off the statuary and bronze of the fountains, there was a 1,300-year waterless interval until Pope Sixtus V once more "turned on" the waters of the Aqua Felice, in A.D. 1588. This renewal of the ancient water wonder is said to have cost three times as much as the Sistine Chapel. The ancient Roman fountains honored emperors supposed to be human gods or divine men. Sixtus topped each pagan obelisk (stolen, of course, by the imperial Romans from infinitely older, different religious purposes when they'd once stood in ancient Egypt) with a cross to symbolize the triumph of Christ over the pagan gods. Noxious tastelessness and desecration, but also bad art! Yet Sixtus' plaque over his aqueduct was imperious enough: "He gathered the waters from afar to bring them into Roma." In the intervening four centuries, more than 3,000 fountains (nobody knows the exact number) have been erected.

Alas, we are fast approaching the end of Rome's modern fountain era. The squares in which they plash and tumble and soar have today become monstrous, overcrowded parking lots, and the sound of roaring automobile motors has almost drowned out the gentle music of the fountains. Typical of the new "colorfulness" of the motor city was a 1969 edict that the 3,000 black and green taxicabs must be repainted *canary yellow* within the next three years. The ancient stonework of the fountains will fade into still further tawdry obscurity beyond and behind the blatant new cab colors.

The Fontana di Trevi is the most impressive of all—a mass of irregular rocks, cascades, and statuary that is the quintessence of baroque art and the finest example of the exquisite Roman use of water in motion. "Whoever will go to the great fountain when the high moon rays dance upon the rippling water, and drink, and toss a coin far out into the middle, over the left shoulder, backward, shall, in offering to the secret water spirit of the place, surely come back to Rome again some day."

In many of the Roman fountains the waters simply gush out into a basin as at the Trevi. But in others the builders sought a more dazzling effect by throwing jets high into the air. Handsomest of the simple jets unquestionably are the two that rise 46 feet above the pavement in the Piazza San Pietro before the Vatican. They are supplied by the ancient Traiana aqueduct constructed by Trajan in A.D. 109 and renewed many times, finally by Pope Paul V. The water is somewhat chalky, and Roman citizens view it rather than drink it. The left fountain was installed by Pope Paul V, the right by Clement X. Either Kaiser Wilhelm of Germany or Queen Christina of Sweden, upon being shown the two fountains playing full force, after a royal examination was said to have then suggested, with typical royal condescension, "Oh, splendid! Now you may turn them off." To those of us who have been reared to turn off faucets so as to constrict the free flow of happy waters, the thought that thousands of Roman fountains are gaily gushing twenty-four hours a day is a wonderful—or else an appalling—thought.

Most water wonders are best seen at odd hours and alone. H. V. Morton, in the historic *The Fountains of Rome*, described a visit to the Piazza Obliqua di San Pietro in the small hours of the morning: ". . . strange experience to be the only person in that mighty reassembly of the marble and travertine of ancient Rome. To stand there at three o'clock in the morning in the light of the lamps round the obelisk, with two arcs of reflected light curving right and left from the colonnades, was to experience a sense of solitude which went beyond loneliness. Fortunately the fountains, cheerfully shooting their shafts of Acqua Paola into the night, link the piazza with normality."

A third variety of Roman fountain attempts to combine statues, basins, and jets into a unified composition. The master of this technique was Giovanni Lorenzo Bernini, the seventeenth-century sculptor and architect who was responsible for the colonnade enclosing St. Peter's Square. His most successful fountain is in the Piazza Navona, the long open oval that occupies the site of the ancient Circus of Domitian. One of these fountains, the Moor, represents a fierce giant struggling to hold a squirming dolphin. Water sprays from the dolphin's mouth, and the pair seem intensely alive and wholly at home in the moving waters. The other great Bernini work, the Fontana dei Fiume, Fountain of the Rivers, represents the Ganges, Nile, Danube, and Plata (all once under Roman control) as water gods grouped around a 50-foot obelisk, each god surrounded by the plants and beasts appropriate to his respective riverbanks.

Natives of Rome treat their fountains with a certain affectionate derision. The Fountain of the Naiads in the Piazza dell' Esedra, for instance, a "recent" work completed in 1901, is lighted at night, an agreeable sight for non-Romans perhaps unaccustomed to seeing naked bronze ladies laved in flowing water. But the sly singers of ballads in the late-hour trattoria sometimes point out that there is also an equally naked man in the fountain, wrestling with a great dolphin. "Oh, what is he doing with that big fish?" they ask.

It is difficult to pick favorite fountains: The tortoises? The papal crowns of the Fontana della Tiara? The sea horses of the Cavalli Marini? The Aesculapius? The bees of the Fontana delle Api? All have personality, and attract or even repulse. One can return to view a favorite with renewed enthusiasm, and few can regard the flowing waters with utter apathy.

Rome is today suffering a strange change, with storage reservoirs under construction for the first time. Since the moving waters have always also served to keep the underground conduits flushed free, one cannot picture how any public waterworks officials would ever dare to begin shutting off fountains in order to "save" water. In Rome? Yet they *were* shut off once before, for some 1,300 years, and a twentieth-century barbarian might again commit the same wicked antiwater crime against these legendary fountains.

In the Vale of Kashmir, during the same seventeenth-century era in which the Popes of Rome were reopening the ancient Roman fountains, the great Moguls were constructing fantastic gardens made beautiful by fountains and cascades of water. Srinagar, sometimes called the Venice of the East for its wide array of water traffic, has the Shalimar Bagh, the Garden of Love, for especially reverential viewing by a North American who wants to lean about the beauty of fountains and flowing water—as well as the Nishat Bagh, Garden of Pleasure, and Nasim Bagh, Garden of the Morning Breeze. To examine the progress of work in construction of these lovely water wonders, the Muslim emperors had themselves carried about on field thrones that resembled closely the sedilium palanquin of the Popes.

"Make it as beautiful as she was beautiful," the Emperor Shah Jahan is said to have commanded his architect, Ustad Isa, in ordering the construction of the Taj Mahal as a memorial to his favorite wife, Mumtaz Mahal, or Mumtazul-Zamani (Wonder of the Age.) It is still an honest pleasure to revisit the Taj gardens in the florid prose of Richard Halliburton's *The Royal Road to Romance,* because he had the vagabond sense to hide "in a darkened grove" while other, less dedicatedly romantic visitors were shooed out. He later emerged (here come Lancelot and Guenevere again) "to see it floating above me, not only a symbol of matchless feminine beauty but an expression of the adoration of the Shah-in-Shah for his chosen one. . . . The moon floated upward from the trees to commune in secret with the phantom Taj. . . . Barefoot I waded in the flowered ponds. On a marble bench I sat beside the deepest lily-pool and looked at the great white blossoms drifting among the reflected stars of an Indian sky. There seemed to come a call from its depths: 'Come to my caress, oh, mortal—bathe your body in my coolness—float upon my tranquil mirror—wash your mind of consciousness.' Only an insomniac owl watched me remove my clothes, or heard the faint ripple as I dropped into the alabaster pool."

In spite of the constant accompaniment of prose that reminds one of TV commercials today ("A page from the *Arabian Nights*, this, at last, was Romance"—which might have caused gruff Dorothy Parker to "thwow" up), one may still find much of Halliburton, the 1920's romantic wanderer, delightful, if one just edits out the excesses along the way. His adoration of a feminine fountain is in a wholly correct spirit. For the more Asian complete understanding of the Taj, one may turn to Rabindranath Tagore, who called it, more tersely and objectively, "a teardrop on the face of time." The sentient enjoyment of sentiment is forever a two-way proposition that encompasses the uttermost extremes of both love and hate. Shah Jahan, who created the greatest monument to man's love for woman, was a record fratricide—he murdered all his brothers—and after his beloved "Mum" died, he consoled himself with an infinite number of substitutes.

Fountain felicity is one of the more gracious of human happinesses. Ada Louise Huxtable, who goes far beyond interpreting architecture in exposing her views for the New York *Times*, has called water "the wine of architecture." Whether as an extravagant baroque torrent or a serene Oriental pool, "the character of water is primarily sensuous, and its pleasures are visual and auditory. It adds extra dimensions—motion, sound and the manipulation of light—to the customarily static three dimensions of building. It is a performance and a show. There is perhaps no more solid, stable and material art than architecture, and no more ethereal, evanescent and volatile element than water. When the two combine, it is for effects of singular magnificence and mystery. Water is spirit to architecture's substance."

Leonardo da Vinci called water "the drive of nature, so one

might say that it changes into as many natures as are the different places through which it passes." And Goethe on water's spirituality for man, wrote:

> A mortal's soul seems
> Like the water,
> From heaven coming
> To heaven rising
> Again renewed then
> To earth descending
> Ever changing.
> Soul of man mortal—
> Thy likeness to water,
> Fate of man mortal—
> Thy likeness to wind.

Ernst-Erik Pfannschmidt, in a 1968 work, *Fountains and Springs,* claimed that today "a new aesthetic, new methods and new materials have created undreamed-of possibilities of water architecture. No longer need water be an accessory to architecture—it can function as a contrasting element within the organic whole of the composition."

Minor L. Bishop, in introducing a 1965 exhibition by the American Federation of Arts of Fountains in Contemporary Architecture, suggested that fountains are "separate works of art as in a studio, moved into an appropriate location in the landscape or interior scheme, a form of 'collaboration' that serves to project the free expression of both individuals, or else very emphatically conceived as an extension of the design of the building." We can see this difference, in viewing any fountain anywhere. Perhaps the uses of moving water are better expressed in the warm countries: for example, in the thirteenth-century fortified Moorish palace the Alhambra (a palace made, surprisingly, mostly of wood and plaster, alas!), on a hillside near Granada, Spain, that has splendidly plashing fountains amid gardens, notably the Court of the Lions alabaster pool, which is supported by great white marble lions. But there are also chill rills of water running coolly down grooves hollowed in handrails alongside stairways; convenient for dainty finger-dipping, or maybe even sipping in the days of the harem—wives higher up, concubines lower down? Abu Abdullah Mahommed Ibn Ahmar, who moved into the Alhambra in 1238, knew the beauty of water sights and sounds. Even Christian Isabella and Ferdinand, who ruined most of the Alhambra, had sense enough to leave many of the water wonders free to continue flowing.

In the Red Fort, constructed by Shah Jahan at Agra, India, not far from the majestic tomb he created in memory of his wife, is the most fantastic use of water as an integral part of the *interior* of a palace—flowing through the great open courts in tranquil streams and pools, in a sense—water at home with man within *his* home.

My favorite fountain—which I have yet to view for the first time—is within the Topkapi Palace, in Istanbul, Turkey. Around this fountain an entire harem once disported during the great days of the Ottoman empire; any man, upon seeing the bare fountain today, must inevitably dream a small dream, joyous and polygamous. Does a lady also envision a scene here, but polyandrously—of many naked youths and men plunging about in the pool, her numerous husbands and lovers at play? Waiting—for her to join each one, alone. Sculptors recognize that flowing water does something to statuary of marble or bronze, transforming the stone or metal to life. There's an especially fine example at Arnheim, Holland, that symbolizes the Lowlanders struggling with the North Sea. But the presence of *living* human bodies within the fountains would make for much more realistic beauty, with the miracle of water's beautifying effect performed on flesh rather than on stone and metal.

The most famous little-boy statue in the world is the Manneken-Pis of Brussels, Belgium, "little squirt," the kid with excellent kidneys who has been relieving himself in a public square now for at least 700 years. Petit Julien is somehow the perfect expression of naughty innocence, the child who left the bathroom door open: every man, seeing him (perhaps noting that the lad is sinistral), immediately senses a fatherly sympathy or even empathy with perpetual animal need "to make water," and every woman, seeing the small boy, feels an inevitable motherly sense of fond protectiveness. In his never-completed micturition, the little kid has given forth wine, beer, and other fortified liquids upon special Bruxellian occasions—in fact, *everything but urine*. He's also been kidnapped many times, so that the city must keep a supply of extra small bronze stand-ins or pee-ins. The present fountain lad is perhaps the dozenth replacement.

The once Austrian Archbishop Markus Sittikus was so enamored of water pranks that he constructed, at Hellbrunn Schloss, a whole series of *Wasserpiele,* water toys, where today figures still move about, air escapes through water so as to create sobbings and gurglings that resemble bird sounds, and there are trick fountains that wet unwary visitors. There's a similar series of water tableaux at Caserta, built in the eighteenth century by the kings of Naples, and also at Peterhoff, which the Russian Romanovs constructed, and the Communists still operate, prankish surprise drenchings and all.

All of the classical and Renaissance fountains operated on gravity alone running downhill like rollercoasters, even the most ornate with high jets. Today's fountains, contrastingly, have an infinite variety of additional possibilities because of the submersible pump, electronic controls, and the use of colored lights thrown at night on the moving waters. Every great modern city has its fountains—in Paris' Place de la Concorde and Lisbon's Rossio Square, spout splendid copies of Italian Renaissance fountains, complete with sea and river gods. From Stockholm to St. Louis are handsome modern jets peopled by the slender fountain sculptures of Carl Milles. Columbus, Georgia, proudly calls itself the Fountain City because of the number of modest jets that spray over marble and cast iron imagery in the town's numerous parks.

In recent years, new fountains have begun to jet decorative high waters forth all over the United States, in part perhaps in counterpart to the visual sterility of so many of the new steel and glass skyscrapers. A New York fountain engineer, Richard De Cew, has called this upward watery revolution "a renaissance of fountains." Because of fear of water shortages, many of them (like those of Louis XIV at water-poor Versailles Palace) make use of recirculating waters. Some of the creators are Edward Durell Stone, Philip Johnson, Isamu Noguchi, and Lawrence Halprin. And their works—Halprin's Drumheller Fountain in Seattle (largest jet fountain in the United States);

François Stahly's Golden Gate work, with bronze sculptures; Johnson's Lincoln Center fountain in New York, with its night lights and dramatic cutoffs between water surges.

Halprin's Portland, Oregon, cascade is a remarkably joyous use of water based on his long study of natural cascades in the High Sierras. It's been compared to Rome's Trevi Fountain, into which the *ragazzi* and *scugnizzi* little-boy waifs of Rome plunge to gather coins whenever the local police are not defending the loot in behalf of the fountain-cleaning contractor. Here the small Portland children scurry about or "engage in ecstatic immersion." Lovejoy Plaza is the area's name, and it's designed for use rather than the usual awesome look-but-do-not-touch. A small child collected comments about the place: "When I first saw it, I came on like a seven-year-old"; "It's groovy, it sings, it screams, it whispers"; "I hate baths, but when I come here, she don't make me take one"; "If I couldn't see, I'd come here just to listen. It's a living creature."

World's fairs have always given most spectacular exhibitions of waterworks. New York had two outstanding exhibits, in 1939 and in 1965; I had the orgiastic joy of viewing both, many times; the great stainless steel world globe still tops its 1965 fountain in the Flushing Meadows today. 1970 has brought a watery breakthrough to new heights of wetness in the jets thrown up at the Expo '70 World Fair at Osaka, Japan: its largest exposition building has been set beneath a transparent roof with a water screen 800 feet long, and fronted by a fountain reaching up 164 feet; elsewhere is a "solid" mesh fountain on which illuminated entertainments can be thrown, as on a movie screen. A Japanese firm, the Kurita Industrial and Company, Tokyo, specializes in the large-scale creation of stainless steel, seamless pipe, aluminum, *eternit,* ceramic, Plexiglas, glass fiber, and other new materials for remarkable illuminated water ballets and programmed electronic color-and-height-changing water fountain shows all over the world.

The tallest of all water jets is the 1891 Fountain in the Harbor in Lake Geneva, Switzerland, a mammoth spurt that soars up 427 feet. In 1969, the Delacorte Geyser began spouting 400 feet skyward over Welfare Island, in New York City's East River alongside the United Nations headquarters. Simon Breines, the fountain's architect, stated that there are two powerful pumps that operate separately or in tandem to throw 4,000 gallons of water per minute into the air (in planning his fountain, he found that the Swiss were as secretive about their famous *jet d'eau* as about their mysterious numbered bank accounts). The august New York *Times* produced a stuffy editorial, in January, 1969, denouncing the "cosmetic spectacular, the last thing this city requires. A *jet d'eau*, measured against genuine environmental opportunities for beautification, is a lot of water, and not much else." This sort of outraged objection was being raised in the 1730's when the great Nicola Salvi was installing the Fountain of Trevi and other water wonders in Rome that many simple tourists still enjoy so much. As a water worshiper, one can only express gratitude to George Delacorte for his high-flowing gift, and of course, a gentle *ha-ha* to the *Times* antiaesthetic editorialist.

Water and fire are the two extremes of the Planet Water's self-creating activity. At Yosemite Park, bonfires were once thrown over a cliff to create a "firefall" for visitors to witness along with the famous waterfalls. In 1960, the pulsating lava fountains within the Kilauea Iki crater, on Hawaii, must have been a fountainous supersight to behold and never forget—jets of molten rock thrown a thousand feet high in the sky. Alas, Hawaii's volcanoes are today considered no longer explosive.

Prometheus, the Titan who fashioned mankind out of clay, one day flew to the top of Mount Olympus and there stole a few sparks of *fire* from the great wheel of the sun, carrying them down to earth for the use of mankind. His cousin, Zeus, was enraged, and in order to punish men for their use of the stolen godly fire, sent Prometheus' own sister-in-law, Pandora, as nosy a female in-law as ever lived, down to live among mankind. She soon opened up a box in which all of the ills, plagues, and evils of the world had been carefully locked away. And so today mankind has Prometheus' fire and Pandora's woes, and also one other delicate little wisp that emerged from the box, *hope*.

A great golden fountain in Rockefeller Center, New York City, depicts and memorializes Prometheus' arrival on earth with the gift of fire in a sort of Olympics torch, and, of all things, he has splashed down with his torch in the midst of an immense fountain, a joyous center of bounding waters against a backdrop of high jets on which colored lights play at night.

The fountain is especially well placed, with the RCA Building directly behind it, a soaring skyscraper that carries the viewer's eye symbolically skyward to some distant place in space from which fire must have originated.

Today's new buildings are often designed with a brand-new set of multiple uses for water. Since water plays a key role in air-cooling (or water-conditioning) buildings, progressive architects have begun using the cooling-system waters also to beautify the environment with pluming fountains that are often also floodlit at night. The new waterscapes are now appearing all over the land. One especially attractive one is, appropriately, around the new headquarters of the Los Angeles Department of Water and Power. Daytimes, the skyscraper floats, in an oriental fashion, in the midst of a man-made lagoon. At night, it glows in the midst of throbbing, floodlit fountains. It is forever important that water, which is used for drinking and washing and air-conditioning, should also be used for a higher purpose, *to look at* and to enjoy. All work and no play is as dull for water as for Jack: fountains are the finest form of water at play.

VII Underground Waters and Hot and Cold Springs

ALL of the Planet Water's surface waters may have originated and emerged, down through the billennia of its existence, as primeval, primary waters rising from the interior —all the water that is presently contained in the atmosphere; all the waters that circulate in the great hydrosphere of the global oceans; all the freshwater lakes, rivers, and streams that course over and rest upon much of the terrestrial surface; the frozen waters that form ice caps and ice-river glaciers; and the hidden underground waters that form a vast water-table reserve in a vadose layer of mixed air-and-water over a layer of water-saturated rock that reaches as far as ten miles downward.

Virgin water continues today to escape from the planet's interior, most dramatically in the form of steam, which is the principal form of gas that emerges out of the eruption of volcanoes. "The main force in a volcanic eruption is gas, especially steam," Frank W. Lane has said of the wild violence of this explosive emergence. "Underground water is heated by hot rocks and red-hot magma. The physics of water explain the rest: when it turns to steam its volume increases about one thousand times. It is as if vast stores of dynamite were suddenly exploded inside the volcano." The Biblical description, "And the Lord went before them by day in a pillar of cloud, to lead them the way; and by night in a pillar of fire, to give them light," also fits Stromboli, the Sicilian volcano known as "the lighthouse of the Mediterranean" because its regular eruptions have guided sailors past the Lipari Islands in safety now for thousands of years;

the escaping steam forms a curtain of high clouds upon which the boiling lava below casts a golden glow of reflected light.

Any volcano in violent eruption is one of the Planet Water's most spectacular sights. The 1400 B.C. explosion of Santorin, in the eastern Mediterranean, may have caused the destruction of Knossos and other Minoan cities. In 1883, the detonation of Krakatoa, in the Sunda Strait midway between Java and Sumatra at the very center of Planet Water's greatest volcanic activity, has been recognized as the greatest explosion and loudest noise that has taken place within historic times. More than 4 cubic miles of rock and ash were hurled into the stratosphere, the volcanic dust caused the sun and moon to appear blue, green, copper, or silver, and the planet enjoyed fantastically beautiful sunsets for several years thereafter.

Since Krakatoa was a small island remnant of a tremendous volcano that must have blown up in prehistoric times, the dedicated eruption viewer can only dream of the planetary super-holocaust that took place back then when that prerecord gigantic thing exploded. In 1963, the volcanic island of Surtsey was born off south Iceland, in a titanic struggle between the subterranean fires of Vulcan and the overhead seawaters of Neptune that vulcanologists have been studying ever since. One can imagine that ancient scholars had an opportunity to study many similar battlegrounds between water and fire, for "volcano" is named for the island of Volcano, off northern Sicily, which mythologists thought contained an entrance to the under-island godly (sacred) blacksmith forge of Vulcan.

The average water content of freshly extruded igneous granite rock is 6 percent (by weight). No one has yet visited a magma chamber, one of the subterranean melting pots whence molten rock pours into volcanic conduits for upward ejection-distribution into the planet's atmosphere, but sightseers have always dreamed of doing so. Who has not taken the imaginary journey with Jules Verne's Professor Lidenbrock and his nephew Harry down the dead crater of Snaefells (Hekla) volcano to the center of the planet? "No proof has ever been adduced as to the earth's internal heat," Professor Lidenbrock suggested. We disillusioned folk of the 1970's no longer consider the possibility of a hollow center (how convenient a target this would have been for ambitious speleologists!), and most scholars accept the theory that increasing heat (rock temperature rises one degree for every 100 feet down) pressure makes for a center temperature of from 4,000 to 8,000 degrees Fahrenheit. In the depths, the great heat and pressure create such treasures as diamonds and gold, which, if they get pushed into a volcano's conduit tube, suddenly surface to start a gold or diamond rush among greedy men.

And so, along with virgin magma or virgin gold, no man shall ever see virgin water.

There are three outstanding areas for viewing hot springs and geysers (pronounced *guy*ser, not *gay*ser, the British have funny hot-water heaters pronounced "geezers"), the jets of steam and water that are surface reminders of the superincandescence below. Iceland, which is a big island of basaltic lava, has numerous hot springs, among them the most famous of all time, the Great Geysir for which geysers all over the planet are generically named. When I visited the famous place, in 1969, she was no longer functioning, but a nearby daughter hot spring performed admirably. The most famous of American geysers is Old Faithful, "guardian of the valley" in Yellowstone National Park, who was given her name a century ago in 1870. Old Faithful shoots up every 64½ minutes—or so—to a height of 110 to 160 feet. Lieutenant Gustavius C. Doane, a member of the 1870 investigative expedition that enthusiastically paved the way for creation of this first national park, was ecstatic: "Rainbows play around the tremendous fountain, the centers of which fall about the basin in showers of brilliants, and then rush steaming down the slopes to the river." The third great hot-spring area is in New Zealand, where at Rotorua one may view the skyward-spraying waters in a verdant setting. My own favorite valley of fumaroles and solfataras is on the West Indian island of Dominica, a small, high private mountain valley wherein a discreet waterfall tumbles over a cliff and sulphurous waters move smokily within narrow brooks: a very secret, and also very hellish place where the visitor cannot think flow-gently-sweet-Afton thoughts alongside brook water that is boiling and has the rotten-egg odor of sulphur. The pleasure of this quiet place is uncertainly divided between the childish live-dangerously expectation that the entire valley just might suddenly blow up (as Mount Pelée did in 1902 on nearby Martinique Island, surprising to death the 40,000 citizens of St.-Pierre) and the also-childish sweet-innocent assurance that this sort of disaster *couldn't happen to me.*

The capital of Iceland, Reykjavík ("smoky bay" in English), was named because the Norse chieftain who founded it in the ninth century, Ingólfur Arnarson, saw living steam and smoke rising from nearby volcanoes. "Smoky" is usually a dirty, polluted urban descriptive word today, but Reykjavík is one of the few world capitals that is today wholly smokeless, because the area is heated by natural hot water drawn from hot springs a few miles away. The water tanks on a midtown hill contain water preheated by nature underground, kept at 190 degrees Fahrenheit (at sea level, water boils at 212 degrees). It is piped into homes (at $10 a month) and also into two large outdoor swimming pools where it's kept at 80 degrees for year-round swimming. The aqueduct that carries the heated water into town is a two-pipe "hot line" that lies on the surface of the earth. If only there were a valley or two to cross, it would be additionally sightworthy in this volcanic land: arches made of basaltic rock carrying hot groundwater!

Geothermal heating is used at Larderello, Italy (40 miles from Florence), and at Wairakei, New Zealand. In 1960 the first United States commercial geothermal power plant was built at the Geysers, in Sonoma County 90 miles north of San Francisco, California. Since internal-combustion-engine automobiles today account for 60 percent of all air pollution in the United States, up to 90 percent in urban areas, there's a strong movement afoot to reintroduce "steam cars," steam-powered autos which could make American cities like Los Angeles and New York almost as pure-aired as Reykjavík.

Yellowstone National Park has more than 3,000 hot springs, of which only a fifth or so have ever been named. They vary in content, in temperature, in color—adjoining springs may be ice cold or boiling hot, iron-flavored or alum-flavored. Although much of the steam that shoots into the sky from a geyser is water that has been heating in the ground to the explosion point, the rims of geysers and hot springs show all sorts of "new" metals—silver, tin, zinc—that have come up from the depths to join the earth's metallic crustal surface richness. A powerful earthquake shook up the *terra infirma* of the Yellowstone geyser basin just before midnight on August 17, 1959, altering and topsy-turvying considerably the fire-hole formations, turning fumaroles into steam vents, steam vents into hot springs, and even causing Old Faithful to become temporarily Unfaithful. Twenty thousand visiting sightseers were also scared half out of their wits.

When virgin or juvenile water is released from the hot liquid rock to join the Planet Water's atmosphere, it becomes a part of the great surface-water hydrologic cycle that has been in motion ever since the Planet Steam cooled off enough to allow water to rest on the surface. Water vapor, the gaseous form, is invisible and, of course, not even wet. However, as *steam,* on its way back and forth between vapor and liquid, it's a remarkable sight. The amount of water on the surface of our planet is thought not to have diminished at all since it first began emerging from the interior, billions of years ago. Only about one three-thousandth of all the water on the surface is evaporated each year into/through the cycle. According to Raymond L. Nace, Geological Survey research hydrologist, over the contiguous United States annual rainfall is about 1,430 cubic miles, evaporation about 1,000 cubic miles, and discharge to the oceans from surface streams more than 390 cubic miles per year, leaving 40 cubic miles of groundwater that must discharge directly into the oceans by subsurface channels. Elsewhere I've seen estimates that up to 50 percent of total runoff from the hydrologic cycle returns to the oceans via underground routes. Are there huge underground *rivers?* Who's kidding?

It is possible to see underground water within caves and caverns that have been carved out by groundwater mixed with a solution of carbon dioxide, making a weak but effective carbonic acid. Two 200,000,000-year-old American underground wonders are Carlsbad Caverns, in New Mexico, with its sculptural wonders carved by seeping rainwater, and Mammoth Cave, in Kentucky, which not only has stalactites, stalagmites, and helictites but also an underground pond, Crystal Lake, inhabited by sightless fish. Submarine exploration ultimately would reach utter silence and darkness if man could plumb the abyssal depths. Within these caverns, the speleological sightseer can achieve the wonder-horror of total nothingness—silence, darkness, lack of any sense of direction or even of self-being.

Peering down, one may view the openings of wells—such as the "pools" which Holy Land ladies have always visited by climbing down steps into them: Jacob's Well, St. Mary's Well, Ishmael's Well (at Mecca). The Pool of Gibeon is worth a visit; one may descend it by inside-winding steps. At Chichén Itzá, in Yucatán, Mexico, is a sacred well, a cenote, sinkhole, down into which the fervent Mayans once cast sacrificial maidens, well-ornamented with golden adornments, to appease, feed, and delight the underground water gods. (Young men were not cast down, so one may conclude that there are no goddesses down there in need of gigolo entertainment.)

Man is not the only creature who visits and makes use of wells and well water. The high point of any safari among and in pursuit of wild beasts is the view of them all-unaware at a water hole. Many of us first began peering down at various African wild animals alongside Tarzan, in the pages of Edgar Rice Burroughs. Burroughs had never actually *been* there, but the fictional thrill was just as great and real nevertheless. For reality, one must visit the most famous water-hole viewing place of all, Treetops Hotel, with its spectacular sidewalk-café-terrace view of rhino, elephant, water buffalo, waterbuck, and other wildlife in search of the mineral waters in an immense pool (nowadays the minerals are added) below the hotel. Treetops is in the middle of Aberdare National Park, some hundred miles north of Nairobi, Kenya. The hotel, which is 30 feet up among the baboon-infested rockaby tree limbs, houses sixty-five guests who spend much of the night imbibing enthusiastically at the hotel's bar and watching the animals enthusiastically slurping up the hotel-salted waters down below. This is the famous animal-watering place where Princess Elizabeth climbed the ladder up, in 1952, and Queen Elizabeth climbed the ladder down. Her father, the king, had meantime died.

Another treetop safari hotel is Tigertops, in the high Himalayas. Nearer home, there are water holes and ole swimmin' holes used by country boys. In *Raccoons Are the Brightest People*, Sterling North told of his own private water hole near Morristown, New Jersey, which is visited by a surprising variety of local wildlife. However, since most of us are located where we cannot attract many four-footed beast-creatures, birdbaths are a wonderful substitute. They draw the thirsty two-footed wonders that fly in to flutter wings, bathe, and drink, each bobolink or warbler always tending to regard the pool as its own special water hole, which makes for entertaining viewing of the drinking and dunking order among avians.

The underground waters become especially sightworthy when they spurt forth to rejoin the waters at the planetary surface. In the Bible, Moses "smote the rock and the waters gushed forth." Springs are a special kind of mystical, magical experience for the water worshiper. Ponce de León did well to seek the fountain of youth in Florida, for it is in this glorious land of flowers that one finds the greatest, and greatest number of, natural springs on the Planet Water. The greatest water volume fountaining out of any concentrated subterranean source is the 800,000,000 gallons that pour each day from Silver Springs' 150 outlets, which also include a sightworthy population of gars, catfish, eels, and other fish that may be viewed through glass-bottomed boats. Second is Rainbow, with 421,000,000 gallons gushing per day and a similarly remarkable underwater population. Itchetucknee is third, with 300,000,000 gallons per day. The largest single spring is Wakulla, which ejects some 146,000 gallons per minute.

There are many other wonder springs elsewhere; among them, Big Spring, at Huntsville, Alabama, whose 24,000,000 gallons go daily into the local city water supply. In the east Ozarks are such fancies as the Ebb and Flow, Granny Meyers, Pull-tight, and Bear Claw springs.

Though happy marriages are said to be made in heaven, health is often procured or renewed by sulphurous, hellish waters, into which the ailing descend at spas all over the world, hoping to emerge cured and revitalized. All these waters, with their often profane brimstone odors, are recognized as belonging to his satanic majesty. Nowadays, heaven is up/out there somewhere in space, but hell still remains down below, within the earth, and Lucifer's palatial palace of pandemonium is still located at the very center of the Planet Water, a hot place to visit, but nobody would want to *stay* there.

When you visit the hot-spring spas at Beppu, Japan, for example, all the local geysers are called *jigoku*, "hells"—red, blue, yellow, and clear-white hells. In the United States there are Sarasota (New York), Hot (Arkansas and Virginia), and French

Lick (Indiana); in Europe, Wiesbaden, Baden-Baden, and numerous sulphurous others. Among the most noted spas are Karlovy Vary (*vary* means "to boil"), Marianske Lazne (Marienbad), and Frantiskevy Lazne, all in Czechoslovakia. In 1967, Czechoslovakia reopened to tourist-visitors the 430-year-old Jáchymov uranium mine, in northwestern Bohemia—where Mme. Curie once experimented with radioactive minerals, leading to her discovery of radium. The Cradle of the Atom Age, this strange radioactive place is called; here pitchblende has been mined for a half a millennium, and sufferers from rheumatism have long come for treatment with the healing waters drawn from the world's strongest radioactive spring. Every minute this spring supplies the spa with 132 gallons of radium-charged water. At the Marie Curie Sklodowska Institute, also called the Radium Palace, located here, spa patients are given treatments based on individual diagnosis.

"Taking the waters" is still an uncertain experience; many practitioners claim that simply the social environment, the relaxed *endroit*, the away-from-it-all experience, is enough, without any promise of "cures" from the mineral waters bathed in or drunk down. In a 1968 guide, *Pleasures of the Spa*, John Duguid at the outset asks: "What of these mineral waters? Can they really do you any good? The squabble continues among the medical people about whether it is the water or the water plus the contents that do you good," and he adds evasively, "this author is foxy enough not to get embroiled in something way above his head." Far more directly, Helen Papashvily has summed up today's mineral-water treatment picture: "To the rustic bathhouse and wooden tub have been added such refinements as Finnish, Japanese and Turkish baths, whirlpools, Scotch showers, steam cabinets, salt rubs, honey massage, paraffin packs, isometric exercise, treatments with violet rays, infrared heat and ultrasonic waves—but the *greatest* attraction of them all still is the 'half-boiled, all-spoiled' mineral water. Today's customer has basically the same aim as his predecessor —to drink and/or soak his way to health by means of water."

Mineral baths apparently may benefit many patients suffering from diseases of the locomoter system and also relieve certain skin conditions. The waters taken internally improve metabolism, stimulate circulation, and aid certain cardiovascular, respiratory, and gastrointestinal disorders. A major reason why visitors used to go to spas—and have recently begun going again in great numbers—has been to take part in a pleasant social environment and watery experience that is at the same time a sort of "health vacation" away from the tedium of everyday "dry-land" living, a change away from one's immediate neighbors and usual earthly activities.

One of the more remarkable Balkan springs, pouring out of a mountainside cleft in Yugoslavian Bosnia, became famous internationally only in 1969. Local shepherds had long used its waters for their flocks, especially the rams, whose procreative capabilities were said to be remarkably enhanced by mysterious properties of the cold springwater. After a Yugoslav journalist had interviewed a vigorous local farmer, aged eighty-seven, who'd just fathered his twenty-first child, "thanks to the waters of Konjuh," suddenly the human male world—of all ages—began arriving at nearby Kladanj (a bus stop between Belgrade and Sarajevo), bearing empty demijohns and evincing high hopes. Local peasants began selling the water for as much as 10 dinars (80 cents) a liter.

The local business community of Kladanj soon took over, posted a guard, and began to sell the sacred water, now officially called *muska voda* (Serbo-Croatian for "man's water"). Of course, the spring no longer trickles freely into the shepherds' trough for the use of rams; it is now carefully channeled into immense underground tanks and thence trucked daily to the industrial town of Tuzla for bottling. It has become another establishment water.

The Konjuh spring, which now earns more than $250,000 a year, is symbolic of the fate of all "medicinal" waters, once they've gained a word-of-mouth reputation. A Belgrade doctor cautiously diagnosed the *muska* water for male water-takers: "Faith is very important in these matters. Who are we to stand between a man's faith in himself and a cold glass of water?"

The greatest scenic factor at the spas is, of course, people. At most of them, the promenade is the viewing place. However, a visit to a Japanese mineral spring can be truly different, for this nation possesses more thermal waters than any other (more than 10,000 of them, with medical claims for at least 1,000). "The Japanese will wallow for hours, relaxing and gossiping in the warmth," Duguid described them, "from the oldest grand-parent to the littlest tot. A colloquialism for going on vacation is 'we are going to *onsen*,' the word for hot spring. Stay at a *ryokan*, a Japanese-style hotel, and enjoy the baths—mixed, and no bashful nonsense, please. The *ryokan* will let you absorb ever so much more of the spirit of Japan."

Water is the original holy liquid. Every religion and every leftover mythology includes a belief in the sacred properties of certain waters. On the site of present-day Cairo, the 5,500-year-old capital of the United Arab Republic, once stood Heliopolis, a religious water-cure sanitarium of ancient Egypt which was built around a spring of freshwater that to this day is still called the Spring of the Sun. Here the sun was "known" to bathe himself either in the morning or at night, and also to have long ago done so when he was first born at the very beginning of the world, when he arose from the abyss. The Virgin Mary supposedly visited and took delight in the Fountain of the Sun during the Egyptian sojourn of the Holy Family. There is also the St. Mary's Spring in the nearby modern suburb of Mattariya, which was visited by the Infant Incarnate Logos, who was borne to and probably bathed there by her.

Whence springs the *holiest* water of all? The most celebrated Grecian water source is the Castalian Spring at Delphi. It still flows, alongside Mount Parnassus, with the same sacred waters. Higher up Parnassus is the other Delphic spring, Cassotis, whose waters once fed the oracular Temple of Apollo. There are water nymphs here who are most attractive maidens. Eheu! They are dangerous to attractive young human males. For if such a one, a hydrophiliac with instincts not unlike those of a necrophiliac, sets her eye on a young man and desires him, she will drag him into the water where he will drown and thus remain forever hers. These undines (female water spirits) can readily be recognized, as they always sit on banks of rivers and at edges of sacred pools, combing their long golden tresses and making like the Lorelei. Their brothers, *Wassermen,* usually only appear when someone human is soon to die.

There is no river on this planet that, if it once had primitive men dwelling on its banks, did not also have tutelary water gods and goddesses worshiped by the conscientious among them, divinities who dwell in the waters. There is even a Gallic "boiling" god of hydrothermal springs named Borvo. Since the gods, unlike men, never die, you will note that I insist on using the present tense in discussing them. They *are* still there, in their rivers, streams, fountains and pools. The human visitor and sightseer of famous waters will do well to say a brief, propitious prayer, and leave a thoughtful offering (the one that *hurts* to give is the best, the most acceptable), so as not to bring on one of their spectral sudden rages, which have, down through all history and folklore, done dreadful things to unbelievers and defiant miscreants. There are waters of remembrance (Lebadia), of forgetfulness (Lethe), of madness (Cocytus?), and even springs that can put a curse on a visitor (Acheron?).

One must be especially careful never to gaze directly at one's reflected image in any natural pool, for if there is an evil spirit that lives there, it may carry off the reflection and one's very soul with it. On Saddle Island, in Melanesia, there is a pool "into which if anyone gazes, he *dies;* the malignant spirit there takes hold upon his life by means of his reflection in the water." Narcissus, a beautiful youth of watery parentage (his father was a river-god, Cephissus, his mother the river nymph Leiriope), was promised a long life if he never "saw himself." Some say that he fell in love with his own reflection in a spring and pined away or else drowned himself in the despair of never being able to accomplish the "Alice miracle" of going through the looking glass to meet and mate with his own image. However, there is a likelier tale of this sorrow—that his twin sister had died, and that he gazed at his own image only with the brotherly desire to recover her memory most clearly.

It is said to be an omen of death if you dream of your own reflection seen in water. All of this—Narcissus, watery death wishes, dangerous reflections in pools—is a sort of primordial warning that an evil spirit *could* drag one down under. It might turn out to be a snapping turtle or crocodile: strange water pools don't make the best, or safest, of mirrors.

Those whom the gods love die young, and human worshipers have been deifying and venerating former young men who suffered unpleasant deaths—almost always from some form of assassination—since far back in pietistic history. Early cessation of earthly existence, being a martyr to the violence of everyday experience in a destructive world, quickly turns the marked one, the murdered young man, into a god. Thus it was with Adonis, whose river flows into the Mediterranean beside Byblos, still red with the dying young god's blood. In the wooded gorge of Afka, upstream where the River Adonis runs fierce and wild, one has a better realization of that long-ago scene where the boar gored the young god-to-be: it is here that Aphrodite forever mourns her lost human lover. Humans learn to worship, but the goddess regrets and suffers. In the New World, some important young god must once have died far up the River Colorado, in North America, hence the red waters of the river. Indians probably once knew and recognized this and possibly ceremoniously once used to celebrate his demise. When present-day visitors enjoy the excitement of the river's wild activity in a rubber raft, there must still be some faint sense of reverence for this. In classical times, the memory of the murder in a grim back passageway of a California hotel would have been transferred to the high waters of the Colorado which he had once ridden so proudly.

Like Attis and Adonis, the Egyptian god Osiris died young and was appropriately transmogrified on high. The Isis mysteries continued the worship of this young man, untimely "demised." The use of holy Nile water in the lustral rites of the temples of Isis was considered so important that the sacred waters had to be carried all the way to Rome in order that the purification and cleansing rites in the great temple of Isis there might be correctly performed.

Adonis, Attis, and Osiris are still very much with us, since the "true" gods never die. More recently, a young man died, Jesus, who is today more widely worshiped than these others once were. John the Baptist must have already baptized many thousands in the Jordan River before the predestined day on which the Christ came walking along the bank of the sacred river. The Biblical passage Mark 1:9-11 is a simple declaration of the Christian rite or sacrament of initiation by water: He "was baptized of John in Jordan. And straightway coming up out of the water, he saw the heavens opened, and the Spirit like a dove descending upon him: and there came a voice from heaven, saying, Thou art my beloved Son, in whom I am well pleased."

There is a long-standing Christian disaccord as to the correct purificatory rite of water—whether it is to be sprinkled over the head of the initiate or he is to be submersed or immersed beneath the hallowed waters. During the Middle Ages, strong men cried out against one another, each knowing the positive truth that either ducking or sprinkling was the *only* way. In the 1970's, the battle still is waged on the eternally moot point whether infant baptism (sprinkling the unwitting babe in arms at a fount) or baptizing postpubescently (when the adolescent can presumably make up his own mind about his acceptance of Christ) is the correct way.

In the Roman Catholic Church, holy water is "created" by the act of a priest's blessing perfectly ordinary water, causing it to be purified into baptismal water, Easter water, or Gregorian water. The "fall" of our first parents, Adam and Eve, "allowed the evil spirits to obtain an influence not only over man himself, but also over inanimate nature," Catholic literature states. "For any material object to be devoted to the service of God, an exorcism is generally first pronounced over it, in order to banish the evil spirit and destroy its influence." Salt and water are blessed and mixed, the one to preserve, the other to cleanse. Holy water is useful in the casting out of devils and for curing diseases "so that on whatsoever this water shall be sprinkled in the homes or other places of the faithful, it may be freed from everything unclean and harmful. In the spiritual order it quenches the fire of inordinate passions and fosters the growth of virtues."

Each one of us is forever seeking miracles, happy solutions that somehow evolve out of the dreadful series of calamitous events that are a part of each person's life: in other words, happenings that simply could not be without miraculous, divine inversionary interference in the usual diabolical order of events. Holy water seems such an easy, aqueous answer to the dry series of disasters which usually take place that it is no wonder the faithful will sprinkle it upon entering or leaving a room or house, sprinkle protesting infants when they are put to bed, sprinkle old folks in spite of their resentful objections.

The purpose of holy water—sprinkled—is, of course, to drive out evil spirits. How do the evil spirits get there in the first place, to haunt wells and springs? When Roy Chapman Andrews was so casually collecting dinosaur eggs in the Gobi Desert of Mongolia, the oldest continuously *dry land* in the world, during the 1920's, he encountered a horrific experience at the Well of Sweet Water. An ancient Mongol attendant came screaming into his tent in the middle of the night, saying he had seen and heard ghosts of his murdered relatives hovering over the well waters. As Andrews described it: "From out of the desert came subdued indefinable sounds, eerie and unearthly: ghost voices out of another world murmuring and whispering, swelling in toneless waves to fade and rise again. A shape, flimsy as gossamer, formed in the black mouth of the well, and floated upward in a long spiral." Marco Polo and Sven Hedin had reported the same sort of specters and sounds hovering over Siberian wells. The Andrews party was finally able to give a scientific answer: the intense heating of the rocks and atmosphere during the hot day created a situation whereby miasmic mists at eventide would come streaming out of the well mouth, continuing to emerge during the cold nighttime, with the accompanying horrific sounds.

Though it would be most difficult to sight-see this water hole in the desolate Gobi today, there is a similar phenomenal blow-hole in the United States, the Wind Cave National Park, in South Dakota, which was first discovered when Tom Bingham heard strange whistlings. Depending on the weather, the wind blows in or out of the cave opening, surely an expression of the moods of the local gods of nature, requiring only a self-appointed priesthood to open a temple on the spot and begin interpreting the wind sounds to a trusting congregation.

Man has advanced, rather swiftly, from a simple, primitive belief in the sacredness of wells haunted or presided over by kind gods or evil devils, to the scientific attitude that presumes everything must have an instant answer (or several answers), to a recent new science-fiction approach that is sometimes suspiciously like a total circle back to the ancient primitive ponderings. After Gertrude Stein, in her last hours, had puzzled Alice B. Toklas with the eternal "What is the answer?" she amended it with "What is the question?" And not far away is Pontius Pilate asking, "What is truth?" and washing his hands of either question or answer. At the sacred water pool, one is afraid that an evil spirit may snatch away the soul—yet no one knows what a soul may be, for it cannot be seen or heard or smelled or touched. It is like a thought or a prayer or a wish—illusory, psychedelic, touched with ESP, often almost hallucinatory, something about which wise old housewives sometimes know as much—or more, even—than the learned Church Fathers.

One may hope that we have come a long way. From "they gave him vinegar to drink mingled with gall; and when he had tasted thereof he would not drink." From King Xerxes, who gave the Hellespont 300 lashes for a storm whereby "it" had destroyed his bridge of boats, and who also buried nine youths and nine maidens alive at the Nine Ways crossing of the Strymon River to bring good fortune on his invasion of Greece. From the Trojans, who threw live horses into the Scamander for good luck. From the Chippewa, whose old and crippled tribal members once used to voluntarily throw themselves into the Ocqueoc River as a sacred duty of the aged and infirm. Even from the Algonkian, who threw tobacco into waterfalls to bribe Lady Luck if she were resident in the tumbling waters. How much more civilized is the tiny female figure of the Ganges, daughter of King Himalaya and the air nymph Menaka, nestling in the hair of Siva the Destroyer!

"Hey, Rama" (Oh, God!), Gandhi cried out in his death agony. "The thing that ordinary people want," Nathan H. Knorr, president of the Watch Tower Bible and Tract Society, told a gathering of Jehovah's Witnesses at the Yankee Stadium, in New York City, in midsummer of 1969, "is right here on earth, where we belong. This desire of their hearts is not misplaced, for right here on earth is where they will enjoy a peace of a thousand years, and this beginning right soon!" Nearly 3,000 Witnesses were then baptized (a ceremony which also ordains them as ministers) in the chilly waters of Orchard Beach, a total immersion that symbolizes the submersion of the individual's will to the will of God.

A major goal of the Aetherius Society, a new space-age religion, is "to replenish the earth's spiritual power, which is being drained at an alarming rate by the world's present troubles." And so this dedicated group has been collecting prayers in "spiritual storage batteries," then sinking them into the Planet Water at numerous special sacred spots. In July, 1969, for example, a battery was discharged into the Pacific Ocean 16 miles off Santa Barbara, as part of Operation Sunbeam. The group's chief communicator is a Venusian (from the Planet Venus) who first "reached" Dr. George King, the society's leader, in 1954.

All of this *human* activity—sinking concentrations of prayers into the sea, baptizing Witnesses into ordained preacherhood, sending the ashes of the saints and the penitent down the waters of the sacred Ganges to join the immensity of the Planet Water's waters—is as *nothing* compared with the preternatural activity that is just beginning to get under way in our part of the cosmos at this time. We citizens of the Planet Water have entered the Age of Aquarius—a truly pacificatory epoch, if one may believe the astrological seers who describe it—during which *we shall witness the righting of all the wrongs of this world.* Obviously the *anima mundi* of our universe is trying to reach that *penetralia mentis* that lies somewhere behind the cockles of the brutal human heart and to tell it something, to get with it, to recognize that the sad centuries of the Age of Pisces are over and that Aquarius the Water Bearer is at last with us. This is surely a time of baptism—sprinkling or immersion—of joyous and watery dedication to a new and peaceful life on the Planet Water, under the aegis and happy auspices of the eleventh sign of the zodiac. One spiritual lady was so deeply moved by our changing times that she stated to Jess Stearn a reason for all of us to watch the skies: "Just as a star marked the birth of the child of Bethlehem, ushering in the Piscean Age, there would be another sign in the skies, perhaps another unusual constellation, portending His rebirth on earth." Pope Paul VI, reversing the papal outlook of the Middle Ages, came forward splendidly in 1969 to hail the American visitors to the moon. "Science fiction becomes reality," he proclaimed, along with giving his weekly blessing to pilgrims and tourists. "Science and technique manifest themselves in such an incomparable, audacious manner as to indicate the peak of conquests and to presage others of which even the imagination cannot now dream."

We simple mortals of the present generation may only hope that we may be—here and now—on the verge of achieving the only kind of paradise possible to mankind, by keeping the promises of the Age of Aquarius the Water Carrier.

VIII Water Bathing and Water Closets

WHEN and why did man first begin washing his body in water? Certain animals and birds are today still licking and pecking away at their fur or feathers, neatening their body-covering growth for the daily encounter with life and meantime amusing themselves and performing a sort of limited narcissistic onanism. We do not know how or why they began this self-indulgent joy. But when he is not on an antihygienic kick (and how a happy hippie may enrage his neighbors if his long locks happen to be even mildly greasy-dirty), man—and even more so, woman—enjoys usually and vastly the abluting of his body in water and the resultant wonderful sense of over-all outside cleanliness and refreshment that ensues. Scientists have traced the "human" family tree back now to as many as 20,000,000 years ago, to a man-ape person who then resided in Africa. Did he wash himself? We cannot interview him, alas. If we could, he might not answer true, like so many self-respecting water-hating small sons who today will often give a false answer when asked if they have washed their hands. Water-laving pleasures, like the ecstasies of sex, tend to arrive somewhat later. John E. Pfeiffer once fictionalized the descent from the trees this way: "Apes at some point were driven out of their prehistoric Eden in South and East Africa, perhaps because rainfall declined and the forests withered. Their new world consisted of great grassy open savannahs bordered by green forests." Did some of the brainier of these new grassland protohuman inhabitants begin to reflect about their lost rainy treetops and then begin sentimentally to wash themselves whenever they could, in memory of the happy heavy-rainfall past?

We do not yet have any idea what generation of man first washed or why: the final answer to that ponderous question of human lavation isn't likely to become available for a long time. But indications are that "civilized" man has always bathed whenever he could. Crude drains have been found even beneath Neolithic structures. I once bathed in an underground pool of water comfortably warmed by volcanic heat in northern Iceland. If the cavemen found warm water, doubtless they used it (especially a heated cave pool), but they would have had no way of conveying their warm-water pleasure in a wall-painting portrayal that might come down to us.

Most of the major religions have dynamic poetic utterances in their holy writings as to water's importance for mankind's spiritual and physical cleanliness. In the Talmud is the inexorable chain: "Guiltlessness into abstemiousness; abstemiousness into cleanliness; cleanliness into godliness." Of uncleanliness, the Talmud also warns: "Poverty comes from God, but not dirt." The Bible says (Isaiah 1:16), "Wash you, make you clean." Muhammad, in the Koran, says: "God loveth the clean." Rama Krishna advises: "Great men can give salvation only to those who have the waters of piety hidden in themselves." *Agoa tudo lava,* water washes everything; *acqua torbida non lava,* dirty water does not wash clean. Ezekiel says: "And I pour upon you pure water, and you shall be cleaned." One hand washes the other or, in the Middle Ages when formal washing at table took place before the meal, rather than finger bowls afterward, *manus manum lavat,* one's hand washing another's preferably with the lady diner to a man's right. Should the washbowl be passed around the table at a Hindu or Muslim feast (which it never was), this would of course have meant washing each other's *right* hand only, since among certain believers the right hand is used for eating, and the left for such necessary cleansing activities as nose-blowing, cleaning eyes and ears, and all the purificatory activities below the navel.

Pontius Pilate turned hand-washing into a lawcourt rite when he "took water and washed his hands before the multitude, proclaiming, 'I am innocent of the blood of this just person.'" Cole Porter's Mrs. Porter and her daughter washed their feet in soda water; high-priced call girls bathe customers in champagne as a final act of washing away their worries and troubles. "Take a hot bath and forget." Curiously, it works very well, for land-creature man.

Bathing—for godliness' and cleanliness' sake, as well as for sheer joy of relaxation. Most civilized people take at least *two* baths daily, the first with water, the second the miraculous "textile bath" of changing their underwear daily. The cleanliness that began as a religious thing was early taken over by kings as a means of associating their royal, well-washed persons with the idea of god on earth, the holy one for whom they wash. "We," the majesties called themselves, and even Tom Jefferson's "We hold these truths . . . We the representatives of" in 1776 didn't manage to wholly transfer well-washed we-hood to ordinary citizens.

The cult of royalty worship continues the antique fiction that there is somehow a superclean elite, an oligarchy of sweet-smelling, genteel superfolk who are not only "nobly born" but also better washed. The big social push, and antipush, would thus seem to be between the aristocratic supercleans and the *nouveaux lavés.*

Diana Vreeland, editor of *Vogue,* christened today's super-cleans "people who are beautiful to look at; it's been taken up to mean people who are rich." Edmund Burke, way back in the 1780's, created the opposite expression for the general run of humanity, "the Great Unwashed." Just as "beautiful" implies wealth as well as cleanliness, Mr. Burke's term indicated what was in the eighteenth century known as the Lower Classes (out of which the *nouveaux lavés* tried to raise themselves).

Mrs. Vreeland and Mr. Burke are both startlingly right, as we move into the 1970's, for bathing is *not* as widespread an activity as one might have supposed, even in the nation whose inhabitants Lyndon Johnson called "the affluent people." Here are statistics from Sylvia Porter, financial columnist, in October, 1967: "One in fourteen American homes today still lacks piped water. One in ten does not have a flush toilet, bathtub or shower." And Lawrence Wright, in *Clean and Decent,* published in London in 1960, warned visitors to that world capital that "even if we bathe but weekly, we should stand fairly high in history; of our neighbours on a London bus today, one in five *never* takes a bath. Many of our cinema managers find it necessary to spray their audiences with *sparsiones* such as once sweetened the Roman rabblement." The *sparsiones* referred to was sprayed over them from the top of the Flavian amphitheater; today's perfumes also come down on the audience from the top of the local orpheum, spread invisibly by the air-conditioning system.

In opposition to our grim present-day determination to judge our neighbors by how often they wash, Isaac Bashevis Singer has made a quietly philosophical utterance: "People have grown up in houses without bathrooms for thousands of years. Did Father Abraham have a bathroom?" Ah, the picture of Isaac and all the hairy Old Testament sons transporting a huge cast-iron bathtub all the way from Ur of the Chaldees to the Holy Land! Louis Bromfield once conjured up a similar journey, made by an intrepid fictional British lady explorer who insisted that her tub be carried all the way across tropical Africa, in order that she might indulge her imperious bones nightly in a relaxing, memsahib bath, while her safari tub-carriers presumably then had their own kind of sudorific relaxation when they got to set the damn thing down. A factual bath devotionist, Hasdrubal, Hannibal's brother and an equally eminent Carthaginian general, whenever he made warlike journeys along the North African coast, was said to arrange his victories so as to arrive nightly at towns with excellent civic bath establishments.

The bath *is* a place of ablution, of nestling within the ambience of embracing waterhood. There need not be, though sometimes this may be so, any idea of return-to-the-womb recidivist escape from present worries. Dr. Karl Menninger once suggested that Houdini's water-escape act, in which the great magician assumed a fetal position in a water-filled receptacle secured with massive locks, was somehow related to the universal water-fantasy of returning to the womb, "to the undisturbed bliss of intra-uterine existence." But one does not require such fishy fancies to enjoy the simple pleasure of the tub. Water is and always has been the all-embracing, comforting, original medium of life, down into which any dry terrestrialite gladly plunges—a trip far back beyond a return journey into our ancestral treetops, back all the way into the original ocean waters out of which our progenitors emerged so long ago. It is part of what we inevitably will always continue to be: lost water babies so very long gone ashore.

There are remarkable bathtubs, some new, some very ancient, to be visited in various parts of the world. In viewing them, one may visualize the joy that other bathers—both the eminent and the unknown—have experienced. One must only look at the *empty* tub and imagine, for actual, immediate viewing, voyeurism, has always created trouble: "David arose from off his bed, and walked upon the roof of the king's house: and from the roof he saw a woman washing herself; and the woman was very beautiful to look upon" (II Samuel 11:2). Presently, as we all know from Bible reading, Bathsheba's husband, Uriah, had been sent to the battlefront for instant elimination, whereupon she became David's wife and gave him that remarkable son, Solomon, who in turn was to beget with the Queen of Sheba a son, Menelik, the ancestor of Emperor Haile Selassie of Ethiopia—all this, mark you, because David strode his roof terrace and peeped at a neighbor's wife in her bath! And Sheba might not have yielded herself to David's son if she had not become thirsty during the night and accepted a tumblerful of water, and so lost a bet to Solomon that she would not accept a gift or else.

A favorite bathtub for American viewers has long been the giant one in the Red Bathroom of Sagamore Hill, the handsome house built only a few miles outside of New York City by Theodore Roosevelt in 1884. The only bathroom for a family of eight that was often expanded to perhaps twice the number by numerous guests-in-residence, this must have been a busy room. But the *tub!* In my memory, it had turned into a mammoth carved-out object of Egyptian porphyry. This is one of the wonderful things that happens within our memories. In reality, when I questioned Mrs. Harold Kraft, Sagamore Hill's curator, she told me it was of heavy porcelain-on-iron, but so immense that the Roosevelt children casually called it "the sarcophagus." Mrs. Kraft even measured the immense thing for me—it was 68 inches by 30 inches, with a depth of 26¼ inches. All her life, Alice Roosevelt Longworth has been telling people about that big tub with the tiny inlet faucet that was far ahead of its time, being hermaphroditic, thus mixing the hot and cold water: "The water trickles in very, very slowly. Whenever I go back to Sagamore, if there is any chance, I always take a bath in it, most sentimentally."

Perhaps one's greatest respect for this fine old tub is that it was able to calm and pacify Princess Alice, something her father never managed. "I can either be President of the United States or father of Alice," he is quoted, "but not both." There is a reminder here of Themistocles' prediction that "the wildest colts make the finest horses," which Mrs. Longworth has so fully filly-wise fulfilled.

Bathtubs have not changed much down through the centuries since they first appeared in the Fertile Crescent palaces of the Near East. A handsome tub has been put back in the Queen's Bathroom at the royal palace of Knossos by Sir Arthur Evans; it must be seen by the universal bathtub fancier, both for its inner, peaceful painted-on decor of reeds and because of the very pleasant surroundings of the queen's apartments. Lawrence Wright pictured this 1700 B.C. tub alongside one manufactured 3,600 years later, and they are remarkably similar in shape, decoration, and air of splendid lavishness. The Knossos queen must have been one of the Beautiful People of the Minoan Age—perhaps a Princess Alice who presently married the Speaker of the House of Knossos.

In 1969, Eugenia Sheppard described a bathroom in a new triplex apartment on Park Avenue, in New York City: "The brown and white marble tub is up two steps and has huge gold and marble faucets. The water rushes in from under marble shells and fills the tub in two-and-a-half minutes, because Charles Revson hates to be kept waiting. Mrs. Revson has already had a couple of near-floods: 'I love the tub,' she said, 'but it's so big I'm afraid I'll drown in it. I can't swim.' " For similar watery immensity, in 1969 the International Hotel, completed in the Nevada desert-town of Las Vegas, was immediately announced as the world's biggest resort hotel "and it contains a pool that is the second-largest man-made body of water in all Nevada." Second only, that is, to Lake Mead, the vast reservoir backed up behind Hoover Dam. For contrast, one may view, on the island of Ceylon, an immense *vapi*, the Sea of Parakrama (Parakrama Samudra) constructed by King Parakrama Bau in the 1160's; it is cleverly divided into three watery areas: one pond for drinking, a second for bathing, and a third for other washing.

The most famous bathtubs are those reserved for use not simply by Beautiful People, but by the *Most* Beautiful People, which gets down to the real nitty-gritty of meaning the most powerful and most important people. Richard Milhous Nixon made it to the U.S. White House in a free election, on January 20, 1969, but he did not *really* get to make it, *water-wise*, on the Planet Water, until on February 24, 1969, he at last got to occupy the most royal of all royal suites at Claridge's, London, the Mayfair hotel that is known around the world to the In, the Beautiful, the Right, and the Affluent People as an annex to Buck House, Great Britain's royal residence.

Auberon Waugh, who has likely no more seen this nonpareil place than have you or I, yearned, "At $95 a day, including service charge, this Royal Suite must be one of the cheapest on offer. It has a sunken bath of pink marble which has received, in its time, the naked forms of nearly every king and queen in the world, of Sir Winston Churchill and Alfred Rosenberg, Hitler's foreign minister who was later hanged at Nuremberg; the skinny body of Sir Alec Douglas-Home, and the gross form of Nikita Khrushchev: no wonder it is pink."

"I hate immersion," the great Dr. Samuel Johnson once solemnized his silly aversion; and intense immersionist Katharine Whitehorn, in the London *Observer* (in 1969), reveled: "I am in my bath. I do not wish to be disturbed. I don't care if the house is burning down, the Government falling, the pound in ruins and all the hogs escaping. . . . I know a man with a gazebo to retire to; there are doubtless some lighthouse-keepers who get a bit of time to themselves; the religious go on retreats and people sometimes get a little enviable privacy, stuck in a lift between two floors. But for the rest of us, the bath is the only refuge." In 1923, Claude William Guillebaud, in the *Encyclopaedia Britannica,* extolled the increase of tubbing a quarter-century ago: "The private bath was one of the greatest luxuries of the Roman empire; today it may be remarked amongst the necessaries of life."

Why do humans insist on washing their bodies in water? From time of birth, a baby born into a "civilized" American family will be bathed regularly and often and, later, trained to

wash himself, and he will then go on throughout life well hab-
ited to thoroughly scrubbing himself daily with soap, either in
the shower or the sit-down bath, but usually one *or* the other. I
once tried to change my mother's sit-down-bath habits by re-
serving a hotel room for her with shower only. Next day, she
admitted she'd not tried, adding simply, "But you know I'm a
tub person." Many shower takers are so for the dreadful post-
Thoreau reason that they live lives of too rushed and noisy
desperation to take the time out to sit and soak. Many of them
honestly hope someday to begin relaxing again in a sit-down
bath.

During the 1950's, psychiatrist Dr. Robert P. Odenwald told
a family life conference: "Freedom to play in dirt, to get thoroughly dirty in face, hands and clothing, is an important privi-
lege in the development of an autonomous human being."
Then, it is always assumed, it is the child's or the parents' obli-
gation, both social and healthwise, to wash up. But why so?
*"People have grown up in houses without bathrooms for thou-
sands of years."*

Of the advantages of cleanliness, Dr. Mark F. Boyd, of the
Rockefeller Foundation's International Health Division, once
stated: "A clean skin is less likely to be diseased than a dirty
one." Dr. Thurman B. Rice, in his *Textbook of Bacteriology,*
said: "The biggest accomplishment of modern times is that a
civilized community takes means to make itself and its individual members clean." A century ago, upon abolishing the British
tax on soap, P. M. Gladstone rumbled that "a clean nation is a
healthy and happy nation." Happiness and health are frequently thus married up with hygiene, and there is of course
also more than a hint of primordial watery spirituality as well,
joined mysteriously with the piece of soap and the towel.

For the opposition, a number of years ago, Robert K. Plumb
warned: "There is an impressive and increasingly convincing
body of scientific evidence that personal cleanliness protects
children from viral infection but that for that very reason they
do not build up immunities early in life. Clean and well-fed
American youngsters, on this basis, are at a disadvantage when
they grow up in a world of alien viruses."

In a remarkable 1969 study, *Life on Man,* the eminent bac-
teriologist Dr. Theodor Rosebury insisted vigorously that

"what is true of wounds is just as true of healthy skin and mucous membranes. Except for hexachlorophene in treatment or prevention of infection with pathogenic staphylococci, the use of antiseptics on the skin or any of the mucous membranes— the eye, the mouth, the nose and throat, the vagina, the rectum —is useless and likely to be harmful. Eyewashes, mouthwashes and douches have no value even as cosmetics, despite certain opinions to the contrary even among professional people, who have merely picked these ideas uncritically out of the ancient lore to which we are all exposed. If washing is occasionally required, plain water serves as well as anything in the mouth, and table salt, a little less than one part in 100 parts of water, on other mucous membranes, including the eye. On skin, soap and water; and, if you really want the truth, not too much soap, and not too often . . . removing too much of the fatty material of the skin with an overzealous use of soap may be harmful. *Know* what you are doing to yourself, and let well enough alone."

Each human being is a miniature Planet Water, with an immense miniature population inhabiting his livable areas. As with the great Planet Water on which he lives, he and his inhabitants are interdependent. Before departing from Dr. Rosebury's remarkable study, here is his statement on skin microbes: "The microbe population on any one of us is undeniably large, numbering vastly more than all the people on earth. Yet they could all be packed into something hardly bigger than an ordinary soup can; and the ones everywhere except within our guts—including our whole expanse of skin— could hide in the bottom of a thimble. These microbes are evidently indispensable to our healthy development and wellbeing."

There is another kind of washing and bathing place that is for everybody together, something, alas, that very few of us ever get to experience today. Even the large resort establishments with immense swimming pools still ordinarily make the tubbing-scrubbing activity a private, solitary thing, divided by sex and also into booths or, minimally, into stalls. This is all very well, but at the same time rather petty and even puritanical.

The golden age of the *group* bath, as of fountains, came in the few, swift centuries of Imperial Rome. The early, unwatered Romans were as puritanically perverse and dotty as the Colonial New Englanders whom we foolishly teach our children to revere—an early-Roman father could not even take a bath with his son. When the Romans at last learned to get with it, with water, they built more and more and larger and larger establishments dedicated to the true *pleasure* of water. If Samuel-Kubla Coleridge-Khan were planning *in earnest* to build the finest of pleasure domes, he would surely have decreed that it be designed only by an architect who'd trained with the engineer who designed the baths, the imperial thermae, for the Emperor Caracalla—six acres of magnificent water chambers surrounded by twenty acres of gardens, with libraries, clubs, nightclubs, and appropriate discothèques and private-party apartments around the perimeter. The place was open from midafternoon to nightfall. Lawrence Wright has described how "wide-span roofs of the past tell us about the people who built them. The purpose is likely to have been their main interest in life. Today it is the aircraft hangar; in the 19th Century it was the railroad station; in the 18th Century the noble mansion (Blenheim); in the Middle Ages, the cathedral. In Rome, it was the public bath, the focus of communal life. Bathing was a basic social duty." Already Wright's statement, made in 1960, has become part of the historic past, since our 1970's "largest" is that great chamber at Cape Kennedy, Florida, out of which emerge the rockets of the space age.

How shall a 1970's sightseer get some idea of the sheer immensity of the Caracallan imperial water wonder? In Rome, concerts are given in part of the ruins, and a large church has also been built among them. A few pieces of the remarkable statuary that once graced the towering halls of water-fun are in museums. Meantime, the grand concourse of Grand Central Station, in New York City, is a careful copy of the central chamber. The replica is ruined by vast numbers of billboards and other money-changer signs that don't belong in a watery temple. But what a fantasy it could be if someday all of the rushed, pushed, upset, hurried, harried commuters hurtling themselves through this great chamber could be invited to relax, let go, stop, take off all their clothes, and proceed calmly to head for the tepidarium, the apodyterium, the calidarium—don't crowd or push, please, there is all the time and the space in the world here—entering each immense facility in correct order and precedence—the laconicum, the frigidarium, and, later, a few hours in the adjoining libraries or gardens, before returning back into their clothes and onto their commutation trains and subways, back from imperial Rome into the pressures of 1970's American living.

Group bathing today is best performed in Japan. When the scrubbing is done and one can relax and enjoy the waters, then comes the water fun. Frank Robertson described a happy group ensconced at a resort hotel in Akita Province, on the Sea of Japan, where "from the large sunken pool, clear glass windows gave a view of the kind dear to the Japanese: angry gray-white seas pounding wet sand a hundred yards away, with gnarled pines in the foreground taking on a mantle of the year's first snow. Deliciously secure against the weather, we lolled in the hot water and light-heartedly composed *haiku*, the Japanese 17-syllable poetry. Even the Romans never had it *that* good." An ultimate, this, in a human companionage of bathing enjoyment.

Sir James Frazer contended, in the *Golden Bough*, that so-called cleanliness among savages was based originally on removal and hiding of personal *attributes* such as hair or nail parings, lest enemies might get hold of them and use them for magic against their owner. Some of the more thermae-struck Roman emperors were said to have gone to the baths seven or more times a day. In a 1969 work about frontiermen living in the Idaho Rockies, we are told of Johnny-Behind-the-Rocks, who never once removed his clothes until just before he died from the shock of taking his very *first* bath.

Few bathers bother with bath thermometers, instead using an elbow or, a better tester, a finger, to gauge. Bath temperatures usually range through five levels: *hot*—102 to 110 degrees Fahrenheit (Japanese bathe in up to 122 degrees in their *yu-dono*, or *furo*, while Scandinavians scald up to 175 degrees in their steam sauna); *warm*—96 to 104 degrees; *tepid*—85 to 95 degrees (the temperature of our skin is 92 degrees, 6.6 degrees cooler than our inner climate); *cool*—70 to 85 degrees; *cold*—40 to 70 degrees. Nobody has yet been able to explain how, in June, 1969, a young Cuban, Armando Socarras Ramirez, was able to endure and survive temperatures down to minus-40 degrees when he hid out in the wheel-pod of a jet air-liner flying from Cuba to Spain. Wearing only a thin shirt, pants, and one shoe, he also survived the acute shortage of oxygen in the 29,000-foot altitude.

Hot baths are soporific, whereas the cold plunge is stimulating. Hot water has usually come from the tap on the left, and is considered to be feminine, whereas cold water is virile, male, and drawn usually from the tap on the right. One of the great miracles of the power of plumbing is observed when one simply flushes a toilet on the topmost floor of the Empire State Building. How can plumbing geniuses make it *flow* so high? One has only to go out on the northern viewing platform, drop a dime into the telescopic binoculars, and peer at the distant structure of Croton Dam—higher than Manhattan—whence flow down, and again back up by hydrostatic pressure (the principle that water will rise to the same level of both arms of a U-tube), the great metropolis' waters, by sheer gravity.

Puritanical extremists have always hinted that Rome fell because her citizens had degenerated into the habit and indulgence of mixed nude bathing. Instead, it seems contrariwise-obvious that it fell after unwashed barbarians had destroyed its great water-carrying aqueducts, much as the Mesopotamian centuries of civilization ended when barbarians from the East destroyed the elaborate waterworks that had made a vast garden of the Tigris-Euphrates valley. In Rome, the obverse wonder is that Romans survived for so many generations the constant use of water carried through pipes that were mostly made of lead. *Artifex plumbarius,* workers in lead, readily wrapped the pipes about underground obstructions (cast iron, or modern ductile steel, cannot, of course, be bent into place). Water carried through lead pipes deposits deadly lead in the human body, which collects it slowly in tiny, accumulated drifts that end with death by lead poisoning. Recent investigation reveals that wealthy Romans also added *melted* lead to their wines, which tasted good but meanwhile also poisoned them and made them sterile. One can always readily identify the drinker of water out of lead pipes: he will have a tinge of gray—which is pure lead—along the lids of his eyes.

Perhaps the most functional piece of furniture ever designed by man was the flush toilet. Down through the ages, many urban centers have had flush systems to carry sewage away, but the first modern flush toilet was patented in 1775 by a watch-maker, Alexander Cummings: the use of the letters WC has memorialized Watchmaker Cummings' name forever, although in World War II Nazis referred to it as the Winston Churchill, and the Worthington Corporation had some trouble a few years ago when they adopted a new logo of WC.

All the elements of today's toilet were present in Cummings' invention—overhead supply vault, pull-up handle, and siphon trap. Only the outlet valve was not reliable. In 1778 a cabinet-maker, Joseph Bramah, patented a valve with a cranking motion instead of a loosely sliding one, improving it somewhat. Then, a hundred years later, the British Board of Trade sent out a call for a more efficient system, and a sanitary engineer, Thomas Crapper, whose name also has become, lower case, a part of bathroom language, presented Crapper's Valveless Water-Waste Preventer, with a float, a metal arm, and siphonic action to empty the reservoir.

The British call a toilet seat a lavatory bowl, whereas in this country the washbowl is often called a lavatory. Americans do not say, "I'm going to the water closet," but "to the bathroom." Japanese consider it disgusting that the water closet is usually put in the same chamber with the washing facilities. Once in Paris, after a long, despairing ride on the metro, a maid finally admitted me to a friend's apartment, and I foolishly asked to be shown to the little boys' room, an accepted, perhaps childish American euphemism. I was promptly shown into a bedcham-ber where two small lads were getting into their pajamas. I've never used the term since. When I tell a friend named John that I am going to the john, he replies no, that I must mean that I am going to the herbert. People named John do not ap-preciate that the rest of us often call the place john.

"Comfort station" was once the attractive name for a public john; sometimes they've been called "relief stations." A quarter-century ago the foulest, most antifriendly invention of all time came about, the *pay toilet,* whereby a person could not relieve himself without first paying a nickel into an infernal de-vice on the toilet door to unlock it. The price has since risen to a dime, and in some instances a quarter. As dastardly a ma-chine, this, as is the parking meter. Communities using either or both do not deserve to receive free-spending visitors, and their native citizens are likely to be unhappy souls.

Men somehow are usually more hard-pressed in this respect than women (perhaps simply because they usually drink more). At beer parties, it is the men who form a steady caravan that goes endlessly back and forth to the bathroom. Perhaps that is why Paris, a man's town, used to have street-corner pissoirs for men only, the famed iron-fenced *chapelles* which disappeared soon after World War II.

In *Grapes of Wrath*, John Steinbeck described the first encounter of two little Okie kids, Ruthie and Winfield, with flush toilets. "I already set on 'em," Ruthie boasted. "I even pee'd in one." She hadn't, of course. But with her brother present, "in a burst of bravado, she boosted up her skirt and sat down. There was a tinkle of water in the bowl. Winfield's hand twisted the flushing lever. There was a roar of water. Ruthie leaped into the air. 'You done it. You went an' broke it. You ain't to be trusted with no nice stuff.' "

A scholar of public toilets, Jonathan Routh, has "done" the water closets of New York, London, and Paris, under the titles: *The Better John Guide: Where to Go in New York; Good Loo Guide* (London); and *Guide Porcelaine* (Paris). He has not only given locations (for "all those people with nowhere to go, and whose need is greater than ours"), but even rated them, *à la Guide Michelin,* by star clusters. There is a resounding watery victory for Grand Central Terminal, New York City, the railway depot modeled after Caracalla's baths, not only for the flush toilets and such but also for various peripheral goodies such as showers, pants-pressing facilities, and even a quick-self-photo booth.

Alas, toilets are *not* a scenic destination, and Routh found out why not: "All over New York, the johns of the great have been ripped out and consigned to the rubblemakers, and in their place characterless modern fittings installed. What an insight into the lives of some of these people if some of these treasures, as personal to them as their desks or beds, still existed!"

Trying to find a public convenience in a hurry can be an unhappy experience for either man or woman. Each city that expects to receive visitors and sightseers owes it to them to provide a list of comfort stations. In fact, one of these days tourist-minded metropolises with a thought for their own citizens' comfort will also begin to operate city-run for-free establishments for the pleasant and convenient easement of everybody. *McCall's* magazine carried an excellent list of "Plush Places to Powder Your Nose" in New York, in their May, 1968, issue; it included swank hotels, the Central Park Zoo, the 42d Street Library, and a number of splendid specialty stores—with the conclusion: "There's no reason why you can't powder your nose in the fanciest 'comfort stations' in the company of the very best people." Meaning, presumably, the Beautiful People or the Right People: absolutely no reason at all why not.

The best comfort stations of all are preurban, what Bob Hope refers to, when he visits far-out Army posts and stations, as "rooms with a path"—rude earth closets which consist of a simple hole dug in the ground and a rude wooden seat set over it.

The "sanitary seat," set in its arbor or back house, sometimes fancied up so much that it is almost a gazebo percé, is usually a floral retreat as well. One can remember countless such garden hideaways surrounded by hollyhocks, lilac bushes, towering sunflowers, the redolence of roses, and the sound of bumblebees bumbling about in peaceful pursuit of sunshine turned into flowerage.

IX The Sky Waters

WHEN did the great rains first begin to fall upon our planet, the torrential downpours that were to fill the ocean basins with water, that would create a hydrous atmosphere and environment in which life became possible, and that would so clothe the whirling ball with a hydrosphere of water vapor and moving waters that its name inevitably must be Planet Water?

There are two contradictory theories as to the planet's origin: that it was born very cold and that it was born very hot. The hot-birth theory is the more familiar, the genesis of an angry cloud that condensed and compressed into a fiery globe that presently began spewing forth water vapor along with other lighter materials from innumerable volcanoes, thus filling the primitive atmosphere with vast clouds of steam that could not condense into water and fall back upon a planetary surface that was as yet too hot to receive it. At last the planet's raw epidermis cooled sufficiently to receive the rains for the first time. And what a huge, unending, tumultuous rainfall then began to take place! For hundreds of millions of years, down it came, an infinitude of waters; it rained buckets, barrels, magnums and methuselahs, salmanazers and belshazzars, rehoboams, jeroboams, amphorae and *diotae, demigiana* and carboys, sheer infinite *nebuchadnezzars* of water.

This *may* have been the way it took place. One feels drenched, inundated, waterwhelmed, moist, juicy, soaked, saturated, reeking wet, just from reading the words of the scientific poets and poetic scientists. "Never have there been such rains since that time. They poured into the waiting ocean basins, or, falling upon the continental masses, drained away to become seas," Rachel Carson spoke for both schools.

On the other hand, what if the planet began *cold?* It still may turn out to have. What then? In mid-1969, radio astronomers reported the first reception of emissions from outer space that might prove to be astral indications of the birth of other planets around a new star aborning. Along with the usual midwife gases expected to be taking part at such an astral delivery, rapidly moving *water vapor* was also detected whirling about the nursery at great speeds. This was the first time that water had ever been found to exist in interstellar space.

The hot-origin scientific theorists insist that all of our protoplanet's waters originated inside the subterranean mantle and only later began to be emitted through volcanic outlets, remaining as steam in the atmosphere until the surface of the planet had cooled sufficiently to let it rain down and stay down on the surface. Let us have some fun with the "began cold" theory: suppose that our planet began as fantastically *cold,* and that much of the water vapor was not bottled up inside but instead first condensed on the *outside* (the outer edges of Planet Water's atmosphere are today about minus-38 degrees Fahrenheit), creating the biggest spherical ice "cube" ever to exist!

The founder of paleoclimatology, C. E. P. Brooks, once postulated that once icing begins, it will go on freezing unless a much higher temperature reverses the process. And astronomer Ernst Öpik gave future warning, in 1958, indicating what might also have happened in a deepfreeze beginning: if the sun's radiation were to be reduced by a mere 13 percent, "the whole planet would soon be covered with a mile-thick mantle of ice."

What a most appropriate inception for Planet Water! We know that this will not be the end, the denouement, because death of all watery things comes simply with their drying out. Our planet will die when its watery cover goes, just as we depart our physical life when our plump, living bodies wither away to become dried-out corpses.

Let us attend the genesis of Planet Water, a vast, slow, steady liquefying and melting down of ice mountains many miles

high, accompanied by the emergence and egress of the cold pro-
tomass of protoelements from beneath the ice where they have
been condensed and compressed, as ever since that frigid beginning under pressure they have been densened by intense heat.
If Planet Water began cold and ice-covered, then the sheer pressure of the great weight of ice could have triggered the first
slow beginning of internal heat within the planet's core.

Biblically, for fundamentalists, this would come somewhere
between Verses 5 and 6 in Chapter 1 of the Book of Genesis:
"Let there be a firmanent in the midst of the waters, and let it
divide the waters from the waters."

Phase two of this kind of planetary beginning (very cold to
very hot) may be viewed today in that newest mid-North Atlantic Ocean land of Iceland, where vast icy glaciers may be seen to
glister unbelievably above portentous, torrid volcanoes—ice
and fire performing their separately succeeding and successive
functions in the evolutionary activity of the planet's development.

Let us consider this possibility, then, of an alternative to the
hot-surface-cooling theory: not virgin raindrops trying to land
on a planet still too hot to receive them; instead, the opposite—
a massive block, lump, mass, a massive and solid accumulation
of the metallic form of water—ice—many, many miles of it,
square miles, cubic miles, miles wide and miles high, multi-
miles in all directions, obdurate, implacable. And then, inevitably, by that old folk-tale wisdom as to whether sun or wind
shall succeed in forcing the peasant to take off his jacket, there
must have come a time when the great ice began to melt—like
a defrosting refrigerator, first drip-drip-drip-drip, then trickle-
drip, and plop, purl, gurgle, guggle, faster-faster, burble, bubble, babble, splash, very fast finally, flow, spout, surge, gush, billow. What a great, wild flow of water must there then have
been, if the planet started cold and covered with ice!

By either cold or hot origin, the surface of the planet was
inevitably to be made watery; the superfices became diffluent,
deliquescent, fluvial, moist, dampish, and, finally, extremely
wet. The enigmatic planet acquired its personality as a whirling sphere mostly covered with oceanic waters: the Planet
Water was born.

The first visit of Planet Watermen to the moon, in 1969, re-

vealed the tragedy of that lost, small subplanet: it has never acquired an atmosphere, and especially the water-drenched aero-
sphere necessary, with surface waters, to the creation of life. Suddenly all of our previous misconceptions of the moon as an offspring of our own planet, perhaps sprung out of the Pacific
Ocean (leaving a conveniently deep "revelatory" basin), fell
apart. In fact, the moon appears to be ever so much *older* than
our own space home, as though if our planet's grandmother had
had a little sister, the moon could have been she. Even her surface pocks, like an old lady's wrinkles, appear to be at least 3.5
billion years old! Poor old childless lady! No waters ever got to
rain down upon her plains, because she never had acquired an
atmosphere. But from our appraisal and future examination of
her dead planethood, perhaps we shall learn to better appreciate the unbelievable miracle of our own planet's retaining not
only an atmosphere but the special kind of watery exteriority
that once assured the arrival, and now the continuance, of life.
In spite of the spirited suggestions made by astronomers (and,
of course, their brother astrologers) that the universe, or cosmos, is overcrowded with peopled planets whirling around an
infinite number of stars, one must have doubts. I still suspect
that ours is the only one that's actually *peopled,* because it is the
only one that we know of that is atmospherically and oceani-
cally provided with *water,* the rich juice of life that has made
possible the only sentient creatures *known* to exist anywhere in
the universe.

Whether the planet started out hot or cold, inevitably the
rains came. And inevitably, I do not think we sufficiently recognize, the rains dominate and always shall influence a major part
of the planet's surface, livelihood, and rhythms. I reside far up
in the northern temperate zone and live in a somewhat "dry"
environment which is relatively rare on the Planet Water's surface. My fellow citizens seek their pleasures in such superdry
places as Arizona, in search of sun rather than rainfall
precipitation. Desert is, one suspects, a sort of dry superaberra-
tion on the Planet Water's surface, an arid excrescence on top
of the insult of continents raised above the juicy oceanic waters.
Dryness is a terrible threat to all that we water creatures believe
in. Aridness and aridity are, in fact, death. Most of the studies
of desert life that Americans read with such enthusiasm tend to

concentrate upon the fabulous ability of various mice and cacti to survive by gathering and utilizing parsimoniously tiny amounts of moisture, notably limited dewfalls, that they somehow manage to make do with for months on end.

The planet's torrid zone—the midriff area between the Tropic of Cancer and the Tropic of Capricorn—constantly receives the greatest amount of heat from the sun, and consequently the air in the narrow belt of rainy low latitudes just adjacent to the equator is constantly rising, air streams in from the trade winds of the higher latitudes, and there is daily torrential rain. One should visit the equator to experience what the primordial planetary rains must have been like. The area embraced by the turbid tropics includes not only the rain belt but also the great rain forests which grow so thick that all life and greenness is in the upper branches, and the ground beneath is without underbrush or animal life: most life is here arboreal, and monkeys, lemurs, and reptiles live the swinging life in the upper branches. "Jungles," in contrast, have plenty of lower-level vegetation and animal life.

H. M. Tomlinson, in *The Sea and the Jungle,* described the oppressiveness of the rain forest: "We found ourselves on a bare floor where the trunks of arborescent laurels grew so thickly together that our view ahead was restricted to a few yards. We were in the forest. There was a pale tinge of day, but its origin was uncertain, for overhead no foliage could be seen, but only deep shadows from which long ropes were hanging without life. In that obscurity were points of light, as if a high roof had lost some tiles. This central forest was really the vault of the long-forgotten, dank, mouldering, dark, abandoned to the accumulations of eld and decay. The tall pillars rose, upholding night, and they might have been bastions of weathered limestone and basalt, for they were as grim as ancient and ruinous masonry. There was no undergrowth. The ground was hidden in a ruin of perished stuff, uprooted trees, parchments of leaves, broken boughs, and mummied husks, the iron globes of nuts, and pods. There was no day."

Thus, a rain forest, called "the utmost or climax condition of forest growth," is relatively easy to walk through but not at all a pleasant experience. Ivan Sanderson, whose *Book of Great Jungles,* written a half-century after Tomlinson's rather simple diary, was based on many expeditions to all parts of the world, knew the right way to view a rain forest: he simply climbed the nearest giant tree. "The uninterrupted view of so much forest was unique in my experience. The sun shimmered on the leaves, and shafts of glaring light reflected back from the shining surfaces. In the hot air, brilliantly painted butterflies flitted among exotic flowers. Clouds of bees hummed and buzzed while flies of all shapes and sizes darted about or suspended themselves above some tempting morsel, motionless except for the beating of wings too rapid to be visible. Birds of many colors fluttered in and out of the treetops. Hawks and eagles soared and swooped, their eyes obviously seeing things within the foliage which mine could not. I do not think I ever felt myself so remote from the world of men!"

The rainiest season of the Planet Water is during the monsoons of northeastern India, which drop more than 400 inches of rain annually. In most tropical paradises, rainy season is a time when showers begin abruptly, sometimes when there is not even a cloud visible in the sky, and stop as suddenly. Describing Dominica, the most primitive of Caribbean islands (and my favorite of all islands after Manhattan), Stephen Haweis, a resident admirer, commented: "Dominica is a wet island, but terrifying figures about rainfall are very deceptive, because the earth here is well-drained and the sun is never far away even upon the dullest day. When the rain stops, it is over. It does not rise up again in miasmic mists which settle upon your shoes in the coat-cupboard, or grow vegetables on your pigskin suitcase." Dominica's jungles are far more exciting and fun than, for example, the rain forest atop El Yunque in Puerto Rico. Most of the islands of the West Indies have beautiful tropical gardens in their capital cities where one may view the most exotic flowering trees growing in opulent profusion, the vegetal offspring of heavy rainfall in the tropics.

The currently most rained-on spot on the planet is Mount Waialeale, on the Hawaiian island of Kauai, where the record fall in 1947–48 came to 624 inches! "The nearest thing to Eden," this garden island, with its numerous waterfalls and year-round flowering vines, shrubs and trees, has been called. Long before the Polynesians arrived, in A.D. 900, the island was inhabited by distant relatives of the Irish wee folk, the two-foot-tall Menehune, who sailed away long ago from Kauai-a-mamo-ka-lani-po, which means "the-fountainhead-of-many-waters-from-on-high-and-bubbling-up-from-below." And Waialeale means "rippling water."

The temperate zones have many notable rain forests, none more impressive than the largest of all, the Olympic National Park, which contains nearly 1,000,000 acres of mist-shrouded woodland on a great peninsula projecting into the Pacific Ocean. Mount Olympus has the greatest precipitation of any spot in the continental United States, most of it falling as snow. Here the most impressive trees are giant Douglas fir. This great rain forest is also "watered" by the steady flow of 60 living glaciers within its high country.

Because of the limitations of human vision, when we visit these great forests we do not get to sight-see the most remarkable watery spectacle of all—the rivers of invisible water vapor streaming *upward* into the heavens from the trees. No matter how tall a tree may grow, or how immense it may be, only about 1 percent of it is ever "alive": the root tips, leaves, flowers, and a thin layer of busy cells just beneath the trunk's outer bark. All the rest is interior deadwood. Trees drink a vast quantity of water, supping it up through their root tips, sapping it up trunk and out branch to the highest and outermost leaves, using only 1 percent and fountaining up into the atmosphere the other 99 percent. Because of this great upward transpiration of moisture, the great forests of the world have come to be called the "oceans of the continents."

The hydrologic cycle, the endless circulation of the Planet Water's aqueous environment up out of the oceans and land areas into the atmosphere, by evaporation and transpiration, then back down by way of condensation and precipitation, is a living, breathing process comparable to the intake-outgo of any other living creature's bodily life operations. Only a small part of the total waters is ever in motion in the cycle at any one time —of the total 326 cubic miles, never more than 3 percent taking part. But this antigravity power machine, energized by the sun—and affected by cold fronts, anticyclones, high-level jet streams, and circumpolar whirls—operating in the great ocean of atmosphere, is still only superficially known. "We see and feel rain, snow, dew, fog. We use water for drinking and washing. We irrigate our lawns and fields. We talk about the weather, but actually our knowledge of it is pretty skimpy," the confession was made in the U.S. Yearbook of Agriculture, 1955, *Water*. But, simply, there is no prettier view, for a man's amazement, than a skyful of rich clouds. One may envy friend dog his nosy joys of rooting among leaves and grasses, but he, like so many creatures constructed so as to look *down* their noses at the world, has no idea of the superjoy of a head constructed so that the eyes may easily gaze skyward. Perhaps that is why dogs and wolves bay so sadly up at the moon.

James Ray, an eighteenth-century chronicler, gave the damp-day advice that if there were no clouds we could not enjoy the sun. And Thomas Fuller, that old gnomological worrywart, was annoyed that one cloud is enough to eclipse all of the sun. Such is the power of rain clouds and rain!

The imaginative fun of weather itself was suggested by a Carib man on the off-side of Dominica Island, who once imparted to me through an interpreter, "Please, I should like to experience snow and a winter storm *once* before I die!"

Shakespeare wrote: "When clouds appear, wise men put on their cloaks." I first misread "For every cloud engenders not a storm" by leaving out the "not." Perhaps I have read the skies, in this case, better than the master. It is the storms that make for activity, for interest, for excitement, for what Shakespeare himself perpetually put into his plays. Storm, tempest, that is what brings excitement into our lives. Bobby Burns' "The tempest's howl, it soothes my soul" soothes all our souls.

An empty sky, the pure blue of emptiness, is a desert for viewing, in contrast to a cloud-rich sky, just as blue seas are empty in contrast with the plankton-rich green seas. The highest ascending collection of water droplets, the rare nacreous mother-of-pearl, may go upward well beyond 80,000 feet. Ordinarily, clouds float about in a range from a few feet to up to about 5 miles. The scholarly hygrology sightseer can readily name all of them—cumulus, strattus, nimbus, cirrus, cumulonimbus. Most of the beauty is created simply by the interplay of atmospheric humidity and sunlight, with minimal aid from dust and ash particles. Imagination turns clouds into great caravans, pilgrimages, prides and tribes of animal shapes, ever so many strange forms and proud personages moving across the sky in entrancing formations. Cloud watching is a perpetually fascinating vocation. Small children should learn while very young to lie on the hilly sides of pastures and look up, telling each other and their often less observant elders what they see with their mind's eye. "I wandered lonely as a cloud," said Wordsworth; his pondering does not make sense unless he uses "lost" or "maverick," because clouds tend usually to be as gregarious as cows, covering at least half of the planet's surface with clusterings of strange, puffy nebulosities. There just *aren't* many "lonely" clouds. Shelley did it better, so much more beautifully, in "The Cloud": "I bring fresh showers for the thirsting flowers," to the sound of departing Thor-like laughter, as "I pass in thunder."

When the rains come down, then is a time of surcease from worries, of aural pleasure in giving oneself solely to the sound of the downpour, on the porch roof, on the tree leaves and needles, even spanking down on a nearby cement sidewalk. This is our North American temperate-zone kind of shower that one is at home with. James Whitcomb Riley's quietly religious song still has immediacy today: "My empty soul brimmed over, and my heart drenched with the love of God. My very soul smiles as I listen to the low, mysterious laughter of the rain." A botanist, who must also be a naturalist-poet, discovered that vitamin B_{12}, manufactured by microorganisms in the air, rains down so richly out of thundershowers that to relieve pernicious anemia symptoms, he suggested sufferers should "stand in the rain, with their mouths open, for ten minutes or so." That's a good idea for an additional crowd of rain people beyond poets and botanists. In fact, rain-walking, with uncovered head or, best of all, naked, is good for any poet's soul. John Muir, the greatest of mountain-rain-walkers, explained: "Every raincloud, however fleeting, leaves its mark, not only on trees and flowers whose pulses are quickened, and on the replenished streams and lakes, but also on the rocks are its marks engraved whether we can see them or not." But, better than all else, is the decoration of simple *bonheur*, sheer gladness, that it lays upon the hearts of persons who walk joyously through it. It is nice to have sunshine brought into our lives; yet, not surprisingly, rainshine is every bit its equal, and as vital to each sane man's accord of living pleasure.

For this reason, I've always been opposed to using an umbrella. In the country, these vast circular demidomes are fine for the person afraid of getting his/her hair wet. Recently a lady even expressed their use for keeping sootfall out of her newly set hairdo; originally, umbrellas were designed in the Orient to be carried over the heads of royalty as a protection against the sun's rays.

Today, a *parapluie* used in our crowded cities becomes not so much an antiraindrops device as an aggressive and offensive weapon for use against all other urban rain-walking pedestrians, who are also carrying the same offensive weapons—vast, eight-*pointed,* circular things that are not held high above the head against the downpour, but like a combined spear and shield of a medieval knight advancing into battle, pointing in front of the sidewalk warrior. A nonumbrellaed man is at the mercy of these pricky keep-dry assailants.

I am not opposed to the "carrying" of umbrellas, but to their antiquated design. They were originally intended for use in a more spacious age, when drymen could endeavor to keep a big circle around them temporarily rainless as they moved forward, one knows not why. Umbrella firms, notably Knirps, have performed wonders in packaging the unopened umbrella. But push the button and, snap, out comes that same monstrous, huge, circular offensive weapon. Someday somebody *must* invent a new, narrowly rectangular umbrella, perhaps pointed, front and back, like an upside-down steamship—or maybe it could be reduced to the circular dimensions of a small frying pan.

Somerset Maugham described tropical rains in a fashion that no temperate zoner can ever forget: "Not like our soft English rain that drops gently on the earth; it was unmerciful and somehow terrible; you felt in it the malignancy of the primitive powers of nature. It did not pour, it flowed. It was like a deluge from heaven, and it rattled on the roof of corrugated iron with a steady persistence that was maddening. Sometimes you felt that you must scream if it did not stop, and then suddenly you felt powerless, as though your bones had suddenly become soft; and you were miserable and hopeless. . . . You felt that the heavens must at last be empty of water, but still it poured down, straight and heavy, with a maddening iteration."

We human animals are terribly dependent upon the elements, and we need especially to *hear* the rain when it rains. One of the sad things about big-city apartments is that, between the big glass and concrete blocks that row on row mark the places where we live our "home" lives, there is no place to let the *sound* of the falling rain in, except for the penthouse or duplex on the top floor: everybody else listens to the tread of the human footprints or the muffled sound of furniture being restationed on the floor above.

"Rain, rain, go away, come again some other day!" Anybody except a farmer with crops or a duck born to wetness is likely to pray the old nursery rhyme, because happy times are usually lived during sunshiny weather. But it is impossible to pin down proof that stormy weather begets doldrums, depression, dejection, riots, murder, and even suicide. Helmut E. Landsberg, former director of climatology of the U.S. Weather Bureau, has both faced and dodged the issue, in 1969, in *Weather and Health*: "Our mental attitude and our attention span change with the changes in the air environment. There is reason to believe that this is not entirely an effect of the constellation of temperature, humidity and wind. More subtle forces may well be at work at the same time. Some scientists have given such attributes to electromagnetic waves, originating from thunderstorms. Others have invoked the ions in the atmosphere. . . . One hypothesis surmises that there is an interaction between fluctuating electric fields and human brain waves." Dr. Landsberg's cautious overall gentle knot, tying us in with the sea of atmosphere at the bottom of which we dwell, is nevertheless a binding, powerful one: "Weather is proverbially fickle and each change in the weather requires an adaptation of the human body." One wonders, then, forever: Was it I, by mine own will and decision, or was it merely and greatly some supernal power of impersonality, that made me do this, that made *us* do this? How one hopes to be an individual, and how greatly meantime one despairs of the possibility. The brief poem "Love's Philosophy," by Percy Bysshe Shelley, is a remarkable explication of the hydrologic cycle that also relates mathematical, musical, and other scales and cycles to one another:

> The fountains mingle with the river
> And the rivers with the Ocean,
> The winds of Heaven mix for ever
> With a sweet emotion;
> Nothing in the world is single;
> All things by a law divine
> In one spirit meet and mingle.
> Why not I with thine?

The ultimate grand diapason performance of the sky waters is a thunderstorm, that great outpouring of lightning, rain, and sound that purifies the atmosphere and "fixes" nitrogen by combining it with oxygen and then raining its richnesses down to reimburse the earthlands and the seas. The 80 percent of nitrogen in the air that we breathe is inviolate—we cannot get at it, though it goes in and out of our lungs constantly, and we "bathe" in it by moving about. And so Father John Martin Scott expressed it, in *Rain—Man's Greatest Gift*, with fine fervency: "We are *fed* by lightning! Every time you see lightning-in-action, you are witnessing the continuing miracle of creation. Each time lightning flashes, it combines nitrogen and oxygen with the rain, which carries the 'fixed' nitrogen to the ground, where it helps enrich the soil."

The greatest wonder of the lightning-storm display is the realization that it can and often does kill and destroy. Shall one hide behind the door, under the bed, in the closet? Where are mama and papa? Let us hasten to crawl into bed with them and be safe!

From the first time of hearing lightning-thunder's *son et lumière,* clamor and lights, someone must gently lead us out to view the great electrical display. The simplest start, with a child, is first to make it a fun game: the sight of lightning reaches the viewer almost instantaneously; the thunder's sound travels at about 1,000 feet per second; so one can begin the introduction-to-lightning sky show by learning to count seconds after the terrifying flash until the thunder's rumble is heard, and thus guess the distance away. But one cannot try this mathematics game without remembering childhood terror, if it scared one back then. Usually the sound of the thunder does not reach more than five or six miles.

"Cloud electrification" is not yet thoroughly understood. In 1938 five sailplane enthusiasts rode their gliders up over the Rhön Mountains, in central Germany, straight into a mass of thunderclouds. They were sucked violently upward; all five parachuted out, and were then again carried up still farther, to perhaps 50,000 feet. Only one man lived—the other four lifeless bodies, after experiencing the heart of the thunderstorm, frozen stiff and probably encased in blocks of "living" ice, later hurtled down as part of the "rain" released by the tempest.

The forked, line-discharge lightning is the most familiar, but there are strange other kinds, notably ball lightning. My grandfather once came in out of the pasture after a "ball of fire" had passed over him and into a grove of trees, where it exploded gently.

Professor M. Toepler, a lightning specialist, has said that this type is relatively harmless, its current strength even below a single ampere. The puckish Ariel of lightninghood is St. Elmo's Fire, tiny blue lights that flicker harmlessly about high objects such as ships' masts when a lightning storm is imminent. Though usually innocuous, St. Elmo's Fire may have triggered the hydrogen-fire conflagration (hydrogen oxidizing) that destroyed the dirigible *Hindenburg*—showers of *rain* fell, the result of the "burning."

The usual death-dealing lightning flash reaches temperatures of up to 30,000 degrees Centigrade.

After the storm is over, the princess of all watery spectacles, a rainbow, follows. This is the loveliest of sky sights, a thaumaturgic miracle that perhaps only human eyes and senses are able to enjoy. Carl B. Boyer, in *The Rainbow from Myth to Mathematics,* wondered: "Does man, then, see the most beautiful rainbow? This question is difficult to answer, for sensitivity to light and color varies considerably from species to species. Insects, for example, presumably see colors in the rainbow which for us are not there, and they probably fail to note some of those familiar to us. . . . If fish pay any attention to the rainbow, they are more attracted by the inner colors." Dr. Boyer's final guess was that "no one can boast that the perception of the rainbow colors is satisfactorily understood. The whole question of what goes on between the eye and the brain when one sees a rainbow is pretty much in a state of flux. Will mankind tire of the endless search for understanding concerning the nature of reflection, refraction, interference, diffraction, and the physiological processes which operate when one views the rainbow?" I tire, very much, and would rather just go out after the storm, look up at the sky, and see one. In French Canada, a man once kindly wrote down for me the more lovely name for it, *arc-en-ciel,* and warned me that it is useless to get into the auto and begin driving frantically toward the end of the bow, seeking the pot of gold. It is as unreachable as the bluebird of happiness: the pot you should already have inherited from your papa; the bluebird you must catch for yourself.

"And it shall come to pass when I bring a cloud over the earth, that the bow shall be seen in the cloud, and I will remember my convenant; and the waters shall no more become a flood to destroy all flesh." The rainbow was God's awesome pledge to Noah: the beautiful *arc-en-ciel* meant no more need to construct arks. One can never remember the exact sequence in which the seven sacred colors appear—in the order of the spectrum, from the inside of the bow outward: violet, indigo, blue, green, yellow, orange, and red. To the Buddhists they stand for the seven planets, to the Christians the seven sacraments: world wonders are always counted by sevens, perhaps because of rainbows.

There are other miraculous seven-colored sky arches— fogbows, moonbows, and lovely waterfallbows, all faintly miraculous and unbelievable. Far more real are mirages—those shallow lakes of fictional water that appear on the hot summer highway, and that as mysteriously dry out and evaporate as we drive closer; the rich, green oasis that looms up over the sands, as you and your camel pursue an endless desert journey, and disappears as you lope over the nearest dune; the weird Fata Morgana that causes sailors to see a beautiful seaport way up in the sky sometimes when they are passing through the Strait of Messina. In the Arctic and Antarctic, explorers dogsledding over ice fields have often beheld distant, towering ice-covered peaks, which fade and flatten out as they approach. And in Paris, *citoyens* sometimes see a second Tour Eiffel standing on its head directly above the usual one. Now *there* is a prestidigitatorial sight which, if the French National Tourist Office could guarantee to produce for all visitors, would double the number of *curieux* visitors to the Ville de Lumière!

Nature had whirling dervishes twirling long before men began the sacred dances. Updriven rotating updrafts of air, triggered by daytime heating of the ground, are called thermals. Most cannot be seen, since they are but wind; but dust devils *can* be seen. They start rotating, either clockwise or counterclockwise, by mere chance, a gust of wind moving around some object on the landscape. Suddenly the dance is begun, and you can watch the whirling mystery of dust and sand as it twirls up-up-upward as high as a mile. Sea gulls and other heavy-bodied birds learn in their youth to glide freely on the uprising thermals, and someday men of our new air age will have learned some secret avian vision so that men wearing wings can learn to take advantage of the thermal convection and convective air currents over the high places.

Tornadoes are the dust devils' older and more dangerous big brothers, towering funnels of water droplets mixed with dust and other debris. Almost all tornadoes spin counterclockwise, sometimes as fast as 400 miles per hour, meantime making a racket like "a thousand railway trains" or "a million bees," to which will soon probably be added "a flight of 747's." When an ordinary passenger gets accidentally trapped on the edge of a big jet plane's windy discharge, there's some faint idea of what a tornado's force may be. Will Keller, a Midwestern farmer residing in "tornado alley," had the honor—and horror—of observing the *inside* of the tube of a tornado. When it passed over his storm cellar in 1930, the siphoning end had "lifted" momentarily, and so was not sucking in, else farmer Keller would have performed a Judy Garland sky act on the spot. It was hollow, he said, maybe 100 feet in diameter, and the inner vortex walls were lighted by constant lightning flashes that zigzagged from side to side; the walls kept giving birth to smaller vortices that then broke away. Nobody yet knows much about tornadoes, for obvious reasons. Maybe the air inside that great, puissant, twisting, uncomfortable, searching tube is even *dry* and perhaps even being rushed downward. Nobody knows yet, and nobody has yet got up the foolish courage to investigate *in situ* the inside of this perilous tube. As exciting as this inside view sounds, it doesn't appeal to the sightseer in search of the unusual: there's too much danger that the landscape, in this case, might actually engulf and intromit the investigator. It is like attempting to peer down into the very esophagus of the watery sea-god Poseidon—something any god would surely resent.

The worst of all the strange termagant sky-storm creatures ever bred up out of the South Atlantic Ocean witches' cauldron was a hurricane misnamed Camille. She came down like an Assyrian on the U.S. Gulf of Mexico coastline-fold for a billion-dollar disaster take in 1969, and wound up causing a flood on the James River, in Virginia, before finally taking off to die at sea. "The greatest storm of any kind that has ever affected this nation," said Dr. Robert H. Simpson, chief of the National Hurricane Center in Miami, giving recognition to this watery monster from the South Atlantic deeps. The sheer power of water vapor drawn up into the skies, when it goes awry according to human standards, is something that has to do, apparently, with the normal functioning of the Planet Water's economy. The oceans' verges need room along the shore to play around with, and rivers require margins for flood and other fevers; perhaps the huge sky-water economy also requires its own kind of extra, marginal living space.

Camille was a misnomer for such a vicious storm. When dealing with a shrewish virago of such superlative, windy force, why not name her for the most historic female character who really warrants the comparison? For example, Xanthippe, the wife of philosopher Socrates, who was the great no-prize, antiheroine of all the ages—as nagger, crosspatch, fire lady, and supremely unpleasant wife to come home to. The 1969 hurricane could well have been named after this historic lady as a symbol of her perpetual clashing contrariness.

On the other hand, since there is always the suspicion that an Amazon is a mannish woman, a warrioress who in her heart would much rather perhaps be a warrior, it is meantime an insult to all elegant, soft, and genteel femininity to name these superstorms after the ladies. Rather, they should be called after male warriors—Achilles, Bolivar, Charlemagne, and so on. The 1969 superhurricane could perhaps, rather than Xanthippe, have been named after the most evil of male warriors and antiheroes—Attila, "the scourge of God."

Every schoolchild has read John Greenleaf Whittier's "Snowbound." It is a wonderful come-to-life experience to visit the old farm, in Haverhill, Massachusetts, where he lived the experience. He expressed perhaps as well as anyone, in that strange, terse, puritanical vein of poesy, the magical form of water that so mysteriously and suddenly turns our world into winter:

> In tiny spherule traced with lines
> Of Nature's geometric signs,
> In starry flake, and pellicle,
> All day the hoary meteor fell;
> And, when the second morning shone,
> We looked upon a world unknown. . . .
> The old familiar sights of ours
> Took marvellous shapes; strange domes and towers. . . .

After we have beheld water in the form of clouds parading through the sky overhead in as many remarkable forms and shapes—paladins or prodigiosities—as our own imagination can relate it to, now suddenly we get to see our own everyday surrounding world of mundane objects and places turned into a magical kingdom of differences, merely by being clothed over with the fragile metallic form of water.

Today's proponents of various drugs for quick trips, journeys, and visits to a make-believe land of beautiful wonders claim that we need not even look out the window to behold a pleasure dome in Xanadu. After all, that's how S. T. Coleridge created his most beautiful of all poems, on drugs. But like Picasso, who knew first his classical art, producing it exquisitely for long years before he set off into the world of the abstract, Coleridge had studied and lived with nature for an interminable time before he ventured to hit the hemp and, in almost frightening beauty through its use, create a domicile for Kubla Khan. Then someone rang the doorbell, in mid-written-down mid-creation, and the rest (he said much more was in his head) vanished. Even the fragment is a rare treasure, like Greenleaf's mirage make-believe glimpse through the window at a world transformed by snow.

Whittier's father, a strict man of little humor, put him to work digging out paths, whereas most kids set out for pleasure either sliding down hills or ski-hiking across the strange, changed countryside. With snowshoes you must clump-clump-clump along through the snow, whereas with skis you slide-glide—ever so much easier and more fun. Corydon Bell has expressed the difference: "The simplest of early snow-travel equipment were snowshoes, which merely supplied the traveler with a webbed, oversize shoe-sole snow cover. The swift flight of runners attached to the feet, as they glide over the frozen surfaces, involves a bit more of physics. In skating, the weight of a man's body is concentrated over the tiny area of the runner. The pressure of the runner on the ice creates enough friction to produce thawing, and the thaw-water provides continuous lubrication between skate and ice. The mechanics of skiing are entirely different. On skis, body weight is distributed over a relatively large area. Friction from pressure is seldom sufficient to melt a track. When skis glide lightly over powder snow or over a cover of granular firn snow, loose ice crystals roll past one another under the ski tread with somewhat of a ball-bearing action. On the other hand, the sharp points of newly fallen stellar crystals offer amazing friction and resistance to a ski surface, no matter how carefully waxed."

Skis are holy wood. The fact that new plastics have nowadays taken over (in their manufacture) does not alter this: skis may even be the very oldest of all man-the-toolmaker's inventions. After all, he began to become a high-class, superior-to-ordinary-animals sophisticate, a sentient being capable of deductive reasoning, abstract perplexing-out, and ratiocination of problems only after he had moved physically way up north from the tropics into the cold-climate latitudes, and begun to chase the little foxes and the gigantic mammoths through snow country.

Skis just *have* to have predated hoes or plows, since man the hunter hunted for many long ages before he got around to teaching his languid wife to get out of the cave and plant gardens. ("But I have to stay home and do nothing else but raise the kids," one can hear the cave walls ringing to her nesty nonsense.)

In various Scandinavian museums there are skis still in existence that are more than 7,000 years old—not made of leftover barrel staves, but remarkably like the present-day thing in careful design and beautiful turning of the wood flesh. Alas for the barrel-stave concept, for this may prove that venery, the pursuit of game, long predated viniculture, the enjoyment of the wine of the vine.

The beauty of winter and snow has always been associated, in our strange Christian-commercial society, with the extraordinary beautification—approaching beatification—of the Christmas season. St. Nicholas and St. Christopher may have been derogated and desanctified in 1969, but by now Sts. Nicholas and Bing of Crosby have become too integral a part of our White Christmas legend and annual revelry to be put down.

Not many years ago, country folk went to the woods for Christmas greens to decorate their homes. More and more, we turn to artificial greens, even make-believe Christmas trees and artificial snow. Perhaps this is as well, for thus the wildwood does not get torn to bits annually. So much of Christmas is genuinely make-believe, to begin with, that one cannot too casually or caustically holler about calling a halt to the industry of Christmas giving. Most department-store sales are made in the period just before Christmas, when the spirit of free spending and giving is healthily rampant. But however did the Holy Child, Jesus Christ, born in a smelly stable in the hot Holy Land, ever get associated with that North Pole character Kris Kringle, who, as St. Nicholas, also originally lived in the warm climate of the Near East—and with the winter world of fir trees, snow and notably reindeer?

The world dreams of a White Christmas, what Clement C. Moore dreamed up in the beautiful "Visit from St. Nicholas." One's heart begins to beat faster, just reading:

> When what to my wondering eyes should appear,
> But a miniature sleigh and eight tiny reindeer
> With a little old driver, so lively and quick,
> I knew in a moment it must be St. Nick.

The sleigh is "full of toys and St. Nicholas too," but what interests one most, as a snow student, is the reindeer. How and when did the Christmas myth ever expand so as to encompass reindeer, those far-northern branch-nibbling tiny lovelies who do not have wings and don't fly? *But for St. Nick they do!* Snow is somehow especially associated with make-believe. A "snow job" is the lies people tell you. But "snow" is also a slang word for cocaine or heroin—the ultimate in dangerous drugs that always end by taking-destroying those who began by enjoying (and being enjoyed by) them. A travesty, this use of pure snow's innocent name! And snow all alone is dreary without Santa. Robert Service's far-north trapper's Christmas was awful:

> It's mighty lonesome-like and drear
> No Santa Claus to make believe
> Just snow and snow, and then more snow.

Christmas envelops everybody but old Scrooge (finally even getting to him) in a great welter of snowy sentiment, with usually the Villon wonderment, *"Ou sont les neiges d'antan?"*—Christmases aren't as snowy as they used to be.

Reindeer are an important part of existence (more commercial than Christmas) all around the snowy Arctic perimeter of human activity—ordinary-sized deer from Scandinavia across the Siberian wilderness and over northern Canada (called caribou there), but tiny in far-north extreme Arctic places such as Novaya Zemlya and Spitsbergen. These delicate creatures, who surely belong to the lore of landing gently on rooftops, were most likely the first domesticated of all wild animals after dogs. In Lapland, reindeer go out to graze all day, returning (on their own) to their human masters at nightfall.

Most far northern animals exult to roll in the snow. For if no enemy is about, here is a time for fun and play. Perhaps man, along with learning to milk reindeer and ride on skis, also first learned to *play*, by living in and sliding on the northern snows.

Much of our snow voyaging is vicarious, like most human experiences (since we know how to read and to listen). And so two of my best snow trips ever were made with a little girl named Heidi and with a snowbird named John Fry. You may have taken the same journey with Heidi and will remember. Otherwise, hold on tight, Marie, and listen to Johanna Spyri's 1880's description of the little girl high in the Alps: "The grandfather got into the hand-sleigh and lifted Heidi onto his lap; then he wrapped her up in the sack, that she might keep nice and warm, and put his left arm closely round her, for it was necessary to hold her tight during the coming journey . . . the sleigh shot down the mountainside with such rapidity that Heidi thought they were flying through the air like a bird, and shouted aloud with delight."

In Janaury, 1969, Mr. Fry, editor of *Ski* magazine, described a way-out midwinter journey into the Bugaboo wilderness of the Canadian Rockies by helicopter. Think of it! Nobody is building a highway. No visitors are altering the local ecology of nature. Just visitors as from another planet landing on the frozen portion of the Planet Water, in a mountain fastness where awaits "for skiers what bagging a polar bear in Alaska has come to mean to hunters: the end, the nirvana of the sport, the inmost thing to do."

"Some of our skiers are probably scared silly at first by the steepness, the crevasses, the avalanche potential and the sheer isolation of the place," Mr. Fry's host, Hans Gmoser, described this miracle of arriving at the top of a snow-covered range of mountains unvisited by other human creatures, and then joyously cavorting downhill—60,000 vertical feet of skiing in a few days, with a helicopter to carry you back upstairs every time, instead of waiting in line for a ski tow amid the typical slope congestion of any ski resort complex. This *is* way out and away, a grown-up experience of what little Heidi enjoyed in her grandpa's protective arms.

Snow is the poetic form of water, making what Emerson called "frolic architecture" in the strange shapes and imagined air castles given to everyday things. Poetry has been called the gay science (*gai saber*), because of the sprightly poeticizing of the gallant troubadours of Provence. And what contrast is the gay science to the dismal science, which economics is contrastingly recognized to be. The best proof of this is to read any line written by an economist—even so jaunty and knowledgeable a wit as John Kenneth Galbraith, and then turn to Francis Thompson's brief rhapsody to a snowflake: "What heart could have thought you? Fashioned so purely, fragilely, surely, from what Paradisal imagineless metal, too costly for cost?" The gay science and the frolic architecture have it, obviously, all over the dismal sciences of economics and engineering!

In the basic structure of snow, the individual hexagons, none alike, of stellar, starlike crystals, are formed by sublimation within high, cold clouds, the free molecules of water vapor turning directly into snow crystals, gas into solid, with no in-between liquid, watery, raindrop state. This simplest form of snow is still 98 percent air, and when it falls, it lies loosely, the ends of the ice particles barely touching. "Wild snow," as it is called, is an excellent insulation, in which rabbits and field mice may nestle in snug warmth, protected from the real winter cold outside their dainty igloos.

In all our world, made possible by water, nothing ever actually touches anything else. None of the billions of cells in our bodies ever touch one another; they're separated by a thin layer of intercellular liquid. Corydon Bell, in *The Wonder of Snow*, explains that this watery phenomenon is also true of snowflakes, that "the ice surface of a snow crystal is always surrounded by a microscopic 'atmosphere' of freely moving, restless water molecules."

Wild snow in time settles somewhat into powder snow, losing some 20 percent of its air, finally turning, via firnification, into old snow, firn, granules that have 20 to 50 percent air, which continues to diminish as the snow slowly settles and turns more and more into ice. About 12 percent of the planet's surface today lies beneath glaciers and ice caps, which represent only about 4.5 percent of the planet's total waters, an amount quite reduced from the massive snow cover of perhaps a fourth of all land surfaces during the last Ice Age.

Eighty-five percent of the permanent glacier lies over Antarctica, the snowy continent, and 10 percent atop Greenland, the snowy island (or pair of islands), with the remaining 5 percent on the highest peaks of mountains all over the planet—each a sight-seeing lagniappe for mountain climbers who reach the top. Few of us are likely to attempt Mount Everest, Planet Water's highest, or McKinley, North America's highest, but it is far more interesting to climb, or even just to *look at* and dis-believe in, the high ones near the equator, where somehow per-petual snows exist beneath the strongest rays of the sun, up on Kilimanjaro, in Africa, or Ixtacihuatl, in Mexico. Up—up—up one climbs, presently crossing the timberline, presently crossing the snow line, above which lies permanent, perpetual snow and ice. In Spitsbergen, up ever so far north at 78 degrees north lat-itude, the snow line is right down at sea level, whereas in

India's Himalayas, it is up at higher than 19,000 feet. Snows sometimes beget some sort of madness in otherwise rational men. There's the strange, imaginary creature who haunts the upper levels of the Himalayas, the abominable snowman. Is it or isn't it for real, or is this merely another aspect of snow madness? Sometime when you are in New York, go up to 319 West 107th Street and look at some of the strange, mystical paintings, in the Nicolas Roerich Museum, of high Himalayan snowcapped mountaintops; right out of the paintings, you will be grabbed by something strange, crystalline, hiemal, hyperborean, a sense of shivering ecstasy. Somebody has suffered a snow change into something rich and strange, and if it reaches into you, then *you* are the sufferer—but vanquisher as well. Laurens van der Post, viewing the towering Himalayan skyline— youngest and highest range of mountains on the Planet Water, their very name means "abode of snow"—described them as "grand, splendid and radiant in their jewelry of ice and ermine of snow." A German wonderer, A. Miethe, who went on a zeppelin expedition over Spitsbergen's glaciers, wrote ecstatically: "The abundance of light and radiance pouring over these snow-fields, when the farthest peaks stand out delicately against the greenish-blue sky, when the sun shines warm on face and neck and the soft gurgling of the melted snow fills the air, over the glaciers and precipitous peaks, rouses the heart to delighted enjoyment of nature and banishes all thoughts of the sad past of these regions and their hostility to man." Miethe anthropomorphizes antihuman feelings into the snows and glaciers much as Maugham gave human perceptions and emotions to the tropical rains. In contrast, Admiral Richard Byrd's diary of a 1934 winter spent in icy solitude near the South Pole was almost wholly concerned with a leakage of exhaust gases from his heater, a subject that could as well have been written from within the basement of a garage or an automobile tunnel. Too many of us do our sight-seeing from inside vehicles, so that our experience concerns dirty windshields, not the tremendous Nature thing outside, and we thus all too often get only a mechanistic, Byrd's-eye "look" which actually reveals nothing beyond motor-exhaust troubles, as though pollution had become scenery.

Ice is that other form of water, the solid state that is, almost mysteriously, lighter than liquid water, unlike almost all other substances, which when they freeze become heavier. If water became heavier, and sank rather than floating when frozen, the Planet Water would long ago have become a dead planet: instead, life lives on beneath the floating-ice frozen surfaces of seas and lakes and rivers. Ice is that form of frozen water which was discovered in 1969 to exist in the lower than minus-400 degrees Fahrenheit ultracold blackness of outer space.

Glaciers, rivers of ice, flow unbelievably slowly, yet when one visits their snout, where they drop off, or calve, great icebergs into the sea, things are lively enough. When American explorers asked the Hoonah kwan Indians about the bay of glaciers, which they believed to be nearby, they were told that this was a place of thunderous noises and evil spirits, and to be avoided. But John Muir didn't turn back. It was the end of October, 1879. How one would like to have been with him when he climbed a ridge, the clouds began to clear, and "beneath their gray fringes I saw the berg-filled expanse of the bay, the feet of the mountains that stand about it and the imposing fronts of five huge glaciers . . . with benumbed fingers I sketched what I could see of the landscape, and wrote a few lines in my notebook." Around the campfire that night, his Indian guides talked quietly "in tones that accorded well with the wind and waters and growling torrents about us, telling sad old stories of crushed canoes, drowned Indians and hunters frozen in snowstorms."

The first overnight lodgings for tourists were built alongside the bay in 1966, and today's visitors can explore Glacier Bay's waters (second-largest unit in the national park system) by cruise boat, beholding the birth of icebergs with attendant huge waves, in a world peopled with sea lions, porpoises, and sometimes whales. Upon the rocks and islands of this icy world are vast colonies of cormorants, puffins, and even eagles.

Temperate zoners like to go southward, during the cold winter months, for a bit of torrid sunshine over the edge of the Tropic of Cancer. But as the spring days lengthen into summer, one will gain far more sunshine by turning around and heading northward, up over the Arctic Circle into the frigid zone, where the sun shines 24 hours a day for as long as four months. The best time to go is during the weeks immediately before or after

June 21, the summer solstice, longest day of the year, when the North Pole is tilted to the greatest degree toward the light of the sun. Scandinavia is an especially good place to celebrate this strange season when "the planet has no eyelids." There are midnight-sun voyages and flights to many far north cities. Hammerfest, northernmost town in Europe, has midnight sun from May 13 to July 29; Spitsbergen, that way-north island at the 80th parallel of latitude, from April 20 through August 24. Over on Greenland's west coast, one can bask in midnight sunlight and watch polar bears frolicking and glaciers calving icebergs. Greenland, three times the size of Texas, is seven-eighths under ice, impacted snow piled up as high as 10,000 feet deep—the great white desert, a giant Gibraltar. I flew over it in the wrong kind of light, for others tell me that you can see lovely pastel tints on the upper slopes if the reflected sunlight and mists are right. I saw only virgin whiteness, but with many strangely bright frozen lakes of pastel shades.

The largest icebergs are of frozen sea ice and come loose from the Antarctic mainland. One was once measured to be 90 miles long! Usually these monsters float only into the Great South Ocean, where only the migrating penguins are likely to be disturbed. Down from the Arctic into the main shipping lanes of the North Atlantic come from 300 to 500 icebergs a year; they are traced and watched by the International Ice Patrol. When one sees a western Greenland glacier giving painful birth to a baby iceberg, if one could follow the heifer on her life journey (unlike animals or plants, diminishing all the way), she would lead you northward along the Greenland coast, westward across Baffin Bay, and southward along the Labrador coast, where she would either go sturdily down the ocean side of Newfoundland and out into the shipping lanes or, a maverick, turn in by the Belle Isle Strait between Newfoundland and the Canadian mainland, and wait to wreck or alarm ships within the Gulf of St. Lawrence.

The Ice Patrol was started in 1914, two years after the "unsinkable" *Titanic* struck an iceberg and went down with a loss of 1,500 lives. That was a very bad year, for at least 1,000 icebergs "came down" from the north. Not cold weather or temperature, but heavy winds affect the number of dangerous bergs —adversely; if the winds are strong enough, they will blow most

of the icebergs ashore in the Arctic before they can sail south.
Arctic icebergs run up to 50,000,000 cubic feet of hugeness,
weighing 1,500,000 tons, but will have melted down to about
5,000,000 cubic feet by the time they sail into North Atlantic
waters, where sailors call them by their shapes—"solids,"
"growlers," "flat-tops," twin-peaked "dry-docks," and, in caravans, a "herd."

Waterton-Glacier International Peace Park, in the mountains of *two* nations, is a wilderness in the high Rockies of Montana and Alberta so full of frozen rivers, flowing rivers, and
tumbling waterfalls that John Muir advised visitors to take a
month for viewing: "The time will not be taken *from* the sum
of your life, it will definitely lengthen it and make you truly
immortal." As far as man is concerned, these mid-mountain glaciers are like working ants, since all their waters flow usefully
into lakes and rivers, whereas the butterfly icebergs of Glacier
Bay go straightway off to sea, doing man no definable good.

Many visitors to Glacier Bay request the captain of their
sight-seeing boat to let them toot the whistle, thus turning loose
a million tons of baby iceberg from the nearest glacier, and allowing them to feel like a Napoleon or Alexander the Great.

Alas, Robert E. Howe, superintendent of Sitka and Glacier
Bay national monuments, is faced with the fact that "practically
every boater who visits Glacier Bay has, somewhere or other,
heard about the possible effects of loud or resonant sounds on
tidewater glacier fronts. Naturally, almost everyone tries one
sound or another hoping to induce blocks of ice to fall from the
glacier. In our experiences, most manmade noises have little or
no effect. And so we suspect that an active glacier is most re-
sponsive to things which produce low-concussions such as explosives, earthquakes, thunder, etc. The ice in a rapidly moving
glacier is characteristically unstable. Crevassing produces often
delicately balanced pinnacles (*seracs*) of ice which can be toppled by the slightest disturbance."

What is delusion in Glacier Bay was genuine horror and fear
of instant death in the high Alps. Both Hannibal and Napoleon
passed through the Alpine passes during midwinter on tiptoe
and whispering, lest the mere sound of their troops' voices set
the snows tumbling down. The sight of one in action would be
one of the great experiences, but vicarious awe may be terrify-

ing enough. The master of description of natural violences, Frank W. Lane, wrote: "The snow in a big avalanche may have a volume of over a million cubic yards and weigh a million tons. Its movement is a combination of sliding, flowing and bouncing. This action sometimes pulverizes the snow into such fine particles that it penetrates closed doors and windows, and sometimes suffocates people while they sleep."

"Avalanches come in every conceivable size, shape, and length . . . up to a monster like the Huascaran avalanche in the Peruvian Andes, over three million cubic yards. Depth hoar is one of his most dangerous enemies," Montgomery M. Atwater states in *The Avalanche Hunters* (1968). "Those coarse, rounded lumps of ice have no cohesion whatever, like having a layer of ball bearings . . . depth-hoar avalanches are the biggest and most destructive of all."

During the Dark Ages, as almost from the beginning, the mountains and high places, especially if covered with snow and ice, were regarded as dangerous and to be dreaded because of the evil spirits known to haunt them. Then, sometime during the eighteenth century, came an awakening to the strange, wild beauty of mountains, especially the snow-capped ones. Alpinism, mountain climbing as a sport, began to be practiced in the Chamonix Valley. People made journeys just to *look at* the Matterhorn, Mont Blanc, the Jungfrau, and all the other high wonders—and Europeans took to walking upon the high rivers of ice, of which the most famous was the Mer de Glace—a glacier "sea" formed by the junction of three glaciers on the side of Mont Blanc over the Chamonix Valley.

The most famous glacier visitor, whose journey was described in an 1860 play, *Le Voyage de Monsieur Perrichon*, by Eugène Labiche, wrote a commentary on the grandeur of glaciers (in the "diary" of the inn at Montanvert) that has had French schoolboys (and American students of French) laughing ever since: *"Que l'homme est petit quand on le contemple du haut de la Mère de Glace!"* His faux pas jeu de mots substitution of "mother" for "sea" is meantime perhaps more right than we who've laughed at him. The Ocean Sea is our mother, and the Sea of Ice, away up there in the Alps, in the hydrologic cycle, is the mother of the sea. M. Perrichon, blundering, pompous, uninformed, the sightseer with absolutely *no* scientific, statistical, or pretentious aesthetic preknowledge of what he'd gone to see that might spoil the pristine innocence of his astounded joy in viewing—ah, here is the ideal companion on a trip to the sea, to a river, into a snowstorm, or for a hike upon a glacier! We meet far too few Perrichons in our travels.

The first glacier scholars were curious about *erratics*—rocks which appeared to be out of place, obviously moved there, Biblical students recognized, by Noah's flood.

Noahites have so many things to contend with! "His" flood obviously *did* take place, not once but many times, a thousand miles downriver from Mount Ararat, just as annual floods were taking place down the Nile, the Mississippi, and all the other busy arteries of Planet Water. The wonderful thing about scientific investigators is their discovery of and ability presently to recognize the *new thing*. The "something else" that had been moving erratic rocks around was of course the great ice sheets, a different kind of Noachian experience, *ice* floods.

For thousands of years, the farmers of the Nile Valley lived on the annual flood of the great river, for it deposited silt carried all the way north from the Ethiopian mountains. The vast acres of rich topsoil in the American north-central states were deposited in the great ice flood of the last Ice Age, an incalculable gift, or theft, from Canada. Abraham Lincoln called the great central region "the New World Nile Valley."

The greatest snowflake specialist of all time was a quiet, unobtrusive man who was the same sort of gentle scholar as was Champollion, discoverer of the language of ancient Egyptian hieroglyphics. Champollion's greatest hour came when, as an old man, he got to journey into Egypt and see the long-ago messages, which he had spent a lifetime translating, actually inscribed on temple walls. The Snow Man of Jericho, Wilson Alwyn Bentley, spent a lifetime closely examining his beloved snowflakes. In 1880, at the age of fifteen, he was given a microscope and began examining snow crystals posed along the railing of his family's northern Vermont farmhouse front porch. Thenceforth, this remarkable man was stuck on snowflakes. For more than forty years, he took photomicrographs of them. *Snow Crystals,* published in 1931, contained 2,000 of the more than 6,000 pictures he made. As a snowflake enthusiast, which should one do: look at the book or go up to Jericho, Vermont, and honor the place where he lived? One suspects that the best way to enjoy what he enjoyed, and in the same fashion, is to take a microscope and go out and look at snowflakes on one's own.

There is a funny-sad side story to Bentley's snowflake mania. He at first tried to reproduce snowflakes by his own drawings. He was not a very good draftsman. His situation is comparable to that of Charles Lutwidge Dodgson, who first attempted to make his own drawings (not very good) to go with his projected history of *Alice's Adventures Underground*. Dodgson/Carroll was lucky enough to then encounter John Tenniel, whose exquisite on-target views so well expose visually what the author portrayed in words. Bentley's similar good luck and good fortune was the camera, which made it possible for him to capture the beauty of an innumerable constellation of exquisite snowflakes.

The ice king of all time was Frederic Tudor of Boston, a man who so loved ice that he cut it off the tops of ponds and rivers all over New England in order to ship it to the far *warm* regions of the world. What a paradox this is, that the people of each climate seek a beverage of the opposite temperature, and that this makes for considerable commercial industry—the lighting of fires and the chilling of ice. Après skiers in the Alps and Rockies desire hot toddies, while residents of the tropics take as considerable joy in iced mint juleps and frosty planter's punches. Shakespeare struck the irrationality of the out-of-season satisfaction, "O! who can hold a fire in his hand, by thinking of the frosty Caucasus? Or wallow in December snow, by thinking on fantastic summer's heat?" Robert Service's Sam McGee had been "so cursed cold, chilled clean through to the bone," in the far north that he begged his friend to cremate him. Later, after the friend had stuffed frozen Sam into a fiery furnace, he couldn't forbear peeking. "In the heart of the furnace roar, Sam wore a smile you could see a mile, and he said, 'Please close that door. It's the first time I've ever been warm!' "

It was this kind of joy that iceman Tudor brought, with his Boston ice, to tropical customers who for the first time discovered such pleasures as ice cream and iced carbonated drinks, made infinitely more desirable and enjoyable by the contrariety that they were consumed beneath the rattling of palm tree leaves in a balmy Caribbean climate.

Many citizens of the Planet Water's torrid belt were to enjoy for the first time the delicious surprise of cool and icy nourishments, as Tudor's ice ships sailed farther and farther. In the past, only the great and powerful could afford to have ice carried down from the mountains for their sherbets. Perhaps the most famous sherbet serving of all time was at the meeting between Saladin and Richard the Lion-hearted in the Holy Land, a romantic consummation of icy splendor. No wonder Richard later urged his sister to change her religion and marry Salah-ed-Din, the host with the most ambrosial surprise for a guest wearing a suit of metal in a hot climate. A similar gracious serving of icy sherbets, among today's bitter Near East rivals, at a Sinai Peninsula desert gathering, could create a 1970's miracle!

The first Tudor shipment, 130 tons of ice packed in loose hay, went from Boston to St.-Pierre, Martinique, in 1783. Tudor, who had chopped his first ice off the family pond in Saugus, near Boston, later reached out to "mine" it from lakes and ponds all over New England, even from the holy waters of Walden Pond, as well as from the Merrimac, Androscoggin, and other rivers far about. Ice-cutting machinery was invented, and pine sawdust was found to provide the best insulation.

Oh, the wonder of seeing ice for the first time! A customer in Bombay demanded his money back after his cake of the strange stuff had melted in the hot sunlight. Another inquired of Tudor whether this curious toothsome (tooth-numbing) stuff grew on trees or was perhaps mined out of some permafreeze depths of the earth. The annual shipments grew to 200,000 tons, carried out of Boston, to the East and West Indies, the Far East, South America, Persia, and India. Presently Tudor began also shipping Baldwin apples—what an exotic fruit to eat in tropical Havana! And he envisioned the day when tropical fruits would be reverse-shipped north to Boston. Tudor always took special delight in his title of World Ice King. In his old age he wrote in his *Ice House Diary*: "The frost covers the windows, the boys run in the snow, winter rules and $50,000-worth of ice floats for me on Fresh Pond." Not exactly Thoreau, or

Thompson, but this man also *loved* ice in his own fashion, and he brought its pleasure to thousands.

Today we plug an electric refrigerator into the wall, or turn on a gas one, and so have remarkably quick and extremely unromantic ice, in neat cubes, no matter what climate zone of the Planet Water we happen to inhabit. One does not even need an ice pick anymore; instead, there's that remarkable wand, the ice tapper, which shatters ice cubes by some strange magic that has to do with the metallic form of water's behavior when thumped. In a very small way, this ice-cube shattering is an imminence of power comparable to the false hope of blowing the ship's whistle to start the birth of a million-ton iceberg baby from mother glacier. Ah, the proud insolence of power! Napoleon crowning himself! You and I smashing the perfection of a small cube of ice (as exquisitely square as an egg is oval perfection, a mini-imitation of Mother Planet Water herself), by merely tapping it with a magic wand!

It's all so wonderfully convenient, our age of "artificial" ice, manufactured in refrigerators that resemble our modern skyscrapers of glass. The ice cubes, the refrigerators, and the buildings all resemble one another remarkably—so cold, so expedient, so extremely *unnatural*, so unscenic and unexciting, so *invented*. I love conveniences, too. And so I find thankworthy Jacob Perkins and F. P. E. Carré for their primary inventive skill in bringing about ice-making machines.

X Playing with Water

CHILDREN learn from birth the religious ecstasy of playing in water. Nowadays this is due partly to our mothers' fantastic dedication and devotion to cleanliness. Because the mommies spend countless hours bathing their babies, the newborn inevitably begin to feel as at home and "safe" within their bathwater pools as in their cradles. But tiny kids love *best* of all to be allowed to play in mud puddles—to sit right down and bedeck, bedazzle, and bedizen themselves with the rich goo of the wet earth. A great work for infants, introducing them to the fun of all this, is *A Hole Is to Dig*, in which Ruth Krauss expresses in genuine tot language the eternal verity of childhood: "Mud is to jump in and slide in and yell doodleedoodleedoo." And so it is! Doodleedoodleedoo-oo!

Another impressive Brillat-Savarin type of work for the young, Marjorie Winslow's *Mud Pies and Other Recipes*, gives the real muddy-gritty both for little girls and little boys. For young ladies, dashing recipes for making mud pies: "These mud pies keep indefinitely and are good to have on hand for impromptu entertaining." But for the little boys, recipes for making pie-throwing pies: "Follow the first step in making Mud Pies, only make it gloppier. Throw!" Here's the beginning of modern civilization: haute cuisine, warfare, and, when the Mesopotamians began forming the mud into clay booktablets, high literature! It all began in the mud: the first great modern cities were built upon muddy foundations and of mud.

Egyptians still proudly recognize that "the first men were born of the mud of the Nile."

All our vegetables—the lettuces and love apples and radishes —are grown somewhere "else" in the mud of market gardens, where few of us ever get near the mud anymore; we merely pick up the produce wrapped in neat plastic packages at the local supermarket. How far away the mud is, for civilized people today.

At how young an age does a child begin blowing bubbles, those bits of water and soap that billow up into the sky, opalescent with mystical rainbow colors? When does he start wondering why he cannot cling to them and sail away—oh, power of levitation—into the faraway places of mystery and fun?

Robert Paul Smith's *"Where Did You Go?" "Out." "What Did You Do?" "Nothing"* told of an American water custom that must have pleased the plain WASP Protestant gods of a generation ago: "When I was a kid, you watered the lawn by standing there and holding the hose and spraying it back and forth. In arcs, and in fountains, and in figure eights, and straight up in the air, energetically, and dreamily and absent-mindedly, washing the walk, and the porch and the window screen and your father in the living room reading the paper. You dug trenches with the stream from the hose and filled milk bottles and garbage cans and the back seats of parked cars. And if it was a grownup watering the lawn, you hung around until he said, 'Why don't you kids go ask your mothers if you can get in your bathing suits and I'll spray you,' and you pounded home and got into the scratchy wool bathing suit and pounded back and there, I tell you, was Heaven on earth, getting wet on a front lawn on purpose."

Alas, Smith also presented today's cutoff mechanistic answer to and demise of this kind of lost boyhood fun: "Now we have sprinklers that are scientific and crawl along a hose, spraying a predetermined pattern." Once at a farm in upstate New York, I encountered a man who each night "hosed down" (his term) his two tiny nephews, whom he was tending while his brother and their mother vacationed away, freed from their care. One night, while they were dancing under the hose shower, one little boy discovered fireflies on the lawn and exclaimed, "Look, the stars are down here, and they're dancing!"

Today, big cities cannot afford to let lawn lovers play too casually with water. In mid-Manhattan, in the midsummer of 1969, New York's water resources commissioner warned residents that "excessive lawn watering and illegal openings of fire hydrants can cause dangerous loss of water pressure."

So how could city kids learn to play with water? Only a few days after the "warning," Clark Whelton wrote a stark story in the New York *Village Voice,* "Papo and the Hydrant: Lower East Side Summer," that is an Eastern big-city adventure comparable to the outdoor Wild West serials on TV. "Papo opened the hydrant for the first time on an airless Saturday afternoon. He removed his shirt and shoes and unscrewed the nozzle cover from the smaller of the two hydrant openings. Then he fitted the wrench to the valve nut on top of the hydrant and pushed. The water gushed up and out of its iron well and spilled into the sunlight. . . . The kids came off the sidewalk, dancing with anticipation. . . . A truck came down the block, slowed briefly while the driver rolled up the window on the hydrant side, then picked up speed. Papo jammed a beer can into the hydrant nozzle and as the truck came even with the hydrant a plume of water smacked the cab window and boomed along the aluminum van as the truck roared by." The bad guys must be driving the truck, see? Truck drivers are a kindly lot, and they usually go along with how a young city kid operating a nihilistic hydrant is still in search of his legitimate water gods. In Greece, somehow, an Olympic statue to/of Papo would indeed be part god. How does one properly honor and respect the eternal gods (no matter what you may call them) in a modern, dehumanized, dedeificated urban environment? Small boys become angry when they cannot honor the gods properly, and certainly the gods themselves must become angry, too, when an automated society denies to young boys and girls the means of dancing before them. The holy-fun thing is within them, whether they be suburban boys spraying water on a lawn of green grass or slum brothers throwing a torrent against the window of a passing truck, and how astounded all of them would be if they were told that this is a kind of religious dancing before his Lord. Later they just might begin to think so.

The ancient Greek proto-scientists recognized four basic elements—fire, air, earth, and water—each with an elemental guiding spirit: the salamander for fire, the sylph for air, the gnome for earth, and the undine for water. The human creature was also divided by the ancient rules of physiology into four different kinds of persons, depending upon the makeup of his contained body fluids: blood, sanguine; phlegm, phlegmatic; cholor (yellow bile), choleric; melancholy (black bile), melancholic. Empedocles defined these four "elements," and Thales suggested that all such forms of matter ultimately reduce to "the *moist*," recognizing that moisture *is* life.

Elsewhere I have discussed the tremendous elemental battle royal that is taking place constantly upon the surface of Planet Water among the three spheres of water, land, and air. The fourth primitive "element" has relentlessly and endlessly battled against the other three, and is, somehow, the eternal outsider. Since Prometheus first brought fire down from heaven (or, if you prefer, since man first learned to keep his cave fires burning), this miracle "element" has been our principal source of heat, power, and light, man's most powerful and provident friend—and, when out of control, his most dangerous enemy as well. Incomplete calefaction is a principal cause of pollution.

Everything that man has built, owned, or lived in has usually been made of flammable materials. "Better a small fire that warms than a great one that burns!" "FIRE!" is about the most dreaded and dreadful outcry of warning that civilized man can yawp in horrified alarm to awaken his neighbors. And *water* has always been the salvation from it.

Playing with water is one of the really great fun-things to do. But if one is combating fire, water's dreadful elemental enemy, then something of the gallantry of Sir Galahad, Young Lochinvar, and Lancelot also creeps in. There's nothing nonsensical about this. Fire destroys property worth billions of dollars, and takes thousands of lives annually. And so when a fireman "plays" a stream of water upon a raging fire, he is enacting a supreme gesture of humanity and brotherhood, rescuing maidens and infants from an inveterate and ruthless enemy, and saving homes and property. Of the 24,000 fire departments in our country, more than 22,000 are dependent on volunteer fire fighters. About 200,000 fire fighters are paid, but more than 1,000,000 are still volunteers. Ben Franklin, who started so many other organizations fundamental in American civilization, of course founded the first voluntary fire department, in Philadelphia in 1736. This was not the first fire department. Way back in 300 B.C., Ctesibius, in Alexandria, Egypt, invented a lightweight piston, an N-shaped device for sucking up water from a tub—the ancestor of *all* fire-fighting equipment for more than two millennia until the development of the modern rotary pump.

"Fire is a deceptively simple-looking beast," Paul C. Ditzel explained in a 1969 examination of *Firefighting.* "There is flame. We can feel the heat and see the smoke. Lurking in that smoke however are gases, including deadly carbon monoxide. After only two minutes of exposure to carbon monoxide gas, a person becomes totally paralyzed, even if completely awake. The death of most people who perish in fires is caused not by the flames, but rather by asphyxiation." Man's mightiest water toy, the all-time mechanical St. George for attacking the dragon of fire, is the New York City Fire Department's $875,000 Super Pumper. This monster machine can deliver up to 8,800 gallons per minute at a total pressure of 37 tons a minute, the water horsepower equivalent of twenty regular pumpers! When it was first used, in December, 1965, Deputy Chief Maurice Ratner claimed it made "a mighty splashing noise that sounded like Niagara Falls pouring into the building." A sight to behold, surely, for earnest viewers of water wonders, but fire buffs are begged to remain away from the fire-fighting action. In their own way, sightseers cluttering up roads leading to a conflagration are as bad as the lunatics who turn in false alarms. And so we should be satisfied with viewing Niagara, leaving the fire fighting and fire-conquered-by-water viewing to the firemen.

For smaller fires, it is interesting that firemen nowadays use "spray" streams that spread a fog of water droplets rather than a heavy stream of solid water—thus smothering the fire and meantime absorbing most of the lethal gases.

Fireboats put on the finest of all water displays when they shoot sky-high streams of water in all directions during welcoming ceremonies for a new ship's arrival for the first time in port. Viewers and visitors aren't in the fireboatmen's way. There's a limitless supply of water (fireboats use the brackish salt-fresh harbor waters). And the splendiferous pomp-and-water glory of these showboats, all shooting sprays which reach up to around 375 feet, is one of the greatest of all water wonders to behold. New York City, with the largest port in the United States, necessarily puts on the best of such water shows. Among its ten-unit fleet is the *Fire Fighter,* Planet Water's largest and most powerful fireboat, built thirty years ago at a cost of $1,000,000. It would cost more than twice the sum today, and meantime most waterfront fire departments have shifted to using a new type of small "jet" boat that is faster and infinitely more maneuverable.

The plunge of a diver into water is one of the great human actival mysteries. One's watching friends can tell what's right and wrong about it. Only the diver himself will never get to view his own swift entry down into the watery depths: at the key moment, he even shuts his eyes! At country fairs, men have long been high-diving from way up there on top of a ladder into relatively shallow tanks way down there so far below, while viewers hold their breath in ecstatic horror. Do those in the audience secretly wish he'll kill himself? Since 1966, from Memorial Day through Labor Day, Mrs. Patty Dolan, a tiny, 4-foot 10-inch lady, has been diving on horseback from a 40-foot-high platform into a 10-foot-deep water tank on the famous Steel Pier at Atlantic City, New Jersey. All summer long, she does this five times a day, seven days a week. She was trained by the original horseback diver, Lorena Carver, now ninety years old; Lorena began the horseback water act back in 1889. "I'm no longer afraid," Patty said in 1969, "but I'm always nervous. Whenever I climb up to the platform I say a little prayer that everything will come out all right." Hopefully, nobody in her audience wishes it won't.

The scariest dive is from the edge of the famous La Quebrada cliff at Acapulco, Mexico, out and down 135 feet over the outward-slanting cliff (a 21-foot *jut*), at 75 miles an hour, plunging into a narrow arm of the sea below. The opening chapter of Jim Thorne's *Guide to Adventure* is the outrageous, crazy story of Jim's own mad dive off this cliff. This was one of the outstanding and dramatic water feats of all time: "I gripped the edge of the rock with my toes and extended my arms for balance. Quickly, I bent deep, bringing back my arms. Then throwing my arms forward, I pushed out with all the strength in my legs.

I went into a rigid swan position and watched the water rush up to meet me. An instant before hitting, I brought my hands forward and locked my arms overhead, grasping my thumbs. I hit with incredible force."

Fairs and expositions have a log-flume ride that is experienced midway between the differing pleasures of performer and viewer: you ride this imitation hollowed-out log around a water path that ends with a swift plunge down a steep waterfall-rapids. I've thrilled to it, and puzzled, and find that the difference is that one is here a *passenger*—even as you slide down the cascade of moving water, you are a spectator rather than participant, and yet somehow *both*.

I am not putting down spectatorhood. Rooters and boosters at a game or competition are more *active* than we are when we read a book about an adventure and enjoy a vicarious thrill of personal accomplishment. At least they raise their voices and holler—and the mass sound may often drive a participant onward to victory. But there's no sweat on the hide of the man in the audience unless it be from the fear of losing his bet. Somehow, the spectator is losing out all the way on the fun of *doing the thing himself*, of truly experiencing it directly.

When one gets right down into the water to swim about, then water becomes real living, existence for real—buoyant, relaxed, free. Roger W. Wescott, examining the potential of *The Divine Animal* (man) in 1969, has hit upon a possible reason for the released joy experienced in swimming: "There are some mammals whose exuberant high spirits are rarely matched by any of their free-living wild congeners, much less by our self-domesticated species. The sportive creatures I have in mind are the aquatic mammals—such as otters, seals and porpoises—whose playful enjoyment of their water world is a never-ending pleasure to watch. In their case, physical environment alone explains much of their levity. For the buoyancy of water facilitates and encourages a quite literal buoyancy of behavior not possible to terrestrial creatures like pigs, men or elephants, who must expend a goodly portion of their energy in just fighting gravity. In man's case, the difficulties of sheer weight are compounded by his upright stance, which puts comparatively as much pressure on each of his two limbs as there is on each of the four limbs of a bear."

The first time any of us has ever seen men leaping about with the same joyous abandon as an otter or porpoise was the very far-distant view, through the front of the crazybox in the living room, of Neil Armstrong and Edwin Aldrin taking the "giant leap for mankind" on the surface of the moon in July, 1969— "a two-footed hop, six to eight feet a hop." At gravity one-sixth that of Planet Water, both men, even encased in their immensely bulky spacesuits (that made them resemble little boys clad in winter snowsuits), moved about with an ungainly but remarkable freedom. "We felt very comfortable in the lunar gravity," Armstrong declared. "It was, in fact, in our view preferable both to weightlessness and earth gravity."

Since few of us will get to gavotte on the moon's surface for a long time to come, our second-best means of achieving relatively weightless freedom is to go in swimming. It is remarkable how few vicious fishes ever attack human swimmers, leaving man free to paddle about in safety in most of the planet's waters, fresh or salt. And, oh, how most of mankind loves to take to the waters! Here is poet Robert Browning:

> You know how one—not treads, but stands in water? Keep
> Body and limbs below, hold head back, uplift chin,
> And, for the rest, leave care! If brow, eyes, mouth should win
> Their freedom—excellent! If they must brook the surge,
> No matter though they sink, let but the nose emerge.

And what wild, silly swims men and women make! Each springtime a vast school of nutty natators from around the world arrives in England or France to attempt La Manche, the British Channel; many of them accomplish it, too. Richard Halliburton swam the Hellespont, as had Lord Byron before him. In September, 1952, U.S. Ambassador George McGhee (to Turkey) and Senator Russell B. Long swam the Bosporus, from Europe to Asia, but denied they were trying to imitate love-sick Leander or Lord Byron or Halliburton, since the Hellespont is at the *other* end of the Sea of Marmara in the Dardanelles. Christopher Marlowe's *Hero and Leander* is a fragment of the tale of these unfortunate lovers—a splendid "imitation" of a work by a sixth-century Greek, Musaeus— (Leander swam the Hellespont nightly, guided by the light

in her tower, until the night the light blew out, when he
drowned), especially of Leander's struggles, that is full of lovely
imagery:

> Leander strived; the waves about him wound,
> And pulled him to the bottom, where the ground
> Was strewed with pearl, and in low coral groves
> Sweet singing mermaids sported with their loves
> On heaps of heavy gold, and took great pleasure
> To spurn in careless sort the shipwreck treasure.

(This was composed in 1590, at about the same time that Marlowe also wrote that passionate shepherd's plea, "Come live
with me and be my love, and we will all the pleasures prove.")

The greatest recorded distance ever swum was a 292-mile
journey down the Mississippi River by a St. Louis butcher—to
Caruthersville, also in Missouri, in 89 hours, 48 minutes, in
1940. The greatest number of swimmers in a competition has
been more than 7,000 in the annual Dead Sea swim in Israel.
Up to 5,000 Israelis also annually swim across the Sea of Galilee
(Lake Chinnereth) each September, in remembrance of the
Feast of the Tabernacle, Socoth, during Passover week.

Fastest of all swimmers is Hans Fassnacht, who achieved
4.04 miles-per-hour at the A.A.U. national championships in
Louisville, Kentucky, August, 1969. Johnny Weissmuller,
whom most of us have seen swimming jungle rivers as Tarzan,
won more Olympic water titles—five—than any other individual. In the Burroughs books made into movies, Weissmuller
truly became Johnny Merboy, as much at home in the water as
on land. Skinny-dipping, dog-paddling, floating, a swimmer
must keep his legs moving gently in order to keep his nose
above water. It's been observed that if our necks were only
about six inches longer, we could be properly buoyant; meanwhile, because of our swivel or ball-socket joints in shoulders
and hips, we nevertheless can most marvelously swim on our
front, back, or side, in four-limbed motion, and also move forward and backward. Remarkable, for a terrestrial biped.

Symbolic of the national pollution of natural waters, James
Whitcomb Riley's famed "old swimmin'-hole" in Greenfield,
Indiana, was closed to kids in July, 1968, because its "gurglin'

worters" were no longer safe. A local lady, questioned by a *Sports Illustrated* writer, Bil Gilbert, regretted that the mythical waters were contaminated but added a comment that's typical of today's artificial approach to landscape, in the sense that man-made things are more properly to be used than nature's: "There is really no reason why children should have to use the creek; they have that pool in the park that was *made* for swimming."

Last year, more than 70,000 new residential swimming pools were constructed in suburbia, U.S.A., more than the total number in existence a scant dozen years before, and the number seems likely to go on increasing multifold. A great number of them are simply vinyl-lined holes in the backyard (an average 16-by-32-foot sprayed-concrete pool costs $7,000, and an average vinyl-liner about $3,500, fully installed in only three days). There are even vinyl "aquadomes" that make for year-round backyard swimming. We are today living in a golden age of American skinny-dipping.

At the International Olympics, in Mexico City, October, 1968, Americans won two-thirds of all the swimming medals, at the same time breaking numerous records, in spite of the "altitude monkey" that tormented all competitors at the 7,349-foot height above sea level.

A Mexican housewife, waiting hours in line to purchase a ticket for one of the swimming programs, explained: "We love to see good swimmers, it doesn't matter if they're Mexicans or Russians or Americans. We love to swim. We teach our children to swim. And we like to watch the champions." Most lovely of all to behold was sixteen-year-old mermaid Debbie Meyer, from Sacramento, California, who won three gold medals; *Sports Illustrated* described her: "about to be beautiful, not old enough to wear makeup—well, maybe just a tiny hint of eyeshadow—with a businesslike tawny haircut and the posture of a coiled spring." Comparing today's "water babies" with the swimmers of the past, Arthur Daley, of the New York *Times,* wrote: "These modern gals would leave the peerless Johnny Weissmuller wallowing halfway up the pool. That's how phenomenal the rate of improvement has been." Daley called the 1968 Mexican Olympics "the most grandiose display of the aquatic art in Olympic history," notably because of the five new men's and six new women's events never scheduled before. Denver, Colorado, and Vancouver, British Columbia, are contending for the 1976 Winter Games; the 1972 games will be held at Sapporo, Japan.

The Hawaiian Islands surely offer the best surf on Planet Water, as they get both the big ones tumbling southward from the northern storms during winter months and the big ones tumbling northward from the southern storms during summertime. In *Surfing: The Sport of Hawaiian Kings,* Ben R. Finney and James D. Houston have gone into another aspect of the ancient sport, a component of almost all competition that the puritanical forever try most feverishly (in a sort of puritanical gambling fever) to proscribe and prohibit: the joy of *gambling on who will win.* Most professional sports, meets, competitions, and matches couldn't take place before a large audience if there were not also a chance of betting on who the spectator/speculator hopes will win. An amateur gambler is rarely hard-minded; he is a special kind of romanticist who puts his money on his candidate, thereby giving him some extra sort of magical propulsion, mystical and spiritual, toward winning.

Finney and Houston stated of the premissionary sport: "Contests were a large part of the game. And the wagering on such matches . . . was a favorite and often fanatic pastime that could overshadow the sport itself. Hawaiians were inveterate gamblers, known to bet everything, down to the last article they possessed. Overcome by the excitement of a surfing contest, a chief might wager canoes, fishing nets and lines, tapa cloth, and sometimes his own life or personal freedom on the outcome of the match."

Alexander Hume Ford, Jack London, George Freeth, and Duke Kahanamoku made Waikiki the world center for wave seekers, and surfing soon spread around the world.

Body-surfing comes first, then canoe-sliding, and finally surf-boarding—belly-boarding, kneeling, standing, even standing on one's hands. Ron Haworth, resident guru of surfdom in Oahu, wrote about "the best and biggest ridable waves": "Surfing challenges man to gamble skill, mind and physical fiber against nature, and has its ultimate achievement in courage. Some big-wave surfers look to such fearsome breaks as Avalanche, far outside of Haleiwa, or Cloud Break, far beyond the familiar Maili surf. Big-wave specialist Buzzy Trent likens surfing Kaena

Point to landing an astronaut on the moon. Felipe Pomar, 1965 world champion, says, 'One reason Kaena has yet to feel the bite of a board is because the waves are not accessible and the lava coastline is not hospitable.' George Downing and Fred Van Dyke agree the biggest ridable waves roll into Castles, off Diamond Head, during the summer. . . . Castles has the biggest ridable waves off Hawaii. It has been slowed by a more gradual bottom change, thus producing a sloping wall which offers more hope of the surfer beating in his race away from the tumbling hook."

Surface surfing reaches an annual high point when the International Surfing Championships take place at Makaha Beach annually during Christmas school vacation; the Duke Kahanamoku Classic, the greatest prestige surf contest, usually takes place at Sunset Beach, on the north shore of Oahu.

Water-skiing, in which champions are towed at regulation 36 miles per hour by 100-horsepower engines, calls for a different sort of skill and sense of balance, and gives another kind of thrill. The spectator can get a better view of skiers moving over smooth water than he can at seaside, where surfing contestants may be moving in front of 30-foot-high waves. Mike Suyderhoud soared to a 155-foot record at the Masters Water Ski Tournament at Callaway Gardens, Georgia, in 1968; other places at which one views the champions are Cypress Gardens, Florida, the Dixie and All-American; Berkeley, California, the nationals; Paris, France, the internationals.

Surfing and snow skiing involve the let-go of gravity, whereas water skiing is accomplished by the drag of being hauled behind a power boat, the way children used to ride their skis and cling to a rope held out over the back of a horse-pulled sleigh; one can go all the way back to childhood, when an adult kindly pulled a whole string of children on their sleds down a country road that had not been plowed. A sail, on a waterboat or iceboat, gives a kind of mystical power that's much nearer the push of gravity than the pull of horses and motorboats. Having read *Treasure Island* when very young, I still have a fear of being dragged by a rope: Long John Silver (turned hideously into a sweet old man, they tell me, in a TV serial) had two guns slung about him—one before and one behind—besides the great cutlass at his waist and a pistol in each pocket of his square-tailed coat.

The crazy parrot, Captain Flint, perched upon his shoulder, "gabbling odds and ends of purposeless seatalk." And young Jim Hawkins "had a line about my waist, and followed obediently after the sea-cook, who held the loose end of the rope, now in his free hand, now between his powerful teeth. For all the world, I was led like a dancing bear." Oh, the nightmare terror of being dragged, towed, hauled, pulled behind a motorboat or horse and sleigh that turns out to be John Silver ("whipped the crutch out of his armpit, and sent that uncouth missile hurtling through the air. It struck poor Tom, point foremost, and with stunning violence, right between the shoulders in the middle of his back. His hands flew up, he gave a sort of gasp, and fell"), and then to be given the business by that evil old mafia-man-pirate! If a man wants to express himself as an athlete, to be *sportif,* must all the energy of his activity be his own? Is virility expressed in its purity only by a person's expenditure of *his own* muscle power, with no use of sail wind, of ski slope, of powerboat ropes, all these other power aids: are they just so much *"cheating"?* Is surfing in high Hawaiian waves the sport of a godlike hero, whereas being dragged by a motorboat at the end of a rope the mechanical exercise of a perpetual schoolboy?

James Dugan wrote *The New Pioneers* shortly before he died in 1965, and *Oceans,* the most refreshing new magazine to visit Planet Water in decades, excerpted it in 1969. Here is part of Dugan's description of underwater sports: "The unique, wholly new adventure of our time is underwater swimming and exploration beneath the sea. It is a sport that leads to science. What does one learn about the planet from skiing, either on water or snow? Or from routine games?

"Free diving thrusts you through the looking glass into a netherworld which waits for identifications. You must be especially insensitive if you can avoid wonder and inquisitiveness when you are 'downstairs.' We have very few answers on the enigmas of the sea. In fact, we don't even know many of the questions.

"The mysteries of the underwater realm begin at the place you choose to stick your mask through the surface. . . . Free divers have extended the grasp of science. They invented submarine archaeology. . . . The first impulse was to prang fish. The killing urge passed rapidly, although some people begin by sticking fish and stick them until the last spear misses and lands they-know-not-where."

Young boys have not yet begun fish-walking—the way they have always done bird-walking—name-calling, listing how many they've seen and identified. Just as New York bird watchers visit the Central Park Ramble to identify birds during migration season, there will come a time when fish watchers will do continental-shelf-edge Hudson-River-Canyon rambling (or fish-naming at some other convenient fish-passing place) to study the migrations of major fish schools.

The wonderful part of being a noninterfering observer is that "our" viewing the other citizens of Planet Water pursuing their expected courses has *nothing to do* with them: the birds, animals, and fishes do not recognize us except perhaps to note: *These bastards do not shoot or hook us.* We seem to be the only mortal beings on Planet Water that can view the others philosophically and wonder about it all. At one point during an interview conducted by *Oceans* magazine, Philippe Cousteau, fine-honed son of a famous father, exclaimed: "I have one pet philosophical idea. And that is that everybody is trying to justify Nature; people keep saying everything has a purpose. I think it is an awfully unpoetic approach to Nature and to life. The point I'm trying to make is that I hope that some things are just there for no purpose at all. I cannot answer questions on a scientific basis, because I'm not qualified.

"It would be terrible if everything had a purpose. We'd be living in a world absolutely conditioned, absolutely rigid in its laws, and I hope it's not true. Art, poetry. . . . Why should a flower have a color? I still don't understand. Maybe so that the insect can recognize one from the other. Maybe so, I don't know. I think it is the same problem in the sea. If you find out why every flower has a different color and a different shape, maybe we'll find out why every alga and animal in the sea has a different color and different shape."

Looking futureward, young Cousteau thought "the normal trend of operation now is to develop equipment that will allow us to live as deep as the sea is and live there for long periods of time. Up to years maybe. And depending less and less on the surface for supplies. This will allow us to use the resources of the sea and maybe also give a new dimension to our philosophy, to our way of living, by constant contact with an entirely different world."

Oceans also interviewed another famous man's son, another great underseaman in his own right, Jon M. Lindbergh, who has found that "a trip into the sea, like a trip into the wilderness ashore, does help bring one into intimate contact with his natural heritage. Man has, in a very short time, evolved a society which is high-pressured, complex, and far-removed from what he knew for thousands of years previously. Daily convulsions around the world pretty definitely indicate he has not yet come to terms with his new situation. Intimate contact with the sea is for me a means of regaining lost equilibrium."

Hanns-Wolf Rackl, examining underwater research, stated the ultimate human reason for searching and researching downstairs, beneath the seas: "The real treasures that archaeologists wrest from the earth are not gold and silver, but information about man. Relics reveal to us the empires and cultures of the past, the thought and feeling of ancient peoples."

What is the greatest treasure yet brought up? As far as I can make out, it is a 400 B.C. statue of Zeus found off Cape Artemisium. Rackl described it as "a symbol of a mighty god and at the same time of a free Greek citizen." Years ago, I first saw the remarkable replica of this mature man-god, which stands in the United Nations secretariat foyer, without realizing what a veritable phenomenon he *is*. Women's magazines are forever extolling svelte ladies of past eras who were lovely because they ate salads and also happened to spend endless hours riding horses, thus keeping their bellies flat. Diane de Poitiers, mistress of Henri II of France (and probably of his father before) was such a one ("She would wash her face with well water even on the coldest mornings, and succeeded in retaining her beauty late into life"), and we can gasp at her portrayal of the goddess Diana, in the statue by Jean Goujon, in the Louvre. We stand in similar awe before the male wonder of Zeus in the Athens museum (what godlike model must have posed for it!), the quality of workmanship (we do not know the sculptor) that caused Alexander Eliot, former art critic of *Time,* to call it "the greatest sculpture we possess" and to dispute its being labeled as Poseidon about to hurl a trident: "The traditional thunderbolt of cloud-gathering Zeus fits the hand-positions much better. . . . Zeus's striding form is electric with young, self-renewing energy. His image seems no more 'sexual' than that of a lion or a fighting bull, yet it does radiate virility. Also it looks impassive and implacable, swift as an eagle, firm as an oak, fine-drawn as a spider's web, smooth as a wave, tall as a hill: the statue was intended not only as an object of worship but also as an inspiration to men. The god resembles a man, who resembles a god."

John Erving, Jr.'s *Worldwide Skindiver's Guide* lists shipwrecks as well as saltwater and freshwater diving spots around the planet, surely the first such directory ever to encompass sightworthy places within the Planet Water's below-water-level wet territories. For sport, there's lobster hunting (up to 20 pounds) inside wrecks off New Jersey's coast in the Atlantic, or octopus wrestling in Puget Sound (10 to 80 pounds, and up to 16 feet across—real grabby!), or even skin diving for king crab in Alaskan waters.

Many visitors to the underwaters are pursuing man's perpetual get-rich-quick dreams, especially the gold-rush fantasy. Island governments in the Caribbean have already begun passing laws to protect underwater historic sites from the depredations of fortune seekers. Off Florida, explorers must pay the state a $600 fee and put up a $5,000 security bond for the right to search an 18-square-mile area for a single year, with 25 percent of the find going to the state as well.

Carl Claussen, marine archaeologist with the Florida Board of Archives and History, quotes records to show what a terribly losing investment most underseas treasure hunting turns out to be: "Ninety-nine out of every hundred treasure hunters go broke. You could put all of the gold found in Florida waters in the last five years into two shoe boxes."

But treasure hunting *is* fun; it's one of man's greatest adventures, the individual adventurer's chance to *make it big* and at the same time escape from mundane everyday toil. In September, 1969, Thomas Gurr spoke freely to a New York *Times* reporter, Jon Nordheimer, about his dreams of finding the *Nuestra Señora Atocha*, "after looking at documents in the archives in Spain, which detail her cargo." The principal galleon of a wrecked 1622 Spanish treasure fleet, "the single richest ship ever lost," she had a gold cargo worth anywhere from

$15,000,000 to $75,000,000. Underwaterman Gurr exploded in treasure-hunter ecstasy, "There is so much that if you find her, you don't bother to count it, man, you just go to the bank and stop worrying. It's just laying out down there, already minted, man. If guys get excited about running off to the cold Klondike to dig raw gold, just think of those big piles of doubloons and jewelry out there waiting in the warm water."

Seeker Gurr is the kind of man who will before long begin pioneering the exploration of the moon's mineral and other richnesses—and this wild new-frontier era will dawn within the next decade. Of his present underwater search for a lost Spanish galleon, he expressed dreaming man's ever-living hopes: "If I should go out tomorrow and stumble across the *Atocha*, I'd be the most confused person in the world. Why, I'd have to hire people to help spend the money for me!"

Paul Tzimoulis, editor of *Skin Diver*, recognized that "the term *skin diving* is undoubtedly one of the biggest misnomers ever foisted upon the English language. No one can come up with a logical explanation as to why we're called skin divers, but we are stuck with it." For a while, after the invention of the aqualung, *free diving* came into vogue, and back in the early 1930's there was *goggle diving*. *Frogmen* are military, and *underwater recovery teams* are police or fire department specialists. (The Los Angeles Fire Department puts swimmers' platforms on small fireboats, to help scuba fire fighters to enter and leave the water more easily for underdock attacks on fires.) Science writers refer to *aquanauts*. Tzimoulis found that commercial companies hire *mixed-gas specialists,* but "these technicians are not doing it for fun. It seems hardly logical to accurately describe them as *skin divers,* a term identified as a pleasurable sport." Skin divers can indulge in: snorkel diving, with face mask, fins, and snorkel; scuba diving, with these devices and a portable untethered breathing device; hookah diving, in which the breathing device is connected to a surface compressor.

Riding upon the surface of the waters is a quiet happiness men accomplish in sailboats, and also noisily with motors. When Mike Todd was a small boy, he and his brother once tried to set out on the upper Mississippi River to sail down to New Orleans in a bathtub. In 1969 a Michigan man actually piloted a motor-driven bathtub across Lake Michigan. Men even row across the North Atlantic: in 1969, John Fairfax rowed 4,000 miles west to Florida; and Tom McClean rowed east 2,000 miles from Newfoundland to Ireland. By canoe, bathtub, sailboat, motorboat, and more recently by the new Cushion-flight—35 miles per hour over land and water and through snow, swamp, or beach—or Circraft, a completely round hydroplane that is steered by body weight alone.

James Ramsey, editor of *Sierra Club Bulletin*, described how a canoe is, "in a sense, a time machine," as a means of getting back to the Nature of Planet Water, places, "some near to civilization, some far—where man's arbitrary definitions of time do not exist; where all living things owe their allegiance, not to man, but to nature. Older than the wheel, the canoe *is* the existential mode of transportation!"

Racing adds another dimension to travel by sail or power-boat. And fishing for fun is one of man's most carefully thought-out contests with another kind of creature. The angler may be a small boy after a sunfish or a Hemingway old man contending against a great game fish far out at sea. The fun line is drawn very closely here. If a farmer lays out a fishpond, planning to use the catch as part of the family's food supply, it spoils the play fun of his son to be ordered to catch some fish for dinner. The deep-sea fisherman who brings home a mess of cod for the deepfreeze is happier if it is considered not as work fishing but, instead, fishing for fun. And when a man goes ice fishing, when the flag goes up, there's a great excitement to rush to the hole and pull the fish in, without getting involved in soul-searching as to the fish's suffering from the hook, or promises to goodwife at home that her husband is hard at *work* fishing for her supper. A man should enjoy his work, but sport is an absolute *separation* of play from work, whether it be fishing or racing or sailing for fun. That's where *professional* sports may confuse and challenge all the usual standards of strife for fun. Professional sportsmen get such huge salaries that spectators always feel that the amateur sportsman must "go professional" while he can still make a big "killing" with his athletic skills. Meantime, of course, each of us is supposed to "enjoy" the work we "live by."

On ice, skating is a wonderfully different kind of locomotion, so unlike walking, swimming, or flying that each one of us becomes an utterly different creature when we begin to glide across water's metallic form. My worst and most thrilling experience as a small boy was to be the end man in the "whip"— the game in which everybody on the pond takes hands and all go around and around in a windup, the end kids being let go and spinning wildly up against the banks. "The grandest team game of them all," Brian McFarlane has called ice hockey, because it combines "skating, shooting, stickhandling and the crunch of body contact." A postscript to the gambling quality of hockey's virility is the sports columnist's footnote that this is "the most productive money-maker in the entire history of athletics."

Man is, outside of a few man-trained bears, the only animal that learns how to skate, and the gambling instinct perhaps reaches its zenith in watching this frenetic sport. Handsome young stick-swingers, such as Derik Sanderson of the Boston Bruins or Jean Beliveau of the Toronto Maple Leafs, are as maddeningly beautiful to behold, for ladies in the audience, as the finest of gladiators were for the ladies of ancient Rome. We live in so prurient an age that one does not learn the successes of hockey heroes among the lady viewers. Roman gladiators, reported J. Bryan III, were "rewarded, coddled and adulated far beyond the actors, actresses and star athletes of today. Their portraits decorated vases; poets hymned them; noble ladies wooed them."

After fun on ice comes snowmanship. Handsome Jean-Claude Killy, the young Frenchman who won the World Cup the first time it was at stake (from Grenoble, *le beau* Jean-Claude came away with all three Alpine-competition Olympic gold medals around his neck), has told us, "The first thing I did was ski from the roof of our house. In Val-d'Isère, everyone skis, even the pastor. It would not be *normal* if they didn't. Older people shouldn't be afraid to start either. The first run down a little hill—with legs so stiff—is thrilling. You fall. You are in a knot of skis and poles. At night, maybe you are a little sore, but you have never felt better—the deep, warm relaxation. Soon you are skiing the whole mountain, in all snows, in all weather. You have made contact with another world."

Levitation—Icarusing up into the air without artificial help— is every water or land creature's dream, and ski jumpers achieve this, especially at Planica, Yugoslavia, site of the biggest "ski-flying" hill in the world. At first skiers "flew" there more than 100 meters before touching down, then records were made elsewhere, notably 154 meters on Vikiersund, a Norwegian hill, in March, 1967, by Reinhold Bachler. But in the spring of 1969, Janez Gorisek opened a new hill at Planica, from which ski fliers right away began to ride the sky 160 and more meters— the Vikiersund record was immediately broken by nineteen ski fliers. Gorisek, the hill maker, has predicted that before long he'll build a mountain off which skiers will "fly" up to more than 200 meters—roughly *an eighth of a mile*—before they come back down to earth!

Ski flying? Who wants to fly, when one can move swiftly downhill on a snowy surface at, say, 83.8 miles per hour? That's the speed Flight Lieutenant Colin Mitchell of England, one-man bobsledder, reached on the Cresta Run at St. Moritz, Switzerland, in February, 1959. Sleds, like skis, are also terrifically old. A Finnish museum has one dated 6500 B.C. But toboggans are, of course, American: *tobaakan* is a Micmac word.

All emotional motional fun sooner or later has to become motorized, simply because an engine can drive the vehicle much faster than can gravity or the wind or a sun-and-moon-driven wave, and the motion and "exercise" involve little exertion on the part of the sportsman. Into the "old-fashioned" world of skiing came, in the mid-1960's, the new sport of ski bobbing, a bicycle on skis that makes time downhill by means of a whirling motorized in-front ski. Ski bobber Erich Brenter established a speed record of 102 miles per hour, only 6 miles per hour slower than Luigi de Marco's old-fashioned downhill-gravity ski speed record. Brenter expressed the neat dichotomy of ski bobbing for those who want a kind of adventure that combines excitement with safety: "Ski bobs remove some of the danger of skiing—but none of the thrills."

The ultimate in modern, mechanized oversnow travel appears to be the snowmobile, the remarkable invention of Joseph-Armand Bombardier, a mechanical genius resident in the isolated Quebec village of Valcourt—the ideal place in which to conceive a vehicle to end the isolation of snowbound winters for far-northern citizens. Bombardier's Ski-Doo is for the formerly shut-in stir-crazy victims of winter doldrums what

Thomas Edison's electric light has been for all human citizenry in enlarging their hours of living. Spring-through-fall used to be their dimension, way up north, just as dawn-through-dusk was the expected routine for mankind before the arrival of artificial lighting.

Bombardier's great breakthrough was in part due to the death of an infant son of appendicitis in 1934, when he could not reach a hospital in time by the old-fashioned horse and sledge. Then he went to work in earnest.

Snowmobiles have become fundamentally useful as business machines for far northerners. For example, *Reader's Digest,* in a roundup piece on "The Cats That Conquered Winter" in December, 1968, found a Finnish reindeer nomad who's been able to stay in business only because of snowmobiles. But nine out of ten of them are used for fun by people who love to whiz over snow in winter, snow-playing where it isn't all keep-to-the-right-of-center-line, where *there is no center line!* You are free to travel cross-country, and for the lazy human animal, you *do not have to use your feet or your personal energy!*

Snowmobiles go up to 100 miles per hour. The Winnipeg-to-St.-Paul snowmobile race is the classic marathon, 565 miles.

The heroes include both the winners of races and those who have lived through extravagant adventures. One such snowmobilist was a Salem, New Hampshire, brewery worker who slid off his Snowcat on an ice-covered road near the summit of Mount Washington and was found unharmed 1,200 feet below. The Snowcat was still topside. A companion was later quoted in Boston newspapers: "Everything is coated with ice up there, and there's nothing to hold you; besides, the road slopes away from the mountain." The paper reported that this was the third Mount Washington accident to be reported within a month. In contrast to drag racers on city streets, this seems an ideal way for adventurers to experience the great thrust and competition against Nature—without endangering others. As a motorized adventure, it's comparable to mountain climbing with pitons and ropes: your problems are your own.

A vast objection to the use of snowmobiles has chiefly to do with the fact that they have not yet been provided with adequate mufflers. Automobiles once had something called a "cutout," whereby the exhaust could be thrown directly out of the motor, creating a great, loud noise that would make the driver, and the young lady accompanying him, immensely proud of the racket he was creating.

This raucous pride has ruined the highway countryside, racketing out of scooters and motorcycles, for decades now. Even in formerly remote fastnesses like Yosemite Park, the midnight sound of the motor scooter, pride of a young man's showing off, ruins the quiet pleasure of far too many visitors who are assembled in expectation of quietude beneath the trees.

Overnoise was formerly confined to highways. Now, with the snowmobile, it can explode far out over any distant snowy countryside. The *Wall Street Journal* reported, in January, 1969: "The world has seen some lousy inventions, like air horns for trucks and booties for dogs, but none is as ill-conceived as the snowmobile." The publication went on to report a new kind of thieves "who use snowmobiles for get-away cars: they break into well-furnished resort cabins, pile the loot into trailers hitched to snowmobiles, and then count on fresh snow to cover their tracks."

In October, 1969, at a hearing held at Johnstown, New York, by the Joint Legislative Committee on Environmental Management and Natural Resources, Michael Nadel, assistant executive secretary of the Wilderness Society, urged that snowmobiles be subjected to "vigilant regulation" because they can more readily than the automobile "penetrate sanctuaries of quiet, silence and remoteness to which the public is entitled in its parks and other natural areas, and to destroy these qualities in a moment."

Most motor vehicles are strictly controlled, whereas snowmobiles roam at will. Noise is the big problem: their sound is likened to that of a loud outboard motor or a chain saw. Most motors have this sort of sound, a proud thing to bray forth if a driver is a primeval animal. Among civilized people, silence, quietude, and good manners are the comportment of considerate behavior: and it is a difficult thing for any young man full of rip-roaring instincts to conform to.

"How shall I enjoy thee in the finest fashion?" Water to drink is man's happiest enjoyment of the universal solvent. Sloughing it down, even as pure and simple Adam's ale, is forever something special. One of man's most superior talents is the ability to lift a glass and quaff. Cats can only lap. One almost regrets, in reading Joan Wilentz's *The Senses of Man*, her calm appraisal of the possibility that "frogs, toads, cats, dogs and even monkeys apparently have distinct water taste receptors. Man and rats do not. The charms of branch water, or the sweet, pleasant taste you may associate with your local supply, is either the contribution of minerals or additives or else an aftereffect sometimes experienced after tasting something sour. If anything, pure distilled water placed on the tongue has a depressing effect."

Water, all by itself, is odorless, tasteless, colorless. In this it is like the great "food foundationals" that have little taste all by themselves, but that give widened and diversified richness to all sauces poured over them. Breads, pastas, and rices are bland in taste; add gravies, sauces, dressings, and suddenly they take on splendrous flavors of themselves and add richnesses to the concentrated things spread over them. Butter, of course, begins it.

Water performs this humble enrichment even better than the leguminose taste-stretchers. Captain Smith Grant, head of the firm that produces Scotland's finest malt whisky, Glenlivet, has stated: "I know no one who does not drink whisky with water. There doesn't seem to be much future in just knocking it back: a little water will bring out the nose."

André Simon, in his formidable *Encyclopaedia of Gastronomy*, has indexed sixteen waters: aerated, aesculap, Aix-les-Bains, apollinaris, barley, Evian, Hunyadi Janos, Kissingen, mineral, Perrier, potash, Rosbach, soda, table, tonic, Vichy.

Tomato juice, orange juice, papaya—all the fruit "juices" are composed principally of fresh water slightly flavored with the fruit's own meat. One of the happiest commentaries on the pleasure of quaffing this kind of water was made by Spanish Captain Gonzalo de Oviedo, in 1523, on drinking coconut milk: "These trees brynge furth a frute of greater circumference than the heade of a man. Within celaveth faste to the rynde a substaunce very white, lyke unto almond. . . . In place of the stone there is a voyde full of a moste cleare and excellent water. The which water surely is the moste precious to bee droonke that may be founde in the worlde. In the moment when it passeth the palate and begynneth to goo downe the throte it seemeth that from the sole of the foote to the crowne of the headde, there is no part of the boddye but that feelethe great comfort. It is doutless one of the most excellent thynges that may be tasted upon the earth, and suche as I am not able by wrytynge to express."

Trying to find her way into the beautiful garden that we all desire to enter, Alice in Wonderland found a bottle, around the neck of which was tied "a paper label, with the words 'DRINK ME' beautifully printed on it in large letters. . . . Alice ventured to taste it, and finding it very nice (it had, in fact, a sort of mixed flavor of cherry-tart, custard, pineapple, roast turkey, toffy and hot-buttered toast), she very soon finished it off." As who wouldn't? Only Lewis Carroll did not state, because he did not know (as a sort of human predecessor of the calculating machine, he would have stated if he'd known of it), that water was the *base juice* liquid in the "drink me" bottle. It just *had* to be.

In country kitchens, ladies have always spent an immense amount of time "decocting" all kinds of berries from the garden patch and out of the wildwood—raspberries, blackberries, blueberries—which extends also to the fruits of the orchard— plums, pears, apples—simmering the berries and fruits *down* to create preserves, partway dehydrating to preserve them.

Many drinkers have learned to add the phrase, in ordering a drink, "on the rocks," because of the added "flavor" that is contributed by this extra dimension of water in its frozen form. Jimmy Breslin once described "the sound of ice hitting the sides of a glass. In the afternoon, the ice makes only this gentle, clicking, almost tinkling sound. Yet at night it sounds like gravel being poured into a barrel. Why is ice louder at night than it is in the daytime? Let me put on my shoes and we'll go out and investigate."

Stewart Holbrook, in his *Lost Men of History,* reported that "soda water and ice cream became excellent new menaces for the more excitable clergy . . . powerful sermons were preached against 'sucking soda' and eating ice cream in drugstores on the Sabbath: and in certain Midwest towns laws were passed against the abomination, and the selling of soda water on Sunday was prohibited. Druggists quickly devised the practice of selling, on Sundays, ice cream with syrups added. This *sodaless* soda was called a 'Sunday Soda,' and presently became popular on weekdays as well . . . cynical druggists changed the spelling to 'sundae.' "

Mae West, a lovely woman with startlingly alabaster skin, has always followed a water regimen in her daily living, and it is reflected in her appearance. "I've always washed my face and hair in bottled water," she has said. "In the days when I was 'on the road,' I carried Poland (purified) water with me. They even brewed my tea in it, in the kitchens of hotels where I stayed."

So many of us live, protesting but acquiescent, with polluted air and water that one honors Miss West's statement: "I have all my own teeth; I've never had any arthritis or any of those illnesses."

Under the swinging title *"L'eau—and behold,"* *Vogue* magazine informed its readers, in 1969: "Water works wonders—an idea as old as the hills, and the streams and the spring. THE CURE, it was once called, and to take it one went to sea or to spa. To swim in, wash with, drink of, sail on, or simply gaze at —water! Those who have gone along with this idea are splashed all through history: among them Queen Nefertiti, St. Paul, Emperor Hadrian, Marie Antoinette, George Washington."

Vogue was introducing Régine, *Parisienne bistroienne:* "I am a water girl. I use more of it than anyone. Evian water. Pads for an hour. Twenty-minute foot bath. Sauna. Cold shower." The magazine reported: "She eats very little—seems to live on water made into weak tea. Apparently Régine's water-work works. She is now looking forward to more success—perhaps as a mermaid?" *Vogue* found Evian water to be a world favorite for drinking or for splashing on, notably the fine mist out of the *brumisateur.*

In the uses, blessings, and wonders of water, James Joyce went pleasantly wild in describing Leopold Bloom's putting a kettle on to boil. In *Ulysses,* Joyce caused Bloom first to carry "the iron kettle to the sink in order to tap the current by turning the faucet to let it flow.

"Did it flow?

"Yes. . . .

"What in water did Bloom, waterlover, drawer of water, watercarrier returning to the range, admire?

"Its universality: its democratic equality and constancy to its nature in seeking its own level: its vastness in the ocean of Mercator's projection: its unplumbed profundity in the Sundam trench . . . and surface particles visiting in turn all points of its seaboard: the independence of its units: the variability of states of sea: its hydrostatic quiescence in calm: its hydrokinetic turgidity in neap and spring tides: its subsidence after devastation: its sterility in the circumpolar icecaps, arctic and antarctic: its climatic and commercial significance: its preponderance of three to one over the dry land of the globe: its indisputable hegemony extending in square leagues over all the region below the subequatorial tropic of Capricorn . . . its capacity to dissolve and hold in solution all soluble substances including millions of tons of the most precious metals: its slow erosions of peninsulas and downwardtending promontories: its alluvial deposits: its weight and volume and density: its imperturbability in lagoons and highland tarns . . . its vehicular ramifications in continental lakecontained streams and confluent oceanflowing rivers with their tributaries and transoceanic currents: gulfstream . . . artesian wells, eruptions, torrents, eddies, freshets, spates, groundswells . . . inundations, deluges, cloudbursts: its vast circumterrestrial ahorizontal curve: its secrecy in springs, and latent humidity, revealed by rhabdomantic or hygrometric instruments"—can any man born of woman add to Mr. Joyce's laudation of the watery stuff?

It's a long time between drinks. That first seeking of the mother's nipple by the puckered lips of the newborn baby; "Let us wet our whistles," *tengomenas faciamus,* quoth Petronius; "We'll tak' a right gude-willie waught for Auld Lang Syne" with Bobby Burns; "There's nothing like drinking so pleasant on this side of the grave," Charles Dibdin; "He saith, 'I thirst'; now there was set a vessel full of vinegar, and they put it upon hyssop, and put it to his mouth; when he therefore had received the vinegar, he said, 'It is finished'; and he bowed his head, and gave up the ghost"; "Drink! for you know not whence you came, nor why; drink! for you know not why you go, nor where," Omar Khayyam; and then, the final drouth that is also its own kind of escape from the wetness of our existence, *"Turn down an empty glass!"*

Bibliography

1. Water Wonders

ACKERMAN, E. A., and LOF, O. G., *Technology in American Water Development*. Baltimore, Johns Hopkins Press, 1959.

AZIMOV, IZAAC, *The Fantastic Voyage*. New York, Bantam, 1966.

BEHRMAN, A. S., *Water Is Everybody's Business*. Garden City, Doubleday, 1968.

BOREK, ERNEST, *Man the Chemical Machine*. New York, Columbia University Press, 1952.

COLLIS, JOHN STEWART, *The Moving Waters*. New York, William Sloane, 1955.

COOK, J. GORDON, *The World of Water*. New York, Dial, 1957.

CULLIGAN, EMMETT, *Emmett Culligan on Water*. New York, Crestline, 1965.

CUNNINGHAM, FLOYD F., *1001 Questions Answered About Water Resources*. New York, Dodd, Mead, 1967.

DEROPP, ROBERT S., *Sex Energy*. New York, Dell, 1969.

ECKSTEIN, GUSTAV, *The Body Has a Head*. New York, Harper & Row, 1970.

LAAS, WILLIAM, and BEICOS, S. S., *The Water in Your Life*. New York, Popular Library, 1967.

LEAGUE OF WOMEN VOTERS, *The Big Water Fight*. Brattleboro, Vt., Stephen Greene Press, 1966.

MILNE, LORUS and MARGERY, *Water and Life*. London, Deutsch, 1965.

MOSS, FRANK E., *The Water Crisis*. New York, Praeger, 1967.

REID, VERA W., *Towards Aquarius*. New York, Arco, 1969.

SEEMAN, BERNARD, *The River of Life*. New York, Norton, 1961.

SMITH, ANTHONY, *The Body*. New York, Walker, 1968.

SNIVELY, WILLIAM D., *The Sea of Life*. New York, McKay, 1969.

TUAN, YI-FU, *The Hydrologic Cycle and the Wisdom of God*. Toronto, University of Toronto Press, 1968.

VALLENTINE, H. R., *Water in the Service of Man*. Baltimore, Penguin, 1967.

VERCORS, *Sylva*. New York, Putnam, 1962.

Water: U.S. Department of Agriculture Yearbook. Washington, D.C., U.S. Government Printing Office, 1955.

WENDT, HERBERT, *The Romance of Water.* London, Dent, 1969.

WESCOTT, ROGER W., *The Divine Animal.* New York, Funk & Wagnalls, 1969.

WILENTZ, JOAN STEEN, *The Senses of Man.* New York, T. Y. Crowell, 1968.

WINCHESTER, JAMES H., *The Wonders of Water.* New York, Putnam, 1963.

2. Variety and Dimensions of the Ocean Sea

ANDREWS, ROY CHAPMAN, *Beyond Adventure.* New York, Duell, Sloan & Pearce, 1952.

BARDACH, JOHN, *Harvest of the Sea.* New York, Harper & Row, 1968.

BJORNSSON, SVEINBJORN, *Iceland and Mid-Ocean Ridges.* Reykjavik, Prentsmidjan Leiftur, 1967.

BLUMER, MAX, *Oil on the Sea.* New York, Plenum, 1969.

BRIGGS, PETER, *Mysteries of Our World.* New York, McKay, 1969.

BROWN, HUGH AUCHINCLOSS, *Cataclysms of the Earth.* New York, Twayne, 1967.

CARSON, RACHEL L., *The Sea Around Us.* New York, Oxford, 1951.

CHAPIN, HENRY, and SMITH, F. G. WALTON, *The Ocean River.* New York, Scribner, 1952.

COUSTEAU, JACQUES-YVES, with DUMAS, FRÉDÉRIC, *The Silent World.* New York, Harper & Row, 1953.

COUSTEAU, JACQUES-YVES, with DUGAN, JAMES, *The Living Sea.* New York, Harper, 1964.

DANA, RICHARD HENRY, JR., *Two Years Before the Mast.* Burt, 1840.

DANIEL, HAWTHORNE, and MINOT, FRANCIS, *The Inexhaustible Sea.* New York, Dodd, Mead, 1954.

DE LATIL, PIERRE, and RIVOIRE, JEAN, *Man and the Underwater World.* London, Jarrolds, 1956.

DERREY, FRANÇOIS, *Our Unknown Earth.* New York, Stein & Day, 1967.

DE SELINCOURT, AUBREY, *The Book of the Sea.* New York, Norton, 1963.

DODGE, ERNEST S., *New England and the South Seas.* Cambridge, Harvard University Press, 1965.

DOUGLAS, JOHN SCOTT, *The Story of the Oceans.* New York, Dodd, Mead, 1952.

DUBACH, HAROLD W., and TABER, ROBERT W. *Questions About the Oceans.* Washington, D.C., U.S. Naval Oceanographic Office. 1968.

EDINGER, JAMES G., *Watching for the Wind.* Garden City, Doubleday, 1967.

ERICSON, DAVID B., and WOLLIN GOESTA, *The Ever-Changing Sea.* New York, Knopf, 1967.

GROSS, W. GRANT, *Oceanography.* Columbus, Ohio, Merrill, 1967.

GULLION, EDMUND A., *Uses of the Seas.* New York, American Assembly, Columbia University Press, 1968.

HEYERDAHL, THOR, *Kon-Tiki.* Chicago, Rand McNally, 1951.

LANE, FRANK W., *The Elements Rage.* Philadelphia, Chilton, 1965.

LANSING, ALFRED, *Endurance—Shackleton's Incredible Voyage.* New York, McGraw-Hill, 1959.

LONG, E. JOHN, *New Worlds of Oceanography*. New York, Pyramid, 1965.
MARX, LESLIE, *The Frail Ocean*. New York, Coward-McCann, 1967.
MCKEE, ALEXANDER, *History Under the Sea*. New York, Dutton, 1969.
MELVILLE, HERMAN, *Moby Dick*. New York, Harper, 1851.
MERO, JOHN L., *The Mineral Resources of the Sea*. New York, Elsevier, 1965.
SHEPARD, FRANCIS P., *The Earth Beneath the Sea*. Baltimore, Johns Hopkins Press, 1967.
SOULE, GARDNER, *Under the Sea*. Des Moines, Meredith, 1968.
TELLER, WALTER MAGNES, *The Voyages of Joshua Slocum*. New Brunswick, N.J., Rutgers University Press, 1958.
TROEBST, CORD-CHRISTIAN, *Conquest of the Sea*. New York, Harper & Row, 1962.
TUREKIAN, KARL K., *Oceans*. Englewood Cliffs, N.J., Prentice-Hall, 1968.
VILLIERS, ALAN, *Wild Ocean*. New York, McGraw-Hill, 1957.
WILLIS, WILLIAM, *The Gods Were Kind: An Epic 6,700-Mile Voyage*. New York, Dutton, 1955.
———, *An Angel on Each Shoulder*. London, Hutchinson, 1966.
WRAIGHT, A. JOSEPH, *Our Dynamic World*. Philadelphia, Chilton, 1966.

3. The Battle Royal: Sea, Land, and Air
BASCOM, WILLARD, *Waves and Beaches*. Garden City, Doubleday, 1964.
BESTON, HENRY, *The Outermost House*. New York, Viking, 1929.
CARSON, RACHEL, *The Edge of the Sea*. Boston, Houghton Mifflin, 1955.
CLANCY, EDWARD P., *The Tides: Pulse of the Earth*. Garden City, Doubleday, 1968.
DEFANT, ALBERT, *Ebb and Flow*. Ann Arbor, University of Michigan Press, 1958.
HAY, JOHN, and FARB, PETER, *The Atlantic Shore*. New York, Harper & Row, 1966.
HOLMES, DAVID C., and PITKIN, MARVIN, *On the Wings of the Wind*. New York, McBride, 1955.
MANLEY, ROBERT and SEON, *Beaches*. Philadelphia, Chilton, 1968.
MAXWELL, GAVIN, *Ring of Bright Water*. New York, Dutton, 1960.
OGBURN, CHARLES, JR., *The Winter Beach*. New York, Morrow, 1966.
STOCKTON, FRANK R., *The Casting Away of Mrs. Lecks and Mrs. Aleshine*. New York, Appleton-Century, 1938.
TEAL, JOHN and MILDRED, *Life and Death of the Salt Marsh*. Boston, Little, Brown, 1969.

4. Man Goes to Sea
ANDERSON, J. R. L., *Vinland Voyage*. London, Eyre & Spottisworde, 1967.
ARCINIEGAS, GERMÁN, *Caribbean, Sea of the New World*. New York, Knopf, 1946.
BOLAND, CHARLES MICHAEL, *They All Discovered America*. Garden City, Doubleday, 1961.
BRAYNARD, FRANK O., *Famous American Ships*. New York, Hastings, 1956.

CASSON, LIONEL, *The Ancient Mariners*. New York, Minerva, 1959.

COHEN, PAUL, *The Realm of the Submarine*. New York, Macmillan, 1969.

FREUCHEN, PETER, *Book of the Seven Seas*. New York, Simon & Schuster, 1957.

GRAVES, ROBERT, *Hercules My Shipmate*. New York, Farrar, Straus & Giroux, 1945.

GREENHOOD, DAVID, *Mapping*. Chicago, University of Chicago Press, 1951.

HAPGOOD, CHARLES, *Maps of the Ancient Sea Kings*. Philadelphia, Chilton, 1966.

HERRMANN, PAUL, *Conquest by Man*. New York, Harper, 1954.

HOMER, *The Iliad*, *The Odyssey*.

KNIGHT, FRANK, *The Sea Story*. New York, Macmillan, 1958.

LANDSTROM, BJORN, *The Ship*. Garden City, Doubleday, 1961.

RENAULT, MARY, *The Bull from the Sea*. New York, Pantheon, 1962.

STEFANSSON, VILHJALMUR, *Great Adventures and Explorations*. New York, Dial, 1947.

VILLIERS, ALAN, *Capt. James Cook*. New York, Scribner, 1967.

——, *Sons of Sinbad*. New York, Scribner, 1969.

VON DÄNIKEN, ERICH, *Chariots of the Gods?* New York, Putnam, 1970.

5. Lakes, Rivers, and Streams

BAKELESS, JOHN, *The Eyes of Discovery*. Philadelphia, Lippincott, 1950.

BARDACH, JOHN, *Downstream: a Natural History of a River*. New York, Harper & Row, 1964.

BULLARD, ORAL, *Crisis on the Columbia*. Touchstone, 1968.

CLARK, LEONARD, *The Rivers Ran East*. New York, Funk & Wagnalls, 1953.

COOPER, GORDON, *Along the Great Rivers*. New York, Philosophical Library, 1953.

DEVOTO, BERNARD, *The Course of Empire*. Palo Alto, Stanford University Press, 1952.

EIFERT, VIRGINIA S., *Of Men and Rivers*. New York, Dodd, Mead, 1966.

FREY, DAVID G., *Limnology in North America*. Madison, University of Wisconsin Press, 1966.

HELMERICKS, CONSTANCE, *Down the Wild River North*. Boston, Little, Brown, 1968.

KING, F. H., *Farmers of Forty Centuries*. New York, Hillary, 1968 (1911).

LANE, FERDINAND C., *The World's Great Lakes*. Garden City, Doubleday, 1948.

——, *Earth's Grandest Rivers*. Garden City, Doubleday, 1949.

LEYDET, FRANÇOIS, *Time and the River Flowing*. New York, Sierra Club-Ballantine, 1968.

PENNELL, JOSEPH, *Highways & Byways in the Lake District*. New York, Macmillan, 1901.

RAIKES, ROBERT, *Water Weather & Prehistory*. New York, Humanities, 1967.

ST. CLAIR, DAVID, *The Mighty, Mighty Amazon*. New York, Funk & Wagnalls, 1968.

SCHNEIDER, WOLF, *Babylon Is Everywhere: the City as Man's Fate*. London, Hodder & Stoughton, 1963.

THOREAU, HENRY DAVID, *A Week on the Concord and Merrimac Rivers* (1849).

————, *Walden* (1854).

TWAIN, MARK, *The Adventures of Huckleberry Finn* (1885).

————, *Life on the Mississippi* (1883).

6. Waterfalls and Fountains

BISHOP, MINOR L., *Fountains in Contemporary Architecture*. New York, October House, 1965.

FARB, PETER, *Face of North America*. New York, Harper & Row, 1963.

HALLIBURTON, RICHARD, *The Royal Road to Romance*. Indianapolis, Bobbs-Merrill, 1925.

MORTON, H. V., *The Fountains of Rome*. New York, Macmillan, 1966.

PFANNSCHMIDT, ERNST-ERIK, *Fountains and Springs*. London, Harrap, 1968.

7. Underground Waters and Hot and Cold Springs

DUGUID, JOHN, *Pleasures of the Spa*. New York, Macmillan, 1968.

EWBANK, THOMAS, *A Descriptive and Historical Account of Hydrologic and Other Machines for Raising Water, Ancient and Modern*. London, Tilt & Bogue, 1842.

KEITH, DAVID, *Ground Water Hydrology*. New York, John Wiley, 1959.

McGUINNESS, C. L., *The Role of Ground Water in the National Water Situation*. Washington, D.C., U.S. Government Printing Office, 1963.

WEISS, HARRY B., and KEMPLE, HOWARD R., *The Great American Water-Cure Craze*. Past Times Press, 1967.

8. Water Bathing and Water Closets

ASHE, GEOFFREY, *The Tale of the Tub*. London, Newman Neams, 1950.

FULLER, MAX, *Maytag Encyclopedia of Home Laundry*. Popular, 1965.

GOULDEN, GONTRAN, *Bathrooms*. London, Macdonald, 1966.

KELLER, JEANNE, *Healing with Water*. West Nyack, N.Y., Parker, 1968.

KIRA, ALEXANDER, *The Bathroom*. Ithaca, N.Y., Cornell University Press, 1966.

PETRONIUS, *The Satyricon* (circa A.D. 100, fragment).

REYNOLDS, REGINALD, *Cleanliness and Godliness*. Garden City, Doubleday, 1946.

ROSEBURY, THEODOR, *Life on Man*. New York, Viking, 1969.

ROUTH, JONATHAN, *The Better John Guide: Where to Go in New York*. New York, Putnam, 1966.

WRIGHT, LAWRENCE, *Clean and Decent*. Toronto, University of Toronto Press, 1960.

9. The Sky Waters

BADER, HAEFELIG, et al., *Snow & Its Metamorphism*. Washington, D.C., U.S. Army Corps of Engineers, 1954.

BATTAN, LOUIS J., *The Nature of Violent Storms*. Garden City, Doubleday, 1961.

BELL, CORYDON, *The Wonder of Snow.*

BLANCHARD, DUNCAN C., *From Raindrops to Volcanoes.* Garden City, Doubleday, 1967.

BOYER, CARL B., *The Rainbow.* New York, Yoseloff, 1959.

LANDSBERG, H. E., *Weather and Health (Biometeorology).* Garden City, Doubleday, 1969.

LOEBSACK, THEO, *Our Atmosphere.* New York, Pantheon, 1959.

SPITZ, ARMAND N., *Weather.* New York, Bantam, 1967.

SUTCLIFFE, R. C., *Weather and Climate.* New York, Norton, 1966.

WOOD, ELIZABETH A., *Science for the Airplane Passenger.* Boston, Houghton Mifflin, 1968.

10. Playing with Water

ADAMS, HERVEY, *The Adventure of Looking.* London, G. Bell, 1949.

ATWATER, MONTGOMERY M., *The Avalanche Hunters.* Philadelphia, Macrae Smith, 1968.

BURDICK, EUGENE, *The Blue of Capricorn.* Boston, Houghton Mifflin, 1961.

DIXON, PETER L., *Men and Waves.* New York, Coward-McCann, 1966.

EDBERG, ROLF, *On the Shadow of a Cloud.* University, Ala., University of Alabama Press, 1969.

EKIRCH, ARTHUR A., JR., *Man and Nature in America.* New York, Columbia University Press, 1963.

ELIOT, ALEXANDER, *Earth, Air, Fire, and Water.* New York, Simon & Schuster, 1962.

FINNEY, BEN R., and HOUSTON, JAMES D., *Surfing: the Sport of Hawaiian Kings.* Rutland, Vt., Tuttle, 1966.

MACAULAY, ROSE, *Pleasure of Ruins.* New York, Walker, 1966.

RIENOW, ROBERT, and LEONA TRAIN, *Moment in the Sun: a Report on the Deteriorating Quality of the American Environment.* New York, Dial, 1967.

ROBINSON, BILL, *The World of Yachting.* New York, Random, 1966.

SANDBURG, HELGA, and CRILE, GEORGE, *Above & Below.* New York, McGraw-Hill, 1969.

THORNE, JIM, *Guide to Adventure.* New York, T. Y. Crowell, 1967.

Index